Radical Unschool Love

Sue Elvis

Susan Elvis

P.O. Box 57, Hill Top

NSW, 2575

Australia

ISBN-13: 978-0-9925588-9-5

For Jacqueline and Venisa

True friends are a blessing.

Contents

Radical Unschool Love

Radical unschooling children don't necessarily brush their teeth or shower, and if they want to exist on an exclusive diet of coca cola and donuts, well, that's up to them.

Or so the stories go.

And for some people that might not sound like a very attractive way of life at all.

But what if we forget about teeth and showers and junk food? Perhaps there's something far more important at the heart of a radical way of life.

What if we accept our children with all their gifts and quirks and failings? Treat them with trust and respect, and instantly forgive? Love them just as they are, no strings attached?

What if we love as we'd like to be loved ourselves?

We'd be loving unconditionally. And isn't that a rather radical thing to do?

So how do we live radically? Don't worry about other people's stories (which might not even be true).

Just love.

Part I: An Introduction

The Next Instalment of the Unschooling Story

In my first unschooling book, *Curious Unschoolers*, I said:

> I've got something very important to share with you.
>
> I want to tell you about unschooling: what it is and how it has changed our family's life and why I think everyone should do it. I'm passionate about unschooling. I hope my words are going to make you feel excited about it too!

I also said:

> I believe unschooling is different because it's all about unconditional love. I want to show you how choosing to unschool will result in a love so powerful it will encourage, not only our kids but us as well, to become the people we are all meant to be.

Unconditional love? Surely unschooling is about giving kids the freedom to learn what they like? How do we get from that to love? It's a long story. Or maybe lots of shorter ones. Stories contained in two books:

Curious Unschoolers

and *Radical Unschool Love*

Curious Unschoolers focuses mainly on the educational side of unschooling. And *Radical Unschool Love* is about unschool parenting. The two books do overlap because, in real life, parenting and education are woven closely together.

I hope you will read both my books to get the full unschooling picture!

Both my books? Perhaps you've already read *Curious Unschoolers*. If you have, are you now ready to read the next instalment of the unschooling story? Do you want to know what happens when we let unschooling flow over into all aspects of our lives and not just the educational side?

Shall we discuss radical unschooling?

There are lots of frightening stories about radical unschoolers. Many people think radical unschooling is an irresponsible thing to do. Well, I'm hoping to change this negative image. Set the record straight. Tell everyone what I think radical unschooling is really all about. It's about unconditional love.

By the time you get to the end of this book, I hope you'll agree with me that radical unschooling is something anyone can do. Maybe it's something everyone should consider doing. Is it the right way to live?

But before we dive into radical unschooling, perhaps I need to introduce myself just in case we aren't already friends!

Sue Elvis: An Interview

I receive an email:

Sue,

I saw your book. It's fantastic. And it's now on Kindle. You're going to be famous! Can we meet for coffee? I'd like to interview you.

Octavia

Octavia? I scratch my head for a moment or two, and then I smile. The email must be from Octavia Latte, the most famous book reviewer on the Internet. Octavia has the power to make or break an author. And she wants to interview me!

What sort of questions will Octavia ask me? Perhaps I should get prepared, jot down a few notes.

I start typing.

What's your name?

Sue Elvis.

Any relation to Elvis Presley?

No, but I *am* married to a superstar: Andy Elvis.

How old are you?

I'm about 30 on the inside. (My outside is looking a bit older.)

Where do you live?

In a happy, messy-around-the-edges home that's surrounded by the beautiful Australian bush in a village somewhere south of Sydney.

How many children do you have?

More than I expected. And less than I expected. Andy and I have eight children. Our eldest child is Felicity, who was born in 1987. And our youngest is Gemma-Rose who joined our family in 2004. Duncan, Callum, Imogen, Charlotte, Thomas and Sophie fall somewhere in between.

More than you expected?

Oh yes, once upon a time, I had my own ideas about my life. I wanted to be in total control of it. I thought I'd have, maybe, three or four children. But unexpectedly I had more. Somehow a lot of unexpected things happened. Thomas died, and so did seven of our unborn babies. But other things happened too. For example, I never expected to become a Catholic.

Catholic?

Yes, I said I'd never become a Catholic. Somehow I did. But don't let that put you off. I'm really quite normal. Well, actually, I'm not. But I'll get to that in a moment.

What are you passionate about? What do you like to do?

Writing. I love it. Except for those times when I hate it. When inspiration disappears, and my words stop singing, I say, "I'm never going to write again!" But I always do. Somehow I can't give it up. I might be addicted.

What do you write about?

I write about what I know: my family, my life. Sometimes I turn that into children's fiction. Other times, I share personal stories on my blog. I especially like writing about unschooling.

Unschooling? Isn't that a bit weird? Are *you* a bit weird?

Oh, yes, definitely! But I love being this way. So does my family. Why be like everyone else? You know what? I'd like everyone to unschool. I suppose we wouldn't be different if everyone joined us. But that's okay. I want everyone to experience the love and joy of this way of life. That's why I write about it...

Words are flowing. I've got lots to say. Then I hear a 'ding!' An email notification! Perhaps it's Octavia again. I smile. I open my inbox.

Sue,

I got the wrong book. And the wrong Sue. I won't be interviewing you after all. Sorry about the mix-up,

Octavia.

The wrong book? The wrong Sue? I'm not going to be famous? My heart sinks to the bottom of my Doc Marten boots. But after a moment or two, I sigh with relief. How would I have coped with fame? All those parties and other publicity events. I shudder at the thought. You see, I'm an introvert. Yes, fame just wouldn't have suited me.

But what about my writing? Don't I want people to read it? Oh, yes, I do. I want to share the unschooling message with as many people as possible. How will I do that without Olivia Latte's help?

Well, perhaps someone will read one of my books and enjoy it. She or he might tell someone else, who might tell someone else. Word of mouth, you know.

Maybe after reading this book, you'll tell someone about it. I hope you do!

A Book of Stories

Stories capture the imagination. They create pictures in our minds. As you read my stories, I hope they'll give you a concrete picture of what unschooling can look like in action.

Each story contains a piece of unschooling. Each piece illustrates some principle or thought or idea. Sometimes the same piece appears more than once, presented to you from a different angle in a different story. Does this mean that my stories are repetitive? I hope not! I did consider eliminating some of them. But then I remembered someone saying, "I need to hear things more than once." So do I. So perhaps it's okay to tell the same story in multiple ways. We can approach the same ideas from different directions.

By the time you get to the end of this book, I hope all my stories fit together, like a completed jigsaw puzzle, to form a good picture of unschooling.

Although I wrote a lot of new stories for this book, I've also included some that I wrote for my Stories of an Unschooling Family blog. I edited and expanded many of these stories. But there are a few that I decided to leave alone. Maybe they'd lose something if I tried to update them: my excitement, worries, joy, whatever I was feeling at the time when I first rushed to my computer and tapped out my thoughts. These stories capture moments in our unschooling life in a way that's impossible to replicate when writing from a distance. I have included the ages of my children in these older stories to give you a rough idea of where our family was on our unschooling journey at the time of writing.

I've arranged my stories according to the subject matter. However, a story may belong to more than one category. Everything overlaps, just like in real life.

How should you read this book? You could start at the beginning and read the stories in order. You could head straight to a topic you'd like to know more about. Or you could dip in here and there, reading stories as their titles catch your attention. Any method is good as long as you read my book!

Part II: Radical Unschooling

Not as Wild as it Sounds

Many people think of unschooling very simply: it's a method of homeschooling where a child doesn't use a curriculum or a plan put together by a parent. Instead, parents allow their children to learn, in their own way, what interests them. They trust that their kids will learn all that they need to know at a time when they need to know it.

But unschooling can affect more than the educational side of a child's life. What if, as well as giving our kids the freedom to learn what's important to them, we also let them make their own decisions about other things such as food and bedtimes and clothes? What if we let unschooling spill over into all areas of our lives? If we do that, we'll be radically unschooling.

Perhaps you think radical unschooling sounds like a recipe for disaster. How can kids handle that much freedom? What if they make the wrong choices? Could they become wild and out of control? Will everyone think that we are irresponsible parents? Well, they might if we just step back and let our kids do whatever they like without any input from us. But that's not radical unschooling.

Our kids need our guidance. But we can't just tell them what to do. So how does radical unschooling work? How do we help our kids become the people they are meant to be? We do it by building up strong bonds of connection between us.

When we are closely connected with our kids, we know them very well. They know us. Our kids feel loved and accepted. They trust us. We are the most important people in their lives so they will turn to us for guidance. We'll be able to share what's right and what's wrong and help our kids determine their needs so that they make the right choices.

So how do we become closely connected with our children? It begins with unconditional love. And that's really what this book is all about!

Unconditional Love

If we love unconditionally, we'll accept our kids for who they are: unique people with their own talents and interests, quirks and failings.

If we believe our children's talents and interests are an integral part of them, we will encourage them to use them. We will value what our children are interested in. We'll let them learn about the things that are important to them. We'll respect their choices.

If we love unconditionally, we won't impose our ideas on our children. They don't have to be who we think they should be. They can be themselves. We won't express disappointment with who our kids are. They'll know that we value them just the way they are. We'll also trust that they'll find their places in the world.

We'll let our unconditionally loved children develop and grow and learn in their own time. They don't have to fit into our timetable. We won't compare them to other children.

Our kids can express their thoughts and ideas and opinions. We will listen and take them seriously. They don't have to be just like us.

We won't let other people's opinions about our children affect how we treat them and feel about them. We'll stand up for them and protect them. They don't have to fulfil other people's expectations.

When we love unconditionally, we love all the time regardless of what our kids do. We won't withdraw our love as a way of controlling or influencing them. Our kids don't have to please us. They don't have to do things to keep us happy. We can't use love to manipulate them.

We'll keep on loving even when our kids make mistakes. Yes, we'll love them regardless. Our children won't think, "I got away with that. I'll misbehave again because I know I'll be forgiven." Even though this sounds reasonable, it's not what happens. When we fail and are forgiven, we want to become better people. I know this from experience. When I fail, and my kids wrap their arms around me and say, "Mum, it doesn't matter. We love you!" I want to be the best mother in the world. I also want to make up for my mistake and put things right. Why should it be any different for kids? Some people say we shouldn't reward bad behaviour with love. But love is necessary. It's what gets our kids (and us) back on track again. Love is powerful. It can transform people.

And perhaps bad behaviour is a sign that our child has a need that isn't being fulfilled. Our child doesn't need punishment. She needs our empathy and love.

We love unconditionally and accept our kids for who they are, but this doesn't mean we don't want them to grow in virtue and become better people. We still have to guide them and help them overcome their faults.

When kids are loved unconditionally, we become the most important people in their lives because of the strong bonds that are forged between us. They will love, trust and respect us and so look to us for guidance, especially when they're learning about right and wrong. They will develop an internal feeling of rightness. This will be their guide. If they do wrong, they'll no longer feel right inside. This is why kids will choose to do what is right even when they don't want to, even if it's difficult. Of course, kids somtimes fail. They can choose to do wrong. But so can parents.

When we love our children unconditionally and accept them for who they are, they have no reason to be jealous of their siblings. There will be no reason for sibling rivalry. Siblings will have close bonds. They will appreciate each other as unique people with individual personalities and talents.

A family should be a group of imperfect people who love each other unconditionally. When we fail, we aren't condemned or criticised by our family. Instead, everyone helps us get back on our feet. We acknowledge how hard life can be. We forgive each other. We keep loving one another.

Our family, where we are unconditionally loved, is our safe place, our refuge from the world. It's where we try and fail and try again, love and forgive and become the people we are meant to be.

So unconditional love is essential if we want our children to develop their unique talents and skills which they will use to fulfil their missions in life. It's also necessary if we want them to learn right from wrong and become virtuous people.

That's a lot of thoughts, isn't it? But don't worry. I have many, many stories that expand on the ideas I've just presented. I hope after reading them, you will agree that unconditional love is an essential ingredient of unschooling!

Our Radical Unschooling Story

In *Curious Unschoolers,* I told you the story of how we started our homeschooling adventure as unschoolers. Unfortunately, we soon left this way of life behind, and I never thought we'd return. No, I assumed our unschooling days were over. But one day, I realised we were indeed unschooling.

How can a family become unschoolers without even realising it? Surely I knew what unschooling looked like? Right back at the beginning, I thought I knew all about unschooling. But later, I realised that I didn't understand it very well at all. If I had, I'm sure that we'd never have moved onto other things.

So we are unschoolers. We arrived here gradually and unexpectedly. And for a long time, we were quite content with our lives. We liked being unschoolers. We were happy letting go of control and trusting that our kids would learn all they needed to know in their own time and way. But we were education-only unschoolers. I couldn't see us letting unschooling spill over into all aspects of our lives. No, I was sure we'd never become radical unschoolers.

The words radical unschooling made me feel very uncomfortable. This way of life sounded rather weird and possibly irresponsible. And even if it was okay to unschool, surely only people living an unconventional lifestyle did it?

All the radical unschoolers we'd heard about travelled around the country in combi-vans or lived in yurts. They grew organic vegetables. They were free-spirited people living outside of mainstream society. And although we liked the radical unschoolers we met very much, they were different from us. We didn't feel we belonged. And we didn't want to change so that we would fit in. We were quite happy living our seemingly conventional Catholic unschooling life in our ordinary house on a regular-sized block of land. No, I couldn't imagine us ever going down the radical unschooling pathway.

But strange things happen.

Some years ago, I stopped and thought about where our family was at that moment in time and where we'd come from. And I realised that we'd changed in a big way. Our parenting style had changed. Our relationships with our kids weren't the same. Our unschooling life was different. One day, I realised we'd arrived at radical unschooling without ever intending to.

Had we become wild and irresponsible? Did we buy a combi-van? Perhaps we'd moved into a yurt? Did we dig up our garden and plant rows and rows of vegetables? No, we didn't do any of those things.

What we did do was discover that radical unschooling isn't what I thought it was. It's not a wild and irresponsible way to live. And it's also not something that's confined to a particular lifestyle. Although there's nothing wrong with yurts and combi-vans and organic vegetables, we didn't have to make these part of our life to radically unschool.

Radical unschooling has nothing to do with the external appearances of a family. It's not about how we choose to dress or eat. Or where we choose to live. Or even what we believe. We might live a simple life on the road. Maybe we reside in a city or on a farm. How about a home in a village on the edge of the Australian bush? We might be Christians. Or maybe not. It doesn't matter. Anyone can radically unschool. Maybe everyone should.

Even after I realised we were radical unschoolers, I never used the word ‘radical’ when I spoke or wrote about my family. Why is that? I think I was reluctant to use this word because it implies that what we're doing is strange. It's extreme parenting. Perhaps risky. That's the image the word ‘radical’ conjures up for most people. I didn't want anyone to read my stories and make the same mistake I did. I didn't want people to think radical unschooling is not for them.

No, radical unschooling isn't out there at the extreme edges of parenting. It's actually something that we should consider as mainstream. This is the way everybody should parent their children. Why do I think that? Because radical unschooling involves respecting our children, loving them unconditionally, and making strong connections with them. And shouldn't we all be doing these things? It really is the right way to live.

So we are radical unschoolers.

Isn't it funny how we can change, one step at a time, and end up somewhere we didn't think we wanted to go?

An Active Approach to Radical Unschooling

You might agree that there are a lot of benefits to unschooling as far as education goes. Children acquire a love of learning. They will indeed learn all they need to know when they need to know it. There are no battles because kids are self-motivated. And when we allow children to follow their passions, amazing things can happen. Learning also becomes a family affair. It can be a chance for parents to have a second education. So some families will choose to unschool for these reasons.

But what about radical unschooling? What about letting freedom to choose spill over into all aspects of our children's lives? Should we do that? Perhaps it's time to take one more step. But maybe you've read negative stories about radical unschooling. Could the critics be right? If we give our children the freedom to choose, will they become selfish people and will our lives become chaotic?

Over and over again, I read stories about parents who have tried radical unschooling. They say such things as:

"If you let your kids do whatever they like, they'll become selfish and lazy. You, as a parent, will end up doing all the work of the family."

"Kids will make bad decisions. We can't trust them."

"We've given radical unschooling a go. We gave our kids time to get their freedom out of their system, and they're still not turning around and saying, 'I'd like to help you, Mum.' No, they're just getting used to being lazy."

For these families, life becomes more and more chaotic, and mothers get exhausted because they're doing all the work. And then one day, the mother says to her kids, "That's it. I've had enough. Get back to work!"

Yes, I've read a number of these stories, and I believe them. This is exactly what's happening for many families. And I'm not surprised. Imagine saying to children, "We're going to be radical unschoolers. From now on, you can do whatever you like." Perhaps they won't want to do the chores. They might want to stay up late making lots of noise. Maybe they'll play all day even when they can see there's work to be done. They'll eat what they like when they like even if this means that they're inconveniencing other people. They'll not answer to anyone. Their parents have given them the freedom to do whatever they like, and that's exactly what they're going to do.

But I don't think this is radical unschooling, and this is why I don't agree with the conclusion these parents have come to: that radical unschooling doesn't work. Because I know it does work. It's what we're doing with our family.

How did we get here? How did we become radical unschoolers? Did I wake up one morning and say, "Hey kids, from now on we're going to be radical unschoolers? Unschooling is working, and I want to take the next step. Let's become radical unschoolers. You can do whatever you like. The choice is yours." Did I just stand back and trust my children would make the right decisions, that they would make good choices?

I have already told you how other people have said that saying such things to their kids doesn't work. But maybe I was lucky. Perhaps my kids responded in a different way to other people's children. Could I have a different type of child who wouldn't even think of being self-centred? This is rather a silly thought, but some people do insist that some children are more suited to unschooling than others.

The fact is I never told my kids that they could do whatever they liked. I never even intended our family to become radical unschoolers. But one day, I looked back and realised we'd changed. We'd arrived at radical unschooling without making a conscious decision to do this. I did, however, make a decision. I decided I wanted to be a better parent.

I knew that I didn't always speak to my kids with respect. I ordered them instead of asking. I criticised their clothes and hair and other things:

"What are you wearing that for?"

"That doesn't match."

"I don't like your hairstyle. It looked better the other way."

"You're not going out looking like that."

I always thought my way was better than my children's. I was the parent, and I had more experience. I had set ideas about how I wanted my children to look and what I wanted them to do and even what I wanted them to think. I was in control. At least, I was trying to stay in control. We had our battles.

I lacked empathy. I didn't listen properly. When my children were talking to me, I always jumped in with the things I wanted to say to them. If they said anything I disagreed with, I'd cut them off. I'd tell them where they were going wrong and why I was right. It got to the stage where my kids weren't sharing much with me because, I guess, they knew that I'd lecture them as soon as they asked a question or expressed an opinion.

I think it's very easy to get into a certain pattern of communication. We can do and say things without thinking. Words just fall from our mouths. One day, I stopped and listened to myself, and I didn't like what I was hearing.

I also started questioning my responses to various situations. Does it really matter if kids don't eat all the food on their plates? And why shouldn't they be allowed to choose their own style of clothes or hair? Does it matter if their clothes don't match? And what about bedtimes? Why should they go to bed at a certain time if they're not tired? And did I always have to nag them about doing chores? I never gave them an opportunity to offer to help me.

And so I decided I'd try and change myself. I'm not saying it was easy because it wasn't. I'd resolve not to say certain things, and then I'd find myself saying them and having to try again. But I did persevere, and I got to the stage where I was no longer trying to control my children. And what happened? It was really strange. When I let go of control, my kids didn't do any of the things I was worried about. They made choices very much in line with my own. And I wondered why they would do that. Why wouldn't they rush off and do something radical? They had the freedom to do whatever they liked, and they chose to be conventional, to fit in with the family. They continued to go to Mass with us. They continued to read books with good content. They helped with the chores. They were considerate about late bedtimes and making lots of noise. They ate similar food to the rest of the family. Life didn't become chaotic.

When we work on our relationships, kids feel loved and valued and accepted. They feel connected with us. They regard us as the most important people in their lives. And because of this connection, they're willing to listen to us, they trust our opinions, and it's very likely that they'll end up adopting our values. Kids want to be considerate. They want to be helpful. They want to return the love we show them.

Connection is essential if we want to radically unschool. When we are connected with our children, we can give them the freedom to choose, trusting they will make good choices.

So we arrived at radical unschooling because I changed. I changed as a parent. I changed as a person. I took action.

We can't just say, "You're free to do whatever you like," and expect our kids to make the right choices without any input from us. We can't stand back and let them get on with it. As many families have discovered, this will never work.

What do we do if we want to radically unschool? We need to take an active approach. Look at ourselves. And begin there.

How Radical Unschooling Might Not Look Radical

Have you heard stories of unschoolers who stay up late every night and then sleep in the next morning? They don't move to anyone's timetable except their own. They eat what they like when they feel hungry, and not when the clock or someone tells them it's time for a meal. They listen to the needs of their bodies and respond accordingly. Yes, they do what they like when they want to, because there are no rules. They are as free as the wind, not constrained by anything.

Is our life like that? No, it doesn't look like that at all. Actually, our life from the outside looks rather ordinary. Perhaps we don't sound much like most people's idea of a family who has let unschooling spill over into all parts of life. Could we just be pretending to live an amazing unschooling life when we are, in fact, conventional homeschoolers? Perhaps we're not radical unschoolers after all.

Or maybe we are because radical unschooling isn't about *what* we do. It's not about what time we get up or when we eat our meals or when we go to bed or what type of activities we're involved with. It's all to do with the question: *do children have the choice to do what they want?* They might choose to do things on a family's timetable, rather than on their own.

But why would kids choose to do this? Why would they want to fit in with their family? I ask my children this question. And they reply:

"Our family life is important to us."

"We like doing things together."

"We want to be part of the team."

"We contribute to the family and want to do things together because we love each other and want to help out."

"When our life has some rhythm to it, we achieve more."

So in many ways, it might seem like we're living a conventional life. But we're not. Appearances are deceiving. We are as free as the wind.

Why do we live the way we do?

Charlotte: "Because we want to!"

And so we do because we can.

Part III: Connection

A Fresh Perspective

One of the huge delights of my unschooling life is sitting quietly with my children while chatting together.

I'm good friends with my kids. We're always sharing our thoughts, ideas, stories, dreams, problems, and moments of joy. We don't talk so that I can impress my opinions on my children. I don't tell them what I think and therefore what they should think. Instead, I'm interested in what they have to say. Who are they? What ideas do they have? What thoughts are circling through their minds?

I love listening to my kids. They observe. They think deeply. I am continually surprised by their wisdom.

My unschooling children give me a fresh perspective on life. They help me see things more clearly. Is this because they aren't tied down by those old ideas that sometimes echo in my head?

Our kids can learn from us, but we can also learn from them. If we are prepared to listen.

Guiding Our Kids by Radically Unschooling

Have you heard the stories? The ones about the radically unschooled kids who refuse to eat healthy food and never brush their teeth? Perhaps these stories make you wonder if there's something wrong with radical unschooling. How can parents stand by and watch their children fill up on junk food and let their teeth decay? Surely influencing a child to do certain things is the right thing to do?

Not so long ago, I read a story about a family of children who not only fill up on junk food and don't look after their teeth but also don't wash. Unless they want to, of course, though I don't think they do because their hair has turned into dirty, matted dreadlocks.

"Our kids can make their own choices," said the parents who are proudly living an alternate lifestyle. They're not imposing their beliefs or values on their kids but allowing them to be free. Their children can decide for themselves what is important. They are free to ignore the basics of hygiene. They are free to eat junk food. They are free to do whatever they want.

Stories like this one horrify some potential unschoolers. Sometimes these parents decide not to become unschoolers after all. And this is very sad because I don't think these stories are about unschooling children at all. To me, they sound more like unparenting ones.

So what's the difference between unparenting and unschooling? Unparenting parents step back and let their kids do whatever they like, regardless of whether it's good for them or not. Unschooling parents know that kids have to be free to make their own choices, but that's not enough. They want their kids to use their freedom to make the right choices. Choices that work to the benefit of their children.

Good nutrition and hygiene are essential for the good health of our children. Good hygiene is also necessary if we want our kids to fit into the world so that they can live and work with others. Unschoolers are different. Maybe they stick out. But we're not doing our kids any favours if we encourage them to stick out in a very negative way. And then there's the matter of being considerate. Surely we shouldn't impose our poor hygiene on anyone else?

So do we insist our kids wash their hair and brush their teeth? Do we force them to eat healthy food? No, we can't do that. But we can become so connected to our kids that they will trust us and value our opinions and want to follow our example.

But isn't working on our connections so that we get the desired outcome wrong? Is it really okay to influence our children's choices by guiding them along the pathway we value? Perhaps it's better to step back and not force our opinions on them. Let children make up their own minds without any influence from us about how they use their bodies and what they put into them. Just like the family in the story.

All this sounds okay until we realise that those parents *are* influencing their kids. They are passing on their values. The message they're giving them is that good hygiene doesn't matter. Other people don't matter. We don't need to be considerate. Other people can adapt themselves to us, but we don't have to adjust our behaviour to get along with them. All that matters is us. We can do whatever we like, whether it is good for us or not.

And that's not the way to live life. It's not what unschooling is all about.

If you've heard some frightening stories, don't be put off because you can't accept that it's wrong to influence a child. Every parent influences her child in some way. It really is impossible not to. What's important is how we do it and why we want to.

So forget those stories about bad teeth and dirty hair.

And guide your child with unconditional love, respect and trust along the pathway that's right for her.

Radically unschool.

A Teenager's Thoughts

Sometimes parents tell me that they're afraid to radically unschool. What if their kids choose to neglect their hygiene or refuse to eat healthy food?

I told my teenage daughter Sophie about a family whose children choose not to wash and who eat a diet of junk food. "Stories like these put parents off unschooling. Should they be afraid of letting kids make their own choices?"

Sophie couldn't understand what all the fuss is about. Kids will follow the example of their parents. Teeth cleaning and washing hair don't have to be traumatic. They're just part of life. Growing up, Sophie didn't even think about these things. Everyone did them. She did them. Aren't they things parents naturally share with their kids? They're things essential for good health.

We always showered our babies and toddlers with us. They saw us cleaning our teeth and wanted brushes of their own. We shared food from our plates.

Perhaps we sometimes worry too much about things that aren't likely to happen. Sophie thinks we should just give a good example, don't make a big fuss, and trust our kids.

And trust ourselves. Trust our ability to love and guide our children. Even if we don't parent perfectly, we're still doing okay!

Learning Right From Wrong

It can be hard to let go and trust our children. How do we know that they will make the right choices? Perhaps we should keep control over them just in case because we don't want them making big mistakes.

Perhaps it doesn't sound sensible letting kids do what they'd like, allowing them to choose instead of telling them what to do. And I think it wouldn't be sensible to give our kids that freedom if we aren't connected to them and don't have strong relationships.

If we say to our kids, "Go and do whatever you want," and then step back completely, yes, they might not know the right thing to do. They might end up making the wrong choices. So we can't do that. If we did, we'd be unparenting. Children need guidance from us. But why should they listen to us? I think they will only be open to our guidance if we are connected with them. Kids must view us as the most important people in their lives. The ones they want to follow, the ones whose values and opinions they trust more than anyone else's.

Yes, we must be connected with our kids. But how do we build up that connection? What is connection all about? We have to accept our kids just as they are. Love them unconditionally. Respect them by treating them as we'd like people to treat us. Take time to listen to them properly. Show them empathy instead of dismissing their feelings and telling them how they should feel. Be willing to forgive them when they make mistakes. Admit our mistakes. Ask for forgiveness when we fail.

We have to show our kids that no one is perfect, but that's okay. As long as we all keep striving to do what is right.

I think that connection results in an inner feeling of peace and 'rightness'. When a child does something wrong, they will know because this inner feeling will change. It won't feel good. Maybe you've experienced this. I know I have. We feel unsettled. We're not happy with ourselves. We have to do something about it. Make amends. Get back on track. Regain our inner sense of right.

This inner feeling is so very important. It will guide our kids when we're not around. It will ensure that their actions are dictated from within and not from outside. It will let them know when something is right and when something is wrong.

Of course, there are times when we think our kids have done something wrong, but they haven't.

Imagine a child dropping a glass of milk on the floor. Years ago, when one of my children did something like this, I'd yell: "How could you be so stupid? You should have taken more care. What a waste of milk! You'll have to clean up all the mess." Of course, my child would cry, and I imagine she felt very bad inside. That was the point. I wanted her to feel bad because I wanted her to remember to be more careful next time. I wanted her to be too afraid to drop another glass of milk.

Of course, dropping something on the floor is an accident. We all have accidents. We all do things unintentionally. Instead of blaming my child and making her feel bad, I should have got down on the floor and helped her clean up the mess. I should have said something like, "Hey, it's not a big deal. Anyone can have an accident." Perhaps I could have added that I drop things too.

And regardless of the situation, it's never necessary to make a child feel bad. If she really has done something wrong, she'll be aware of it. She knows what is right and what is wrong.

.

Developing a Sense of Right and Wrong

My young adult son Callum and I went to town to have some mother-son time. As we sipped coffee, we chatted.

"I've been keeping up with an interesting discussion online about spanking children," I said. "The big question is, how do you make children do what you want them to do without smacking them?"

Make kids do what we want them to do? There's something wrong with this question. It seems to be all about us.

"How do you teach kids the right thing to do and remain a gentle parent?" I continued. "I'm not a smacking mother. Except for that time when you were eight. Smacking didn't help."

I thought about that occasion when I smacked eight-year-old Callum. I can't remember what he'd done wrong, but I do remember how frustrated I'd felt. I lashed out at him, and my hand met solid-boy flesh and came away stinging. Callum didn't look repentant at all. My smack hadn't made him reconsider his behaviour, and so I felt even more frustrated.

Callum grinned as he remembered my futile effort to smack him. "Yes, it didn't work."

"Why didn't smacking work?" I asked.

"I was tougher than you. The smack hurt you more than me. It didn't convince me I needed to change my behaviour. Children are clever. If they can avoid punishment, they will continue to do what is wrong as long as they don't get found out. Maybe children have to want to behave because it's the right thing to do and not because they might get caught and then smacked or punished in some other way."

"So children need to develop a sense of what is right and what is wrong and want to live by those standards?"

"Yes."

"But sometimes doing what is right isn't much fun at all. What makes children freely choose to do the right and necessary thing if there is no threat of punishment? Couldn't a child just say, "I refuse to do that and stand his ground?"

"He could, but if I'd have done that I'd have felt bad inside."

"You wouldn't have thought, 'Hey! She can't make me do anything I don't want to do' and enjoyed that powerful feeling?"

"No. It wasn't like that. Do you remember when we were fighting about whose turn it was to do the dishes and you came in and said you'd do them instead of us? We didn't go off thinking, "Hooray, Mum is going to do the dishes. We can go and play.' We felt bad, and all of a sudden, we wanted to do the dishes ourselves."

Callum thinks some more. "I guess it's a bit like how I feel now I'm working and don't have to do the regular chores because I'm not always here."

"I thought you'd like not having to do any jobs around the house."

"In one way it's good because I don't feel overloaded now that I'm working full time, but in another way, I no longer feel I belong. I get up in the morning and see the rest of the family working away together, and it doesn't feel right that I've nothing to do."

"Belonging. Yes. Maybe children need to feel they belong, that the family is a team, and they have a valued place in it?"

Callum agreed. "When children feel loved and valued and have a role within the family, they feel right inside. And they don't just want to be part of the good things in the family. They accept they have to work too and have to be considerate and think of others. It's all part of being a family. Children grow up, expecting to do all these things. It feels normal. It's all part of being on the team. When they misbehave or don't cooperate or pull their weight, they feel they have let the team down. It doesn't feel good."

We were silent for a moment, and then Callum added, "That unhappy feeling has to come from within. It can't result from a mother's reaction to the situation."

"So a mother can't withdraw her love because of misbehaviour?"

"No. Punishments and withdrawal of love can lead to resentment. It can spoil a relationship. You have to do what is right because it is right and not because you have to keep your mother happy. Actually, it feels even worse if you know you have done wrong, and your mother still loves you."

"A mother has to show unconditional love?"

"Yes."

As we finished our coffees, I tried to sum up what we'd been discussing: "A child needs to grow up feeling loved and part of the family. He accepts that a family means both working and having fun together. It's his safe place where he belongs and wants to be, and he will do what is necessary to keep his place in the family and to feel good about himself..."

"... and when he misbehaves, he knows he has let the team down, and he feels bad inside. He will be unhappy until he puts things right," finished Callum.

"So, you did learn to do what was necessary and right even though I didn't smack you?" I concluded.

Callum grinned. "Yes." Then he added, "Not that I'm always perfect."

No. None of us is perfect. We know what we should do, but sometimes we fall short. Children are the same. As long as we all try and do our best.

We were driving home, and I was still thinking about our conversation when I had a new idea. "Unconditional love. That's how God loves us. He doesn't withdraw His love for us when we sin, does He? Maybe because we know He always loves us regardless of our behaviour, we feel worse when we let Him down. We don't feel right inside. Do you think it's because of that great love we want to do what is right and necessary?"

"It could be," Callum agreed.

I think back to the big question I posed at the beginning of our discussion: how can a parent best influence a child's behaviour so that he does what is right and necessary? Perhaps it all comes down to love. A child needs to feel unconditionally loved and valued. He has to feel safe. He has to feel he belongs.

Somewhere to belong? Isn't that what we all need and want? Isn't that we are all searching for?

Can We Be Both Parent and Friend?

I'm scrolling through my Facebook feed when I see a link to a parenting video titled something like *Be a Parent and Not a Friend to Your Kids*. So being a curious person, I take a look. And after I've viewed the very popular video, I am again struck by how differently I think about parenting compared to the friend who shared the link and many other people.

Just for a moment, I wonder: are they right? Is it not possible to be both parent and friend? Perhaps I've got it all wrong. Surely, I need to do my parental duty and demand obedience from my kids? It's good for them. They need to respect me and do as I ask straight away, no questions asked. Yes, they'll be plenty of time to be friends with my kids when they've grown up. Right now, I need to be a parent.

Of course, I only turn these thoughts over in my mind for a very short time. But I'm guessing a lot of parents are watching this video and seriously considering the ideas presented by the vlogger. She's saying something they want to hear:

Parents take back the reins. Forget all this being friends stuff. Show some tough love. It doesn't matter if our kids protest and say such things as, "I don't like you!" Hey, parenting isn't a popularity contest. Take control. The battle is on, and we're going to win.

There was a time years ago when I just wanted my kids to obey me. I'd had enough of encouraging, bribing, threatening, explaining, begging, or turning everything into a game to get them to do what I thought was right. I was tired. I just wanted to shout, "I'm the parent, and you're the child. Just do what I say!"

Is there anything wrong with doing this? If we shout loud enough, perhaps our kids will actually do what we want. Maybe it's good for them to be obedient. They'd be showing respect to us and learning self-discipline at the same time, wouldn't they? Perhaps we'd be doing our kids a favour by training them.

Training them? Those words remind me of our puppy, Quinn. My daughter Gemma-Rose is training her. She demands obedience of the dog. She says, "Sit!" and Quinn lowers her back end, her velvet soft Shar-Pei skin puddling around her Great Dane bottom.

But do kids need the same kind of training as dogs? Instead of being obedient to our commands, surely it's better for them to choose to do what is right? And how will they ever learn to do that if we're always telling them what to do, no questions allowed?

Whenever we say such things as "Just do it!" or "I'm the parent!" or "I don't want to hear another word!" we close down the lines of communication between our children and us. We erect a barrier. We break all connections.

Why are connections so important? When we are connected with our kids, we are the most important people in their lives. They feel loved and respected. They trust us. When they need guidance, they look to us for our opinion. They come to us when they need help. And it's very likely that our connected kids will adopt our values and beliefs, the ones that we sometimes get so anxious about sharing with them.

Working on our connections might take a lot more effort than saying, "Do it, right this minute!" But surely it's worth it? Don't we all want to have strong bonds with our kids? It's these bonds which allow us to be both parent and friend.

Real friends accept us as we are. They don't criticise but instead encourage and support us. They like spending time with us and sharing our interests and involving us in theirs. They cheer us on. They make life fun. They listen when we need to talk and help us through the difficult times without taking over. We can open up and say anything to good friends. They respect us. They trust us.

Everyone needs a good friend. If we're not willing to be friends with our kids, they'll go looking for a friend elsewhere. Someone else will take the place that should be ours.

"Hey, Sophie, what do you think of this: 'We can be friends with our kids later when they've grown up'?"

"Parents can't suddenly turn around and tell their kids that they're now ready to be their friends," says my teenage daughter. "It doesn't work like that. And even if it was okay, think of all those lost years."

Yes, years we could have enjoyed being friends.

So can we be both parent and friend to our children? I know we can.

One-on-One Times

I got up early this morning. The house was quiet until our three cats, and one dog saw me. Meows and pitiful whines accompanied me to the kitchen. Apparently, our animals were on the edge of starvation. It's just as well, I appeared.

Once I'd tossed food into each pet bowl, I filled the kettle. As I waited for the water to boil, I heard a sound. Was my daughter Sophie up? Expecting her to appear at any moment, I placed her cup next to mine and made two cups of tea. I then carried them into the family room, where I curled up on the sofa to check my mail.

Some time later, I realised that Sophie hadn't appeared. Her cup of tea was getting cold. Had I made a mistake about her being up? Was she still in bed?

Two hours later: "What happened to you this morning, Sophie?"

"I was awake in the night because of my asthma. And then I slept in. I guess I was tired."

Sophie and I quite often spend time together early in the morning, while everyone else is still asleep. We sip tea and chat, sharing ideas, enjoying each other's company. I suppose we're having one-on-one time.

Is spending time with just one child important? I think so, especially when there are lots of children in the family. It's something I've always done. And when children leave home? And what if they're married? Even then, we still have our one-on-one times. They give us opportunities to stay connected.

My adult son Callum arrives in his super-charged car to take me to town to have coffee. We fly along the highway, and we're chatting even before we reach the cafe: "What do you think, Mum? Doesn't my engine sound good?"

Once we're settled at a table with our coffee in front of us, I say, "How's life, Callum? What have you been doing?" And soon my son is sharing the latest instalment in his story of hopes and dreams.

I missed chatting with Sophie this morning. But I can always talk with her while we walk the dog this afternoon. That's another good one-on-one time of day. As Nora charges along the bush tracks, her sniffy nose parallel to the ground, my 14-year-old daughter shares all her latest ideas. And I listen, adding a comment here and there.

We'll need our umbrellas for today's walk. It's raining again. I don't suppose Nora will want to go out in the wet. But once she's trotting along a muddy track and jumping over puddles, sniffing the delicious earthy damp air, she'll forget she wanted to stay at home.

Sophie and I won't even notice the rain. We'll be too busy talking. There's always so much to say.

Part IV: Rules

Rules Were Made to Be Broken

There's a common saying:

Rules were made to be broken.

Someone said it. Others repeated it. Everyone knows it.

So why do people think rules are the answer? There's something better than rules: radical unschooling.

What a Day Without Rules Looks Like

My children said, "Sleep in tomorrow, Mum. You're overtired. You haven't had much sleep in the last 48 hours." So I slept in.

When I got up, the kitchen was deserted. Everyone had had breakfast, washed the dishes, cleaned up, and disappeared. I found myself some cereal and made a cup of tea, and then went back to the warmth of my bed to enjoy my breakfast. Gemma-Rose (9) discovered me a short time later.

"Mum! You're awake. I was waiting for you to wake up so I could make you some porridge."

"Perhaps you can make some pikelets for morning tea instead," I suggested. My youngest daughter smiled.

When I'd showered and dressed, I went in search of everyone else. "What are you all doing?"

Sophie (12) smiled. "I've been educating myself. I've written a blog post about my sewing. Can I show you?"

The house was clean and tidy. There was even washing on the line.

"The basket wasn't quite full," said Charlotte (15), "but I decided to do some washing anyway. If I'd left it until tomorrow, the basket would have been overflowing."

I joined the younger girls in the family room, where we worked on our own projects for some time. Mid-morning Gemma-Rose made a batch of pikelets, and then everyone appeared to eat them. When we'd licked the last of the syrup-coated crumbs off our lips, we headed back to work.

"Shall we have lunch?" Imogen asked about 12.30 pm.

"Informal or at the table?"

"What do you think? Informal?"

"Yes. Sounds good."

Imogen and Charlotte collected the orders, and they made lunch. Everyone helped clean up afterwards. Then it was back to reading and writing and piano practices.

"Have we decided what we'll have for dinner?" asked Sophie mid-afternoon.

"I'll make potato and red pepper soup," I offered.

"No, you won't," said Imogen. "You're tired. I'll do it." I didn't protest.

When I noticed the shade overtaking the garden, I snuck outside and brought in the washing. Good thing someone was playing the piano, otherwise, the girls might have heard the pegs falling into the bucket, and I wouldn't have been allowed to do this job on my own.

Soon Imogen will start preparing the dinner. I will wash the afternoon tea dishes. Someone will set the table for dinner. Andy will arrive home from school. Callum might make it back from his day out in time to eat with us. If he doesn't, we'll put his dinner aside for him to eat later. Duncan will appear from his bedroom where he's been studying all day. We'll chat around the table, swapping news. Then everyone will help wash and dry the dishes by hand.

After dinner, the girls will play a computer game or watch a DVD or read a book. Perhaps we'll sit together in the family room and chat while we enjoy the warmth from the gas heater.

About 8.00 pm, Sophie will say, "We'd better get ready for bed," and then she and Gemma-Rose will head off to the bathroom.

I will say, "Do you want me to tuck you into bed now or do you want to read for a while?"

If the girls say, "We'd like to read," and then I don't arrive at the right time to turn off the light, Gemma-Rose will come looking for me. "We're tired. Can you come and say goodnight to us, please? We want to go to sleep." They like a proper kiss and hug before closing their eyes.

About 8.30 pm, Charlotte will appear saying she is tired and is going to bed. She might read before turning out the light. Imogen might join her, but then again she might stay up chatting to Andy, or they could watch a DVD together. I have no idea when the boys will go to bed because I will have headed off to my bed long before they start to think about sleep.

Our day looks very ordinary, doesn't it? We completed the chores. Everyone was helpful and considerate. We all worked and ate meals together. We made a few quick decisions that were mutually acceptable. The girls will go to bed at a reasonable hour. So will I. Nothing interesting at all about our day. Just a quiet, peaceful day.

A day without rules? It's not as exciting or as wild as it sounds. Or maybe it is. It depends on how we look at it. Each day everyone is willing to work together and to help each other so that life runs smoothly and is productive. And we do this without the help of rules. I think that's rather exciting after all. Maybe you think so too!

Rules and Radical Unschooling

If you google the word 'unschooling', it won't take you very long to find someone criticising unschoolers. The most judged unschoolers are those who have adopted a radical way of life: those who do not force a set of rules and regulations upon their children, in the area of parenting, as well as education. The critics are quick to point out that, without parental control and rules, children will go off and do whatever they want without regard to anyone else. They will run wild and be inconsiderate, lazy and selfish. They won't learn right from wrong.

What about my unschooling children? Are they wild and undisciplined? Maybe not, but you're not radical unschoolers, you might say. You limit your unschooling to educational matters and are sure to impose limits and rules upon your children to ensure they are well brought up. You are parenting responsibly. At one point in time, I might have agreed.

When my first daughter was young, we had lots of rules and regulations. I wanted to train my children well. I considered it my duty. It wasn't long before I discovered something very interesting about rules: they result in children and parents fighting for power. It was such hard work staying in control. The result wasn't a well-disciplined child who accepted my rules because she saw that they were in her best interests. Instead, she longed to rebel but couldn't because I was the parent and she was the child, and if she did decide to ignore my rules, she knew I'd punish her.

But somewhere along the way, our parenting changed. Like our homeschooling, we knew things weren't right and gradually, and naturally, rules and power struggles fell by the wayside. The result? Wild selfish children? No, we have hard-working, well-balanced, considerate children who know right from wrong.

We have no rules about such things as TV, computer use, bedtimes, dress codes, and attending church. We do have a radical chore roster, but it belongs to my children, and it has nothing to do with me.

Despite not having clearly set out rules, our children don't watch much TV. They enjoy a DVD here and there. They each have a computer which they use every day, but they don't spend excessive time in front of their screens. They play computer games whenever they feel like it, which isn't that often. They dress appropriately. We've never had even one battle about what they want to wear. They all choose to go to bed at a reasonable time that they have decided is appropriate for their needs. Without fail and without complaining, they contribute to the upkeep of our home. They always come to Mass with us and turn up for morning prayers. Even the issue of appropriate books and movies doesn't seem to be a problem.

I ask my children a few questions:

"Would you ever consider not doing your chores?"

"No, because the house would soon become a mess. I wouldn't want to live like that."

"You might think it's my job to do all the work as I'm the mother."

"The mess belongs to all of us."

"But no one's forcing you to work."

"It wouldn't feel right not to work. We all have to do things we don't particularly enjoy doing."

"You are choosing to do your chores?"

"Yes."

I think that choosing to do what is right is much better than being forced into doing it. Motivation comes from within and so will remain even when parents aren't physically present with the threat of punishment.

So it seems to me that children can learn to be considerate and know right from wrong without imposing rules and punishments. But how do they learn? Could it have something to do with modelling the values, beliefs and practices we want to pass on to our children? Could it involve showing respect to all? Maybe it's about regarding everyone as valued members of the family team, about listening, about acknowledging everyone's needs and responding to them with love and not punishment? Might it be about building up children's inner sense of 'right' feeling? Is it about parenting gently, attachment parenting, maybe?

I used to hear the word 'radical' and recoil. I listened to such words as 'neglectful', 'lazy', 'allowed to do whatever they want' and 'wild' and I didn't want to know. But somewhere along the way, I started pondering new ideas.

I discovered that, contrary to popular belief, radical unschoolers do not practise hands-off parenting at all. They have well-adjusted and well-parented children. The critics are wrong.

That is quite a radical thought.

Principles Instead of Rules

We all know what rules are. Life is full of them. Most families have many rules by which their children must live, such as:

"You are allowed to play on the computer or watch TV for x hours (or minutes) each day.

"You must eat everything on your plate."

"You must never call anyone an unkind name."

"Hitting is not allowed."

"You must do your chores."

"You must be in bed by..."

"You must complete your school work before going out to play."

"Never exclude anyone from your games."

We can modify the rules. We can increase the number of rules. The list of rules could be endless.

Some people might say that family rules are essential because they ensure a child knows what is right and avoids what is wrong, and so he will act appropriately. If a child breaks the rules, he will have to face the consequences, which might include punishment.

"My children know what the rules are. They know what will happen if they break them. It's not always easy, but I have to be consistent and follow through with punishments so that I can teach them what is right and what is wrong."

But do rules teach children right from wrong? Or do they teach children how to avoid punishment? Could it be that the motivation to behave a certain way is coming from outside a child and not from within? Maybe we impose rules on our children because we don't trust them to behave in a way we feel is appropriate, without us controlling their actions. Perhaps we think rules are the only way.

But what if a family decides to live by certain principles instead of rules? Everyone could decide that principles such as kindness, safety, consideration, honesty, and respect are important. If a child is kind, then she will not name call or hit a sibling or tease mercilessly or ignore someone in need. If a child is considerate, he will not play loud music late at night when others are trying to sleep or leave a mess for someone else to clean up or arrive late without a valid reason. With principles, rules are unnecessary.

But how do we encourage our children to adopt such principles?

Does it begin with parents? Is it essential that we put principles into action? I can't just say, "Be kind," or "It's important to be considerate," or "Show love towards your siblings," or "Be forgiving." My children need to see me doing all these things.

I used to think I actively lived the principles I wanted my children to adopt. Then I listened carefully to myself.

"How did you manage to do that? You're so clumsy! You should have taken more care."

"You don't like the taste? Don't be silly! There's nothing wrong with it."

"I don't want to hear any more about it. Be quiet!"

"If you don't finish that work, I'm going to send you to school!"

"In a minute... In a minute... I'm busy!"

"It doesn't matter if you aren't interested in it. You have to do it."

At times, I could be unkind, mean, insensitive, inconsiderate and not show respect and love towards my children. I made excuses for myself. Parenting is hard and tiring, and children don't listen. Or do they? I think they listen very carefully to us and adopt our standards, whether they are good or bad.

So if we act towards our children as we want them to act towards others, they will adopt our principles. Could it be that easy? Or perhaps it isn't that easy at all. Doing what is right can be very difficult. But still, I try. Not only as an example for my children but also because it's the better thing to do.

Guiding My Children Without Rules

We don't make rules in our family, so how do my children know what is right and what is wrong, if there are no clearly stated limits to guide them? Do I believe that my own quiet example of appropriate behaviour is sufficient to influence my children? Perhaps I stand back, hands-off, and let my children behave as they choose?

I decide to ponder a few ideas with my children, in an attempt to find the answers to these questions.

"Should I correct you if I feel your behaviour is wrong?" I ask.

"Oh yes," replies my second daughter Imogen. "Children need guidance from their parents. You can't just let us do whatever we want. We'd grow up to be very self-centred. And we wouldn't know what constitutes appropriate behaviour when it comes to relating to people."

"Should we have rules so that you all know what is acceptable and what is not, or is there another way?"

"Rules aren't the answer. They can be broken, and parents and children end up fighting over them in a power struggle. I like how you do things better."

I ask Imogen to explain. "You take us quietly aside and chat about things as equals. I know we're not equal in experience. You're the parent, and we're your children, but it feels like we're talking on the same level. You don't lord it over us, talking down to us. You don't make us feel small."

When I observe one of my children having a hard time acting appropriately or upset over something, I do try to spend some quiet time with her or him. I try not to make accusations but rather endeavour to show empathy:

"You don't feel like your older sister is listening to you?"

"You're feeling frustrated with the younger kids?"

"You don't feel like smiling?"

Showing empathy usually gives my children an opening to share how they're feeling. They can talk about the issues they're finding difficult. We ponder the situation together and sometimes chatting is enough. If it's not, we usually come up with some suggestions together for dealing with the problem. Often I share my own experiences too. I'm certainly not perfect, so I can talk about my own struggles.

"What if you want to do something I'm not happy about?" I ask Imogen.

"Like what?" she asks.

"Well, what if you want to go out with friends and stay out to the early hours of the morning, and I'm worried about you doing this?"

Imogen smiles. I smile too. This sounds like a very improbable scenario. "Just pretend," I say, before adding, "Should I intervene or just let you do what you like?"

"You should tell me how you feel and share your reasons for not wanting me to do that, and I'd listen," Imogen says.

"But why should you listen?"

"Because I respect your opinion. I trust you because you always trust and respect me."

Twelve-year-old Sophie has been listening intently to this conversation. Now she says, "You always listen to me. You always want to hear my side of the story, so I would listen to you too."

Now, of course, if I saw my children fighting and someone was in danger of being hurt, I wouldn't wait for a quiet moment to sort things out. That would be silly. I'd separate my children immediately and deal with the problem there and then, listening to both parties.

And if a child were about to do something dangerous or destructive, again it wouldn't make sense to say, "When you're finished, would you mind meeting me for a little chat?"

There are other situations where one-on-one conferences are not the answer. Sometimes all that's needed are a few words of empathy, a reminder, even eye-to-eye contact.

"Tired? Finding it hard to cope?"

"Is that mud on your shoes?"

"Gentle..."

As I am writing this story, my young adult son Callum arrives home. Perhaps he has something extra to add.

"I'm writing about rules," I say.

"Rules don't work. Children need boundaries."

"But how can you have boundaries without rules?"

"I don't mean boundaries enforced by external rules. I mean self-imposed boundaries," explains Callum. "The incentive not to step over the line and do what is wrong must come from within a child."

"And what makes a child want to stay within those limits?"

Then Callum mentions trust and respect and love and example, all very powerful motivators for influencing a child to do what is right.

Can parents bring up well-adjusted children who know right from wrong without rules? I believe they can.

The Jeans Wearing Rule

I have seen a few articles online that have titles such as *Rules for Modest Dressing*. The rules consist of a comprehensive list of dos and don'ts aimed at teenage daughters in particular. I'm sure parents write lists of rules because they care. Many people agree. The number of congratulatory comments for such posts is enormous: *You care, so you make rules. I admire that!*

I used to have a set of similar dress rules for my daughters. Well, the rules really only applied to my eldest daughter Felicity as she is seven years older than my second daughter Imogen. Dress codes don't seem to affect little girls as much as teenage ones.

I decided that jeans were not appropriate dress and so I wouldn't let Felicity wear them. I told her my reasons: they were immodest and unfeminine. She was a girl. Therefore she couldn't wear pants. Nice and simple. No arguments allowed.

Actually, I wasn't entirely truthful. The reason I didn't want Felicity to wear jeans was that none of my friends let their daughters wear them. I wanted to be accepted by these women, and so I adopted their standards. I let myself be swayed by others' opinions – adult peer pressure- but when I thought about it, they were right, weren't they?

Felicity did not think I was right. I spent a lot of time trying to make her abide by the rules, rules she couldn't see the value of. We can make rules, but we also need to police them, and that can involve a lot of time and energy and conflict. And rules can lead to deception and loss of trust. I have heard of young girls changing into their jeans when away from home, hoping their mothers will never find out.

But rules are worth the trouble. We make them in the best interest of our children. We need to guide them in what is right and what is wrong. A parent has to be strong enough to make unpopular decisions and stand by them.

Or does she? I suppose it depends on whether the reason behind the rule is valid. And are rules the only way of ensuring our children act appropriately?

When I was a teenager and young mother, I wore jeans all the time. Are they immodest? I guess it depends on the cut. Some jeans are perfectly modest. Are they unfeminine? I don't think they are as feminine as a pretty skirt. Is it a crime to be unfeminine? I don't suppose it is. Is the issue of jeans worth fighting over? No.

I haven't worn jeans for a very long time. These days I am a skirt girl. I like the soft feel of them and the comfort. I always felt rather restricted inside my stiff denim jeans. And yes, I do like to feel feminine.

Do I want my girls to be feminine? I suppose I do. But they have free choice in the matter. I can't force my preferences on them. I don't have the right to control them. To me, jeans-wearing is not an issue worthy of a rule. It's not like it has been written into the Code of Canon Law or anything. And it's not as if skirt-wearing makes us better people.

So we have no rules about jeans. Actually, we have no rules about modesty either. I have never seen the need to write any. (Dare I confess I don't make rules about anything?) All children, boys included, have always dressed modestly. Why make rules? Instead, we have always talked about dressing appropriately:

"Do you think this skirt is good enough for Mass?"

"You might feel more comfortable in cargo pants. You'll be climbing off and on equipment all day."

"Have you seen my shorts? I need them for running."

"I want to look special. It's an important occasion."

"I need to find my board shorts. I don't feel right wearing my swimmers without them."

So what do my girls choose to wear? The daughter who was not allowed to wear jeans prefers jeans (as far as I know). The girls who never experienced 'the jeans rule' wear skirts. They won't go anywhere near a pair of jeans.

Isn't that funny?

The other day a friend gave me a bag of odds and ends that she thought might come in handy for the younger girls. Included in the bag was a pair of jeans.

"Hey, Sophie! These might fit you," I said, handing the jeans to my twelve-year-old daughter.

"But Mum! They're jeans. I hate jeans," said Sophie screwing up her face.

"Just try them on," I encouraged. "You never know when a pair of jeans might come in handy."

Sophie went off to her bedroom, obviously under protest, trailing the jeans behind her. A few minutes later, she appeared with jeans-clad legs and a tortured look on her face.

"They fit perfectly!" I smiled.

"I hate them!"

I guess there's no rule that says a girl has to wear jeans.

These days many of my girls' friends wear jeans. My daughters don't. They are the odd ones out.

"Wouldn't you like to dress like everyone else?" I ask.

"No! Not if it means wearing jeans," four feminine voices reply.

There are probably people who look at my daughters and feel sorry for them. Poor girls! Their mother insists on being old fashioned and doesn't allow them to wear jeans! Others might congratulate me on being a caring mother who insists on her girls dressing as girls.

The truth of the matter is my daughters love wearing skirts, and I see no reason to dissuade them from their preference. As I said, I'm a skirt girl too.

Would Felicity have been a skirt girl as well if I hadn't made any dress rules? What if I hadn't banned jeans? Can rules push children in the direction that we don't want them to go? Not that it matters. I love all my five daughters, whatever they choose to wear.

Imogen walks by, and I say, "Would you like to read my latest story?"

When she finishes reading, I'm struck by a funny thought: "Do you realise that I've written a defence for jeans-wearing, and none of you wears jeans?" We laugh.

"You should have written a story about how jeans-wearing is wrong," says Imogen. "You could have pointed at your daughters: they know they have to follow the rules!" We laugh again.

It's good to laugh. Why fight over something that isn't very important?

I wrote *The Jeans Wearing Rule* a few years ago. Since then, my girls have started wearing jeans. They're part of the uniform of the cafes where they work. My daughters discovered that jeans aren't quite as uncomfortable as they thought.

And we've all discovered jeggings which are a different version of traditional jeans.

These days, everyone wears skirts, dresses, jeans, jeggings and tunics depending on the occasion and how we feel.

Our tastes in fashion have changed. I guess they might keep changing. But there's one thing that will always remain the same: our opinion about rules. We don't need them!

Part V: Trust

All About Trust

What is trust? I looked the word up in a dictionary:

Trust is the firm belief in the reliability, truth, or ability of someone or something.

Maybe, with people, it's about predicting with confidence what they are going to do, say or think. Is it important that the result of trust is positive? We might predict a person will make the wrong decision, but we don't trust them.

Trust isn't something that just happens. We can't say, "I trust you" to our kids and then walk away and expect them to act in the right manner. We have to base our trust on something. It can't be blind.

Trust is only possible because of knowledge. We can't trust someone or something we don't know. We can't trust our children if we don't know them well. We can't trust unschooling until we know a lot about it and understand how it works.

We might already think we know our kids very well, but perhaps we don't. Maybe we don't give them a chance to express their opinions. We might talk at them rather than listen to them. Do we correct them instead of accepting their views? Could we have preconceived ideas about who we want our children to be and not see who they actually are?

If we build up strong bonds between us, we'll be closely connected. Then we'll know our children, and we'll find it easier to trust them. Strong connections enable us to guide our kids. We are the most important people in their lives. They will be inclined to listen to us - just like we listen to them - because they trust us.

Becoming trustworthy doesn't happen overnight. Kids will make mistakes. But this is okay. We should give them the freedom to make choices without fear of retribution if they do happen to fail. Failure doesn't mean we should tighten up control: "See what happens when I trust you? I told you I couldn't trust you." Kids need opportunities to try, fail and learn in a safe environment. Becoming trustworthy involves a lot of time and experience. We have to trust our children will get there in the end.

If we don't trust our kids while they are at home with us, they won't get a chance to use their freedom while they still have us to guide them. When the time comes for them to head out into the bigger world, they'll be ill-equipped to make decisions on their own.

Perhaps keeping our kids safe is so important that we are scared to give them the freedom they need. Instead, we hold on tightly to them. Maybe we worry that if something happens to our children or if they make mistakes and get themselves into trouble, it'll be our fault. We should have controlled them better. This is the responsible thing for a parent to do.

But will controlling our kids keep them safe? Or does it encourage them to rebel as soon as they can? It can be frustrating never having a say in what we do. Even though a parent's intentions are good, controlling kids can backfire. It can push them in the direction that we don't want them to go.

Or instead of rebelling, will overprotected kids doubt their ability to make decisions or to act appropriately or to try new things? Will they be unable to stand confidently on their own two feet?

What would we like our kids to do when we trust them? Perhaps we shouldn't want them to do anything in particular. Instead, we should trust that they are good people who are capable of making the right decisions appropriately. It's not about trusting our kids to follow our directions: "You have to be home by 11 pm." The right choice might be different at different times. Kids need to develop the ability to assess the situation and make the best decision.

When kids are trusted, they want to live up to that trust. It spurs them on to become better people. Kids might be imperfect, but they have good intentions (just like parents). Why do we assume they will automatically choose to do the wrong thing if they have the choice? Children are sometimes more capable than we'd like to believe. And why shouldn't they be? Do we doubt our ability to pass on our values and the knowledge and experiences that are necessary for them to become trustworthy?

When we don't trust, we inflict hurt and pain on our children. It doesn't feel good not to be trusted, especially when we feel we are indeed trustworthy.

Do we say thoughtless things that get in the way of trust? Do the words fall from our mouths inflicting damage without us realising? We could get into the habit of always telling our kids what to think or say or do when we should just trust that they will do the right thing: "While we are at the Jones' house, remember to be polite and offer to help and share the toys." Our kids shouldn't have to ask, "Don't you trust us?" We should have confidence in them.

Perhaps there are times when we aren't honest with our kids or even ourselves because we don't want to get into a situation where we might have to trust. We avoid opportunities to trust: "There's no need for you to cycle down to the shops for me. I need to get out of the house after working on the computer all morning, so I'll go myself."

Does our reluctance to trust have its roots in our childhoods? Perhaps we were never trusted. Did we learn we couldn't be trusted?

Trust should be mutual. It's necessary, not only for us to trust our kids but for them to trust us. Do we have to earn that trust? Are we trustworthy, or do we chop and change and confuse our children? Are we unreliable?

When we're unschooling, do we try and sneak knowledge into our children instead of trusting they'll pick it up for themselves when they're ready? Perhaps when our kids ask us a question, we see our opportunity and give them more than they want or need. Perhaps we use subtle means to test them.

Parents seem to have the most trouble trusting teenagers. Trusting doesn't begin when our kids get older. We have to start when they are small. It's a gradual learning process for both parent and child. If we control our small kids, it'll be very hard for us to trust them when they get to the teenage years. We need to work on our connections right from the start.

If we find it hard to trust, we could think about the consequences of not trusting. Do we really want to live a life of control? That will be stressful. When we don't trust, we become suspicious. How do we know what our kids are doing when we're not around? Will we snoop on them? Is that respectful? We could keep our kids close and not allow them to do anything away from home. But doing that will limit their experiences and their opportunities to grow. We'll prevent them from enjoying the wonders of the bigger world. They won't be able to develop and grow and acquire the skills that they will need to live happy, successful, independent lives.

Can we trust unschooling? Do we have a firm belief in it? Will our unschooled kids really become the people they are meant to be? Will they learn all they need to know? To gain confidence, we need to understand unschooling. We can read about it and ponder it. We can learn from other people's experiences. Perhaps it's even better to observe our own kids and how they learn best. Talk to them about the things that are important to them and what they'd like to do. Respect their opinions and interests and who they are as people. As well, we can look at our childhoods honestly and openly. We have to be prepared to question what we experienced. Do we want the same things for our children? Or do we want something better?

Is there another dimension to trust? Does it extend beyond us? If we have a faith, we have to trust in God. Perhaps unschooling is something that He wants us to do.

I believe in my kids. I believe in unschooling. Unschooling is what we are meant to be doing. So I trust. Do you?

Trusting Dogs and Kids

We look up from our cameras to see two lean and muscular dogs racing towards us. They grin and circle us before disappearing along the bush track. A tall man appears. He pushes his long curly hair behind his ears as he says, "Good morning! You're up early."

We nod. "It's a beautiful morning," we say as we look out over the river. "It was worth getting up early to see the sunrise."

There's a mist hovering above the water. The river bank sparkles with frost.

Our eyes dart quickly towards the man's long legs. They stretch out of his three-quarter length cargo pants. His pale bare toes are visible in his brown leather sandals. And despite our many layers of clothing, we shiver.

"The light is magnificent," we say. The man looks at our cameras. Perhaps he thinks we're taking photos of the sun rising over the river. But we're not. We're filming a music video.

While we chat, a third dog appears from between the trees. This dog is stout. It trots towards its owner. Soon the man and his dog continue along the track. "Enjoy your walk," we say.

When the man is out of sight, I ask, "How will that fat dog keep up with the other ones? Did you see how short its legs are?" We giggle as we turn back to our cameras.

Twenty minutes later, the fat dog ambles past us once again. Its roly-poly body almost brushes the dirt track as it retraces its footsteps. Nose to the ground, it disappears out of sight.

The sun rises higher in the sky. The man strides back towards us with his lean dogs bouncing along by his side.

"We saw your other dog," we say.

"He was heading back to my car," the man tells us. "He knows how far he's capable of walking."

The dog is an unschooler! His owner trusts him. The dog decides how far he can walk. When he's reached his limit, he turns around and heads for home. The dog is quite capable of making a good decision.

If a man can trust a dog, surely we can trust our kids?

Children know when they're tired or hungry or cold. They know what interests them and what they need to know and when they need to know it. We don't have to make their decisions for them.

We can trust our kids. It seems some people also trust their dogs.

Time and Trust

It's 6.15 am. We're walking down the road to the park: one mother, four girls and two dogs. We're the Team. We're going to run through the bush.

As I look at my daughters, my heart feels warm. It's good to see the Team reunited. I can't remember the last time we all ran together. One by one, my daughters disappeared until it was only Gemma-Rose and me, and of course, our dog Nora, who headed out each morning.

I run my usual route along the main fire trail, up and down the hills, around the bends and through the trees. Now and then, I pass a daughter travelling her route. We smile at each other and raise our thumbs in the air. It's like the old days. Yes, it's almost as if we've gone back in time. I feel like I've received a huge unexpected gift.

Time moves so quickly. Girls grow. They get busy. They go to work and do other things. And our days change.

Sometimes I wish I could make life stand still. I want to run through the bush every morning with all my daughters, day after day after day. I want to experience today's joys forever and not move forward. But I know time will march on regardless of my desires. A day disappears and then another. Days form weeks and weeks assemble themselves into months. And then one day, I realise that another year has gone, never to be seen again.

I used to worry about time passing so quickly. Not because I wanted to keep our running team intact, but for a reason that used to seem important: how was I going to teach my kids everything they needed to know? I only had a limited number of years to do this, and we flew through those years never accomplishing everything on my must-learn list.

These days, I'm still aware of time. However, knowing how fast it can seem to disappear makes me want to spend our days doing all the truly important things with my kids. We don't rush from one thing to another. I'm not cramming knowledge into my children's heads in an anxious kind of way. I refuse to waste a moment battling. Instead, we talk and listen and learn, love and run and enjoy our unschooling days together. I sometimes describe our unschooling days as living in the moment. We soak up the joy of each day, and I don't worry. I trust my children are becoming the people they are meant to be. They'll be okay. They'll get where they are meant to go.

Knowing that I can't make time stand still, I savour each day, soaking up all the available joys. And because I've extracted all I can, I feel able to let go of each day and move on.

Deep down, I know I don't really want to control time. You see, I've discovered that change isn't something we should fear. Instead of fighting it, I try to accept it. I know that life will always be okay even if it's different. We have to let go of some things so that we can embrace others. There are always delights to enjoy and adventures to follow in every season of life.

Our run comes to an end. One mother, four girls and two dogs are hot and tired. But we're happy. We feel satisfied. We've worked hard and exercised our bodies while running through the beautiful Australian bush with the people we love best. I raise my hand and high-five girl after girl. "Well done, Team!" I smile. "Time for breakfast." Words from another time. Will I get to say them again? For just a moment, my heart skips a beat. The blue sky disappears as clouds appear. And then the sun returns.

Haven't I enjoyed every stage of my children's lives? Aren't I enjoying things today that I wasn't experiencing last year? Why shouldn't there be new delights ahead of us? It'll be okay. All I have to do is trust.

When Unschooling Doesn't Appear to Be Working

We decide to unschool. Everything is going very well. Our kids are learning, and our family bonds are strengthening. Life is full of joy.

Then one day, things change. Something happens. Maybe a child makes a mistake. She could choose to go her own way. Do something we're not happy about. We begin to doubt unschooling. We wonder if we've made a mistake. Maybe the critics are right: *You should have kept tight control over your kids!* We feel like we've failed.

We hear a lot of positive things from unschoolers. I suppose that's because most parents don't mind sharing the good stories. But I'm sure, despite all the amazing things that happen, no unschooling family's life is perfect in every detail.

Our family has certainly had some difficult times. And those times have seemed even worse because I'm a blogger. I've thought: *what if my readers find out that my kids aren't perfect, that they've made mistakes? Maybe I shouldn't write about unschooling. I might be leading people astray.* So I've wanted to delete my blog and run away. Become an ex-unschooling blogger. Become an ex-unschooling family. Yes, I've questioned unschooling.

But we're still here.

While pondering the difficulties, I have always returned to the idea that we have to do what is right, and I'm sure unschooling is the right thing to do. It's the way we are meant to live. We have to respect our kids and love them unconditionally and not control them but instead trust. We don't have a choice.

And so even if a child goes astray, makes a mistake, does something that we're upset about, we must keep unschooling. We can't change course, choose another pathway. We must trust that, despite appearances, things will be okay.

Trust is a strange thing. It's easy to trust when things are going just as we want: *as long as my children choose to do what I'd like, I'm happy to let go and trust that they'll be okay*. But can we trust when kids don't act according to our plan? Would we rather forget all about trust and grab back control?

So things don't go to plan, but despite our misgivings, we decide to trust. Who knows? One day, things might fall into place. I know about this. I know how it feels. It's very special.

Yes, it's a fantastic moment when our children decide for themselves that they're going to live by the values that are important to us. They return stronger and more committed than before.

Children can make mistakes, whether they are unschooling or not. But I think unschooling helps children get back on track.

We have to keep listening, respecting, and loving unconditionally. We have to keep the lines of communication open. Regardless of what our kids do, we can't risk severing or even loosening the bonds between us. It's those bonds that will draw our children back.

There are times when unschooling doesn't appear to be working. What do we do? Perhaps we need to stay strong, continue to unschool, and trust. I'm not saying it will be easy. But isn't it the right thing to do?

The Wobbly Moments of Life

The doorbell rings. Our puppy, Quinn barks. I look at my daughters, and they look at me.

"Who can that be?" I wonder.

"The postman?"

"A courier?"

"Someone who's lost?"

"We could answer the door and find out," suggests Charlotte. But she doesn't move. No one moves.

The doorbell rings again. And then Imogen sighs and says, "I'll go." She slowly uncurls herself from the sofa. She pads barefoot down the tiled hall. A growling Quinn follows close behind.

A moment later: "It's okay! It's only Amina!"

We all breathe a sigh of relief. Amina's almost family. No need to move into guest mode. We can continue being us.

"How nice to see you, Amina. Want some coffee?" I smile over the edge of my laptop.

Amina ignores my coffee question. She doesn't return my smile. She doesn't even sit down. Instead, she plants herself in front of me and gets right down to business. "What's going on?" She points her finger at my computer. "Your blog has disappeared!"

"No, it hasn't," I protest. "It's still there. You just can't see it."

"And why can't I see it?" Amina demands.

I utter a few disjointed words in a pathetic kind of way before Amina takes pity on me. She says, "You're having a wobbly moment, aren't you? You're questioning all you're doing," Her voice has softened. "Wondering if you should delete your blog? Why should anyone listen to you? It's not as if your family is perfect? So what gives you the right to write about unschooling? It's safer to delete your blog. No one will miss it. They won't even notice it's gone. Am I right?"

I nod my head before mumbling, "I know, I know, same old story."

Amina waves my words away. "Do you want to know what I think?" She rushes on without waiting for an answer. "Why should anyone listen to you? Because you have an important message to share. People need to know about unschooling. Life isn't perfect, but unschooling is the perfect way of life. Isn't that what you're always telling everyone? Well, it's true. Unschooling leads to a life full of love and joy. People need to hear that. You don't want to keep something so amazing to yourself, do you?" I shake my head as she continues, "No one will miss your blog? I missed it."

Amina raises her finger again and points it at my laptop. I reach for my mouse and click it a few times before saying, "It's back!" Amina smiles.

Amina is right. I can share my stories even if our life isn't perfect.

"Unschooling isn't a magic solution," I say. "It's life and life can be difficult."

I think about how it's the hard times that deepen our trust. We question, mull things over, and then we pick ourselves back up and go forward again, stronger than before, trusting we are on the right pathway. Trust isn't worth much if we are only willing to trust when life is good. Things always work out which is just as well because when I look around at the alternatives, I realise we don't have anywhere else to go.

Amina's voice cuts into my thoughts. "Did you say something about coffee?" she asks.

Do you ever have wobbly moments, times when you doubt what you're doing? And do you have a friend like Amina who encourages you, boosts your confidence, and gets you back on track?

If you do, your friend is probably real. Unlike Amina. I had to make her up. You see, we don't have any friends because we're introverted weird unsociable unschoolers who don't even like answering our own front door.

The Risky Business of Trusting Children

Trusting children to make their own choices sounds risky enough when it applies only to education, but what if you extend this trust to other areas of life? Will children decide they don't want to do the things you think are important such as going to church or eating healthy food? What if they want to watch inappropriate movies or play computer games all day? Some parents decide they can't pass control over to their children because it would be irresponsible. They wouldn't be fulfilling their duty of protecting and caring for their children. At first glance, this might all seem very true.

But I wonder: why would children choose to do things parents feel are not appropriate? Can the way we parent influence the choices a child makes? Is it possible to give a child the freedom to choose but at the same time be confident they will make the right choices? I think we can. If I didn't, I would keep firm control over my children at all times, because I regard myself as a responsible parent.

Trust.

I ask Charlotte what it feels like not to be trusted.

"I don't know," she says. "You always trust me."

"I don't think it would be very nice," says Sophie. "I've read books about children who aren't trusted."

"Why do parents think the worst of their children?" asks Imogen. "Why do they assume they will always do the wrong thing if they have the choice? Aren't they confident they have given them the skills to make good choices?"

Maybe there are misconceptions about unschooling. Unschooling parenting isn't hands-off. Children aren't thrust out into the world and told to find out everything for themselves. They don't have to decide what is right and what is wrong without any input from their parents.

Children are brought up within a family. They observe their parents and learn from their example. If they feel secure and respected and valued and are treated with love and kindness, why shouldn't children love and trust their parents and accept their values? Why shouldn't they make the right choices?

Of course, there are some things that aren't worth worrying about. A child has the right to choose what she wears each day and what and how much she eats. She knows how much sleep she requires and whether she needs a cardigan or not. Maybe little children require some help in determining their needs and how to fulfil them, but we can offer it gently, without taking over. We can guide rather than control until we are no longer needed. I wonder if we tend to want to have a say long after that time has arrived.

I think children can recognise when they need us.

"Girls, I've just thought of something else. What if you came to me and said you want to leave home. Should I let you? Should I trust you to know what you need?"

"Mum, don't be silly! We're not ready to leave home. We know that. We still need you."

"I guess there might be some children who can't wait to leave home because they feel their parents exert too much control over them," someone adds.

That makes me wonder: do some parents inadvertently push their children into making the wrong choices by never trusting them? If we hold too tightly out of fear, don't we run the risk our children will rebel? We will lose them, despite our best attempts to protect and look after them.

So is it risky trusting children, giving them the freedom to choose? I will speak for my unschooled children. I don't believe it is.

And just in case anyone is wondering, I no longer have babies and toddlers, but if I did, I wouldn't let them play in the street even if that's what they wanted to do. That would be irresponsible.

But I would let them eat whenever they were hungry, and sleep with me and carry them around if they didn't want to be alone.

Saying Yes

Do you ever say no to your kids because you're afraid to say yes? Perhaps you want to protect them from possibly dangerous situations. Maybe you don't want to put yourself through the agony of worrying about them.

I sometimes worry about my daughter, Gemma-Rose. She likes to run through the bush. We all do. But there are times when my daughter runs alone. And I wonder: what if she meets someone dangerous in the bush? What if she slips on the rocky, steep ground and breaks her leg?

When Gemma-Rose takes a dog or two with her into the bush, I am happier because she has some protection from strangers. Nora might grin at anyone she meets, but Quinn won't. She'll growl in a very off-putting way. So two dogs might deter anyone from harming my daughter. But what if a kangaroo suddenly appears on the track in front of Gemma-Rose? No doubt, the dogs will pull on their leashes and try to chase it. Will Gemma-Rose be able to keep hold of two strong dogs? Will she be able to dig in her heels and prevent them from pulling her along in their wake? Worse, will the dogs pull free and give chase? Will we never see them again?

My imagination goes wild.

I can think of a lot of reasons to prevent Gemma-Rose from going into the bush alone. When she announces she's off for a solo run or a walk with the dogs, I'm tempted to say, "Shall I come with you?" I want to add, "I need some exercise too." But I know that these are the wrong things to say. I'd be trying to deceive Gemma-Rose and even myself. I don't need a walk. I just don't want to trust my daughter's skills and judgement.

But am I foolish to trust? I think: how likely is it that something negative will happen? And if something did, Gemma-Rose does know what to do.

Gemma-Rose carries a phone. She knows she should turn around if she sees someone suspicious ahead of her on the bush tracks. She can run fast. And she assures me she can handle two dogs. I can't, but she can. That's important to remember.

Often we hold kids back because of our fears. We wonder how we'd feel if anything happened to them. We imagine every possible negative scenario. We want to say, "No, you can't do that." We don't want to place ourselves into situations where we might worry.

But are our fears justified? Are the dangers as big as we imagine? And are our kids equipped to deal with whatever might happen? Perhaps we can help our kids gain the skills they need to be independent. We can build up confidence. We can build up trust.

If we can move past our fears and give our kids the freedom they want and need, then they'll grow and develop into confident and adventurous people.

Gemma-Rose runs through the bush on her own. Or she roams along the trails with the dogs. And I don't suggest that this is something that she's not fully equipped to do because that's not true.

I'm choosing to say yes.

Part VI: Respect

Treating Kids With Respect

Years ago, when my husband Andy and I were young parents, we were friends with Harry and Martha, who had similar-aged children to ours. We'd meet regularly on Sunday afternoons, and while our kids played together, we'd sip wine and chat about all the things parents are interested in: our kids.

One day, we mulled over the topic of how we should talk to our children. How do we speak to them so that they'll do what we want?

Harry said, "It's no good asking in a polite tone of voice. Kids won't listen unless we show them who's in control."

Martha nodded, "Yes, we've got to show them who's the boss." Their actions matched their words. They barked orders at their daughters.

I ordered my children around too:

"Stay away from the TV."

"Don't touch!"

"Come here."

"Do this..."

"Do that..."

I had a niggling feeling that ordering kids around like this was wrong, but I continued yelling at mine. I called it training. By keeping up a constant stream of orders, I got my children to stay away from some things and not to touch others and to come to me instead of me going to them. (I wonder if my commands floated over our neighbours' fences.) And then one terrible day, I heard my words falling out of my daughter's mouth: "Go away!"

I sometimes tell our dog to go away: "Go away, Quinn!" I cry as she drools all over me.

My words never upset our puppy. She grins and ignores me. (It would be nice if she obeyed.) It might be okay for me to issue commands to a dog, but what about my children? They're not pets. They are people, just like me. Despite the differences in our ages, we're equal in value and dignity. And so we're all entitled to be treated with respect.

I realised that the way I was treating my children was unacceptable. I knew I had to make some changes. First, I rearranged our house. I made it a safe place for young children. There was no need for me to order them away from dangers. I'd removed them.

Instead of saying, "Don't touch!" I said, "Would you like to hold it?"

I stopped telling my children to come to me. I went to them.

Yes, I stopped ordering my kids around and started talking to them in a respectful way. I didn't just reframe my requests with friendly and polite words. I changed my whole behaviour. I treated my kids as I like people to treat me. It wasn't always easy, especially when I was tired. But it was the right thing to do.

By this time, we were no longer friends with Harry and Martha. We'd drifted apart. But if we'd still spent lazy Sunday afternoons together, sipping wine and talking about our favourite subject, they might have asked, "Do your kids still listen to you? Do they do as you want? Does respecting kids work? Is it worth the effort?"

And I might have thought: they're missing the point. For a long time, I'd missed it. Shouldn't we treat kids properly without expecting something in return? We shouldn't have an ulterior motive. Isn't it the right of every child to be treated with respect?

So how do we show children respect? Is respect about how we talk to them? And our willingness to listen properly and accept their opinions and choices and feelings? Perhaps we ought to adapt our world to suit them instead of insisting they cope with ours. Respect is about accepting that our kids know their needs better than us. And is it respectful to allow our kids to be who they are instead of trying to turn them into the people we think they should be?

In my mind, I answer Harry and Martha's question: "When we're respectful towards our kids, we don't have to order them around. They're willing to do what is right."

And isn't that better than having kids who obey?

When a Child Can't Cope

A few months ago, a family story made big news in a city newspaper.

A married couple decided to take their small son to a restaurant. It wasn't long before the young boy started to make a fuss. He wouldn't sit quietly in his chair and do what his parents wanted, and soon, he was the centre of attention. Fellow diners complained about the child's noise and behaviour, and the restaurant manager felt compelled to ask the family to leave. The parents were very upset. They felt they had the right to stay. They must have gone to the media with what they perceived to be a story of discrimination. When the story became public news, everyone was discussing the situation. Everyone had an opinion.

"The parents should have taken the child out of the restaurant. In fact, they shouldn't have brought him in the first place. People go out to dinner to relax and enjoy themselves. How can they do this when a child is screaming right next to them? The parents were inconsiderate of those around them."

But just as many people disagreed.

"Parents need to get out of the house and enjoy a meal like everyone else. Why shouldn't they be welcome in a restaurant with a child? Other people need to be more considerate of the needs of parents. They should be tolerant and not so concerned with themselves."

The parents. The fellow diners. Why was no one talking about the child? What were his needs? How was he feeling? Was he trying to tell everyone something by screaming?

This morning, a child cried at Mass. It's a familiar situation. You've probably heard all the discussion before. Everyone has an opinion.

"No one can hear a word when a child cries. The parents should remove her from the church. It's the considerate thing to do."

"Children should be made to feel welcome at Mass. Jesus said, 'Let the children come unto Me.'"

But what about the child? Was she saying, "I don't want to be here because I am too young to understand, and I haven't the patience to sit still for so long?"

I've heard some parents say, "It doesn't matter what the child wants. If she can't sit still, she must learn. If we remove her from the church every time she cries, she will only learn that crying gets her what she wants. She will become manipulative. She will never learn to sit quietly."

I wonder if that's true. I took all my children out of the church as soon as they became agitated. And what happened? Perhaps my children never learned to sit still. They probably never learned to love the Mass and pay attention.

I look along the line of children sitting in our pew. They are all quiet and attentive. Yes, I know that they are older. They should know how to behave at their ages. But it's been that way for many years.

Now you might say, "I kept my children in the church even when they protested, and they are all attentive and love the Mass just like your children do." I don't mean to criticise. I don't want to argue about the end result. All I'm saying is this: when a crying child is caught in a situation where she is unable to cope, it's quite okay to 'give in' to her crying and 'indulge' her needs.

I am sure children don't need to be forced to do anything. They will learn to do what is right and necessary when they are ready if we treat them with love and respect.

I remember:

I walk through the church door with Gemma-Rose in my arms. My daughter starts to squirm even before I have entered a pew. Just as I drop to my knees, she opens her mouth wide, and a loud cry hits my ear. I sigh as I gather up my toddler and make a hasty exit. The Mass hasn't even begun, and we are on our way back out the door.

I think: *she'll never learn to sit still if I keep taking her out.* But deep inside, I know that's not true. Today I'm just tired. I don't want to spend another hour looking at the daisies in the presbytery garden while listening to the Mass through the church window. I want to stay in the pew like everyone else. Today I'd like my child to sit quietly by my side. But I try to be patient because I know this phase of my child's life won't last forever.

And it didn't.

Years later, my kids are still sitting quietly in the church. They're still paying attention. And I wonder why. Could it have something to do with the fact that they have always regarded the church as a good place to be? They know they belong. It's somewhere they experience love.

Why I Am My Children's Number One Fan

"You have such good children!" says a woman as we come out of the church. My children smile. They glow with happiness. And then I spoil it all by saying rather hurriedly, "They're not always this good, you know!"

I feel uncomfortable, rather embarrassed. I want to brush off the woman's compliment. I swipe it away as quickly as possible. And then I notice I've also swiped the smiles off my children's faces. I have not only rejected the kind words, but I've also turned them around and used them against the people I love the most.

I can understand the need to be humble. None of us wants to look like we think we've got it all worked out, that we're perfect. Compliments are hard to accept. We may feel we don't deserve them. But is it my right to brush away a compliment that someone directed at my children?

I could justify diverting the words of praise. I might worry that they could make my children proud. I don't want my kids to feel they are special, do I? I want their feet planted firmly on the ground. They need to know they still have a lot of work to do. How else will they be motivated to strive for virtue?

I know this is a whole lot of nonsense. Criticism doesn't result in children trying harder. Well, it might seem to at first. But eventually, children give up: "I'll never be good enough." However, when we praise and encourage and love, children grow and grow.

I wonder how my kids feel when I downplay any praise by denying they're clever, beautiful, funny, helpful or sweet? Then I wonder how I would feel if my husband denied I was a good wife.

My husband is my greatest supporter. And that's what I need to be for my children. I have to be their number one fan.

"You have such good children!"

"Thank you!" I reply. "I'm very blessed to have them."

My children smile. They glow with happiness. And so do I.

Through the Eyes of a Child

"Do you want to watch a movie? We're having a boys' movie night."

A movie night? That sounds like a relaxing way to spend an evening. Someone grabs the popcorn, and someone else inserts the DVD into the player and then waves the remote control. The TV screen lights up. Three boys settle back and start munching and watching. The movie is good, the story involving, the tension is mounting.

And then someone waves the remote control once again at the DVD player, and the TV screen goes blank as the movie disappears.

"What's wrong? Where's the movie gone?"

"It's time for bed. We've all got to be up early tomorrow. We'll have to finish it another night."

"Another night? But I was enjoying the movie. Why do we have to go to bed?"

"If you stay up any later, you'll get overtired. The DVD will still be here tomorrow."

"Time for bed? We'll finish it another night?" There's a lot of mumbling going on.

My sons reluctantly drag themselves out of their chairs. Oops, that's not right! My husband Andy reluctantly drags himself out of his chair. He takes a last longing look at the TV and starts cleaning up. Our boys have already disappeared.

How times change.

And although Andy and I find the whole situation amusing, we also learn something:

Sometimes it must be very frustrating being a child.

Forcing a Child to Do What He Is Afraid to Do

My husband Andy has taken Charlotte (16) and Gemma-Rose (8) to the swimming pool, and I'm sitting here bleary-eyed after a late night. Yesterday evening, we went to a parish trivia event. Our team didn't win, but we ended up with a respectable score. We didn't disgrace the name of teacher and unschooling parent. We were good at answering questions on cars, vegetables, religion and sport, but we were hopeless at identifying celebrities. But we can live with that.

Andy came home, climbed into bed, and went straight to sleep. I lay awake most of the night thinking about fennel and Rolls Royces and the theme music to *Gilligan's Island*. Andy is feeling fresh enough to swim a few laps, and I'm doing what I always do when I'm tired. I'm ignoring the housework and have disappeared into my computer.

Andy is swimming, and I'm thinking about swimming. Swimming has been a weekly event in our lives for a long, long time. I remember taking our eldest son Duncan for swimming lessons years ago. One school holiday, we headed off to the pool for a week-long course of lessons.

Duncan enjoyed the first two days enormously. He must have been about three or four at the time. He wallowed in the baby pool, splashing with the other kids, and playing with a toy crocodile. It was a lot of fun. And then day three arrived. This was putting-your-head-in-the-water day. Duncan didn't want to put his head in the water. He wasn't ready. I expressed my concerns to the teacher, but she wouldn't listen to me. She had a schedule to keep up with. This was day three, so it was time for the children to put their heads into the water.

I begged and appealed and reassured Duncan: "It will be okay. I'll be there. If you want to learn to swim, you have to put your head in the water. Please try." So my little son submitted to being thrown through the water from teacher to parent. But he was frightened. That evening, it was his turn to do the begging. Did he have to return to the lessons? No. I decided that I couldn't put Duncan through all that agony. He wasn't ready. We cancelled the lessons.

Well, Duncan wasn't ready for swimming lessons the next year or the next or the next. I started to get anxious. How could I tell everyone my son couldn't swim? Was I a negligent mother?

When Duncan turned twelve, I wondered if it was time to try and help him overcome his fear of water. I talked to him about the importance of learning to swim. Duncan agreed that we needed to do something about the situation. He could see he was at a disadvantage. A couple of friends had invited him to their swimming parties, and he hadn't been able to join in properly. So with Duncan's cooperation, I organised some lessons.

I explained Duncan's swimming history to the teacher, and she treated him very gently. And Duncan, who had freely agreed to undergo the lessons, did his best to cooperate. I remember the day he put his head under the water. The teacher looked at me, put her thumb in the air and smiled very widely. We both cheered. I felt like crying with joy. The day Duncan swam a width of the pool was even better.

Sometimes I see other children at the pool who are afraid of the water. Their mothers say such things as, "You'll have so much fun when you can swim. Putting your head under the water is easy. Look! Everyone else is doing it. Once you get in the water and do it once, you'll be okay." Echoes of what I once said to my son Duncan.

But will they be okay or will their fear increase?

I found this quote from John Holt:

If we continually try to force a child to do what he is afraid to do, he will become more timid and will use his brains and energy, not to explore the unknown, but to find ways to avoid the pressures we put on him.

Yes, I don't believe it is right to pressure a child to swim or do anything he is afraid of. He'll overcome his fear and learn when he is ready.

Duncan is now a good swimmer. He learned all the different strokes as well as the extras like tumble turns and diving. No one would ever know he had such a rocky start to his swimming career.

Now it's Gemma-Rose's turn to learn tumble turns and how to swim butterfly. She's certainly not afraid of the water. She loves her Saturday mornings in the pool. She's very different from Duncan at the same age.

Yes, Duncan was different. But that's okay. Shouldn't we respect differences? Shouldn't we trust that children will learn when they are ready? They will all get there in the end.

Age and Respect

Maybe most of us don't look forward to getting old. Perhaps that's because we don't want our grey hair and wrinkles to automatically place us into a category of people who are no longer respected and valued. I certainly don't want anyone to look at me and think, "Hey, she's old," before passing over me without even wondering if I have something to offer. I don't want to be classified, put in the old people box, be pushed away.

Yes, older people can often feel like they are no longer a useful part of society. I'm not surprised some end up moaning and complaining about everything in their lives.

"When I'm old, I'm going to sit in my rocking chair in the corner of your living room and complain about everything," Andy says to our children.

"You'd better not, Dad. We'll throw you out."

"You wouldn't do that to me," protests Andy.

"If you want a home with us, you'd better not turn into a cranky old man."

Andy grins. He knows he's never going to be homeless. He's not even going to turn into a difficult older person.

But many people do become unlikeable as they age. Perhaps it's a reaction to a world that seems very unfair. Maybe older people think that everyone should respect them for their wisdom and their age.

"Why don't most young people value older people?" I ask my daughter Sophie. I expect her to say that young people haven't learnt how to show respect. They don't realise that it's important to value everyone, regardless of age. But she says something totally unexpected.

"The problem doesn't lie with young people," she says. "It begins with older people. If they want to be respected, they need to respect those younger than themselves."

"And they don't?"

"Oh, no. Some older people treat young people very badly. They disregard us. They're impolite. They're demanding. They say, 'You should respect me,' but they don't think they have to respect us."

Sophie tells me about some of the older people she knows. "When I'm tired, they say, 'Why should you be tired? You're young.' They don't recognise that I work hard. They don't even ask about my life. They're too busy telling me about theirs: how they've been playing bridge and golf and having morning tea with their friends. (While I've been working.) Or maybe they complain they can't do any of those things because they've been feeling unwell. They like talking about their health in lots of detail. Which is okay, but they don't ask how I'm doing. I'm just young. So everything in my life is perfect."

Wouldn't it be good if all people, regardless of age, took a real interest in each other? If they had a valuable place in each other's lives? If they enjoyed one other's company? If they treated each other with kindness and respect?

Not every older person is grumpy. Some of our older friends have welcomed us into their lives. They share their time and talents in a very generous way. They respect my kids, and my kids respect them. Actually, it's more than respect. It's genuine friendship and love.

So it is possible for everyone to respect each other regardless of age. We just need to begin by giving our young people a good example. Respect them. Show them that they are important. Share with them. Encourage and support them. And in their turn, they will do the same for us.

Should We Push Our Kids to Use Their Talents?

Most mornings as the sun is rising, Gemma-Rose and I stroll down to the park at the end of our road. When we arrive, we place our water bottles on a bench. We adjust our earbuds. Then I say, "Have a good run!" before we head off into the bush.

Gemma-Rose was only seven when we first started running together. All those years ago, I was the better runner. "Can I run with you, Mum?" my youngest daughter would ask. She knew I could run 5 K, and she wanted to run that distance as well.

But that was seven or eight years ago. Although I'm still running strong, Gemma-Rose no longer struggles to keep up with me. These days, I can't keep up with her.

"Gemma-Rose is good at running," Sophie observes.

"I bet she could win a race," says Imogen.

So I say, "Gemma-Rose, would you like to enter a fun run? You might enjoy racing with other people."

Gemma-Rose doesn't even think about it. "No," she says, shaking her head. She's not even a little bit interested. I know I can't persuade her, so I back off.

We watch Gemma-Rose. She runs faster and further than all her older sisters and me. And I think, "Gemma-Rose is a good runner. It's a pity she doesn't want to pursue her running in a bigger way. Is she wasting her talent?" I'm tempted to push Gemma-Rose. But I don't.

One day we decide to take a trip to the city to buy new running shoes for Sophie. The sales assistant measures Sophie's feet, and then she disappears into the storeroom returning a few minutes later with a stack of shoe boxes. While Sophie is busy trying on shoes, I walk around the shop. A poster on the wall catches my eye, and I stop and read it. I store up all the information splashed across it, just in case.

Later, I say to Gemma-Rose, "Did you see that poster in the shoe shop? There's going to be a fun run. Do you want to run in it?"

I expect Gemma-Rose to shake her head, but she doesn't. She says, "Yes."

A few weeks later, Gemma-Rose joins a crowd of fellow runners at the start line of the race. Sophie has decided to run too. The seconds tick down. Then runners are off. Gemma-Rose flies along the course. When she comes over the finish line, she has a huge grin on her face. She has run her best time ever.

"When's the next race?" asks Gemma-Rose.

"You want to run again?"

"Yes."

Gemma-Rose runs again. And again. She increases her distance. She improves her race times. And I'm so glad she's using her talent. Not because I want her to win races and come home with medals. No, that's not important. What I love most is seeing Gemma-Rose doing something that fills her with confidence and joy. Running is her thing.

Gemma-Rose just needed time and space to decide for herself that competing in races is something she wants to do.

There are other things I think Gemma-Rose would be good at, but she's not interested in pursuing them. At least, not at the moment. And maybe never. Or she might do them, but in a completely different way to the one that I've got in mind. And that's okay, isn't it? Perhaps we have to put our own ideas aside. Let our kids work things out for themselves. What do you think?

The Right Words

Callum passes his driving test first go. No problems. He's a natural driver. Now he can't wait to get on the road by himself.

We have a Ford Laser hatchback. It's our teenager-learn-to-drive car. Callum needs transport to get to work, so he takes charge of the Laser even though he's no longer learning to drive.

Then one day I get a call: "Mum, the car's overheated. I'm stuck in town."

It seems the car has more than overheated. The head gasket is irreparably damaged. It's an old car and not worth fixing, so it's towed away for scrap.

"Dad, can you help me find a new car? I need to get one quickly so that I can drive to work."

If Callum can't drive himself to work, Andy will have to take him. He'll have to get up extra early each morning to get Callum to work on time. So there's no time to waste. Andy starts searching and soon Callum is the owner of a nice reliable, safe Toyota Camry.

Andy finishes his Master's degree and gets his first job as a primary school teacher. He is over the moon. There's only one problem. He has to travel 50 minutes along the freeway to his new job at a school in the nearest city. He needs a car. So Andy goes car hunting again and comes home with a green Commodore station wagon.

Callum looks at Andy's car with longing eyes. "That's just the sort of car I'd love, Dad!" His safe Camry has lost all its appeal.

For weeks, Callum repeats, "I'd love a car like that, Dad!" And one day, Andy gives in. He knows all about being a teenager and having dreams.

"Okay, we'll swap cars."

Callum grins. "Really? Do you mean it?" He smiles for days. He smiles while he's driving his big new car.

Duncan passes his driving test, so he also needs a car. Andy offers Duncan the Camry which he readily accepts. A nice reliable, safe car for a nice reliable, safe son. Perfect fit.

Andy needs a car for himself, so he goes car hunting yet again. This time he comes home with a Hyundai Excel, not exciting but fuel efficient. Andy is no longer a teenager with dreams, but a man with a family to support. Fuel efficient is good.

Then one day, Callum's dream car goes wrong. The power steering breaks. Other things aren't working. After getting a quote to fix everything, Callum sadly agrees the car isn't worth the investment of any more money.

So Andy and Callum go car hunting for the fourth time.

"You should see what I bought, Mum!"

Callum has bought himself a Toyota Cressida. It's not really the kind of car I expected him to buy. It's old, but it has leather seats and lots of luxury features. It's the sort of car that an older person might have owned for years. Probably did.

Callum turns his Cressida into a young man's dream car by applying numerous trendy stickers to the rear windscreen and lowering the suspension. Now he can scrape over every speed bump in town. A set of superalloy wheels arrives in the post. "It was such a great deal, Mum! I bought them online for less than half price!"

Callum is satisfied...

... until Andy says, "One day we'll have to buy an old Commodore that needs restoring. It could be a father-son project. We could spend time fixing it together."

Callum's eyes light up, and before long he has bought an old Commodore station wagon to do up.

Soon some huge bright yellow springs arrive in the post (bought on the Internet), and Callum starts pulling bits off his car. But he hits a problem, and the car remains on the driveway without wheels for a few weeks. But he can still drive to work. He still has the Cressida. Or maybe he doesn't.

"Where's Callum?" I ask Andy.

"He's gone to pick up his new car."

"New car? What new car?"

Andy shrugs his shoulders. He's given up. Boys and their cars.

A couple of hours later, Callum arrives home with a wide bright green thirty-something-year-old Holden Kingswood that stretches on forever. How will he park it?

"Where's your Cressida?" I ask.

"I traded it in for this car," Callum explains with a huge smile on his face. "It's a classic."

It's old. It's huge. It will guzzle fuel. Boys and their cars I shrug my shoulders. I just don't understand.

Callum calls the girls. He wants to give them a tour. They have to admire their brother's car. That's what sisters are for.

"What's that?" asks Gemma-Rose pointing to a small electric fan perched on the dashboard.

"Air conditioning," replies Callum.

Air conditioning? I hide a smile.

"Those are strange seat belts," observes Sophie.

"They're not inertia reel belts," I explain. "We had seat belts like those in our car when I was a girl." Years ago.

"What are you going to call your car?" asks Charlotte.

"The Jolly Green Giant?" suggests Imogen.

A few days later, Callum arrives home from work. "Two people offered to buy my car today. One man asked me how much I'd be willing to sell it for. Another man said he'd swap his car for mine."

"What sort of car?" we ask.

"Why didn't you accept the offer?" asks Andy after hearing it was a newish reliable expensive car. "That man's car is worth much more than yours. I would have taken it like a shot." But Andy is a family man with a budget, not a young man with dreams.

"I like my car," says Callum, his smile disappearing. "I've only just bought it."

Andy and I giggle over the thought that anyone would want Callum's Jolly Green Giant. "You should have taken the other car," repeats Andy. We giggle some more.

Callum is no longer smiling. He goes off to the kitchen in search of dinner. A little later, I see him sitting silently at the kitchen table.

"You okay, Callum?" I ask.

"I'm fine, Mum." But he doesn't sound fine.

Later that evening, while I am cleaning my teeth, I think about Callum and his green car. Suddenly a sentence appears in my head. It's a perfect sentence. I go in search of my son.

"It must be really lovely having a car other people want to buy," I say. And I mean it.

Callum's face lights up instantly. His mother understands. I have said the right thing.

"I'm sorry, Callum. I shouldn't have laughed. I can see the car is very special to you.

"That's okay, Mum." He gives me a hug. "You know, I've always dreamt about having a car like the Kingswood."

"I shouldn't have giggled. I shouldn't have made fun of you and your car." I shouldn't have been disrespectful. Callum generously brushes my apologies away. He's happy again.

One afternoon, Callum drives his Commodore station wagon (you remember – the one that's been sitting immobile on our driveway for weeks) to the local workshop for a safety inspection.

He's fixed it. The wheels are back on. The car is back on the road. Callum is now the proud owner of two roadworthy cars, both paid for and maintained with his own money. No loans. No debts.

Boys and their cars. Every boy needs to pursue a dream. Before very long, young men with dreams turn into men with families to support. That's good. They all have to grow up. But for now:

"Any chance of a lift to town?" I ask.

"Of course! I'll take you in the Green Giant." Callum can't wait to show off his car.

"Wow! Listen to the engine. That sounds good!" This time I've said exactly the right words.

Callum grins.

Part VII: Love

Something to Do With Love

We can endure a lot when we love, can't we? Love helps us do things that seem almost impossible.

I remember a winter when I had to nurse seven children all at once. They caught some dreadful bug at exactly the same time. They coughed. They sneezed. They drooped. Their temperatures rose alarmingly. I took a couple of them to see the doctor. The next day I took a couple more. "Are you back again?" the doctor asked. And the day after that: "Do you have a never-ending supply of children?" No, he didn't say that. I made that bit up.

For days, children huddled under blankets while I measured out medicine and popped thermometers into mouths. I held hands, stroked foreheads and read stories. In odd moments, I cooked meals, washed dishes, threw clothes into the washing machine, and swept floors. Oh yes, I also fed the baby. She was sick too. But I wasn't. I knew I was living on borrowed time. These germs were going to get me in the end. Except they didn't.

I tell this story to my daughters, and they ask, "What would you have done if you'd become ill as well?"

"I'd have looked after you regardless."

Why? Because I'm a mother. It's got something to do with love.

When Worry Gets in the Way of Love

Sometimes life can feel very overwhelming. Parenting is not always easy. There are so many concerns and worries.

It starts very early:

Do I have enough milk for my baby?

When will my child sleep through the night?

Will she ever wean?

How long will it be before she's out of nappies?

Then when a child gets to school age, it gets worse, especially if we decide to homeschool:

Will my child learn to read?

Will he ever learn to write?

Will he become addicted to computer games?

Will he learn everything he needs to know?

Sometimes we wonder if we should pass all that worry onto someone else and send our children to school. But we battle on. It's our duty.

Even when a child is almost grown up, the worries do not stop:

Will she get into university?

Will she get a job?

Will she ever leave home and be able to look after herself?

Will she find someone suitable to marry?

Will she always love her faith?

The concerns are endless.

Do our kids know how much we worry?

If we don't talk about our concerns directly to our children, they might hear us mulling them over with our spouses or friends. Even if we never say a word, they can still pick up on our moods and attitudes. And I wonder: how does that make our children feel?

We might assume they feel loved knowing we worry about them all the time. We wouldn't worry if we didn't care, would we?

But recently, I had another thought. What if my children concluded that all these concerns were making me unhappy? Instead of feeling loved, they might feel they were just a problem for me.

Parenting should be a pleasure. Life should be joyful. And our children should feel enjoyed and loved. But, unfortunately, so many concerns get in the way.

I am tucking my youngest girls into bed.

"I really enjoyed spending time with you today!" I say.

My girls' eyes glow with happiness.

"I love you, Mum," they both say as they wrap their arms about me.

"I love you too," I reply. "I love being your mother."

I turn off the light. It's the end of another joy-filled day, a day in which I refuse to be anxious.

My children will get where they are meant to go because God will take care of that. All I have to do is focus on this present moment. I can't worry, even though I'm tempted to at times, because I want to enjoy my children and make sure they feel enjoyed.

And I want nothing to get in the way of love.

Following Our Mothering Instincts

"Did I ever tell you my discipline talk story?" asks my friend Amina. I shake my head before settling down to listen.

"Some years ago, a friend gave me a CD. 'It's a talk about disciplining kids,' she said."

"Did she think your kids were wild and out-of-control?"

Amina smiles. "She didn't mention my children. But who knows what she was thinking? We are unschoolers, you know!"

"Who was the speaker?" I ask.

"I can't remember his name even though he was well-known at the time. He was an experienced family man and was considered to be a parenting expert."

Amina tells me how she took the CD home and decided to listen to it even though she didn't think she needed any advice. "I had to listen because my friend might have asked me about it. Anyway, I was curious. I wanted to hear what the parenting expert had to say."

"So, what did he say?"

"The father must be the authority figure in the family," says Amina. And then she went on to describe the expert's recommended method for disciplining children.

The mother should draw up a misbehaviour chart for her children. When the father returns home from work, he must deal with all the discipline issues that have occurred during the day. If a child has a 'mark' against his name, he must call that child into the privacy of his study. The father should tell the child how disappointed he is with his behaviour. The child hasn't been obedient. He didn't do what he was told. Because he has broken the rules, his father must spank him. It's only fair. After the father has inflicted the punishment, he must take his crying child into his arms and reassure him of both his and God's love. The father has only been tough because he cares. Tough love. (It is just as hard for the parent as it is for the child.) The child will dry his eyes and resolve to do better.

"I felt there was something wrong," says Amina. "How can a father inflict pain and shame on a child one moment and then say, 'I love you' a moment later and expect a child to believe that? I couldn't get my head around that at all."

"So you weren't tempted to follow the advice?" I ask.

"No, I couldn't do something like that. There were other things I couldn't do either."

Amina describes how her friends had used wooden spoons to paddle little bottoms to deter misbehaviour in their children. "That didn't feel right."

"Did you say anything to your friends?"

"No. Whenever they talked about such things as discipline, I kept quiet. They did what they believed was right. Our family did something different. I avoided getting into parenting discussions. I didn't want my friends to know I didn't share their views because I wanted them to accept me."

I understand. Most of us want people to like us. We want the approval of others. We need a group of friends to belong to. It's hard going our own way, isn't it? That can be very lonely.

"I also didn't want to look like I was judging my friends' choices. Everyone has to do what they feel is best for their family." So that's why Amina chose to do what she felt in her heart was right for hers.

"Even though I kept quiet about my views on discipline," says Amina, "everyone must have noticed we were different. Years later, one of my friends said, 'Your kids turned out okay even though you didn't spank them.' Maybe she was surprised."

Yes, Amina's kids are considerate, pleasant and very loving people.

Sometimes it can be very difficult raising our kids in ways different to those around us. We might have to defend our opinions. We could feel alone. There might even be times when we wonder if everyone else is right after all. Why should we know better than our friends? And what about the parenting experts? Surely an expert knows best?

Except he often doesn't. If his advice doesn't feel right, it's okay to ignore it. Instead, we should listen to our hearts and follow our mothering instincts.

"When in doubt, just love," I say.

Amina smiles. I don't need to explain further. That's the wonderful thing about pretend friends. They're totally in tune with our thoughts and feelings. They understand.

Aiming for Love Not Perfection

I had a vision: by the age of 18, all my children were going to be perfectly brought up and educated. I wanted them to fly off into the world without a problem. I was going to sit back and sigh with satisfaction and happiness. Pat myself on the back: a job well done.

To make my goal come true, I spent a lot of time looking for the perfect way of homeschooling and stressing over every little detail. I chopped and changed, both methods and resources, always on the lookout for that one perfect thing. I badgered my children and prodded them along: "You'll thank me one day!"

So what happened?

I realised that my vision was just an impossible dream. None of my children has reached the age of 18 and been declared perfect.

Did I do something wrong? No. It's just the way life is. It's just the way people are. Who can learn everything by this young age? We spend a lifetime growing and learning, both in virtue and knowledge. I know I'm still growing. So why did I expect things to be any different with my children?

I guess all parents want to give as much as they can to their children. We'd like to help them avoid as many problems in life as possible, especially the ones we have faced ourselves. We want to equip them with knowledge and skills, anything they might need to be successful. Our dreams aren't bad. We can give our children good starts in life, perhaps better than the ones we had. But perfection? That's just not possible.

These days, I'm much more realistic about my goals. And I'm relaxed. I now have time to enjoy my children. I concentrate on two smaller goals.

Firstly, I want to bring my children up in such a way that they know without a doubt that they are unconditionally loved, both by God and me.

I also want my children to love learning. There is no way I can help my children learn everything they will ever need to know in a few short years. I can't cover all the possibilities. I can't see into the future and know what kind of world they will be living in, and what particular skills they will need. I remember John Holt's words:

Since we can't know what knowledge will be most needed in the future, it is senseless to try to teach it in advance. Instead, we should try to turn out people who love learning so much and learn so well that they will be able to learn whatever needs to be learned.

Yes, I want my children to love learning and to be independent learners.

My vision for my children's future? It's got everything to do with love, not perfection.

I have a few young adults none of them perfect but all perfectly loved and accepted. They are great people. They will do good things. They have their whole lives to continue growing and learning, discovering and developing and using their talents. They will make mistakes. They will inevitably struggle. They will suffer. But they will learn, and they will love, and they will become the people they are intended to be.

I'm imperfect but perfectly loved too. I continue to grow and to learn. That's the wonderful thing about unschooling. It never ends.

I don't have to be perfect. I don't have to bring up my kids perfectly. All I have to do is love and trust.

I sigh with relief.

What Do Children Need for a Happy Childhood?

Sometimes my children's words warm my heart.

"Don't you love being us?" asks my daughter, Imogen (18), turning to me with a huge smile.

I am surprised. It's not as if we're doing anything special right at this moment. So why does Imogen feel like a big ball of happiness, as Sophie would say, for no apparent reason at all?

"You don't wish you belonged to another family?" I ask.

"No! We have a good life. I've been writing. We have our singing lessons later. But before that, we're going to the library!"

A good life? "Will you look back on your childhood and think it was happy?" I ask.

"Oh, yes!"

"What will you remember the most?"

Imogen thinks for a moment and then says, "Doing things together. We're always spending time together."

There is so much I want to give my children. I want them to have a life full of memorable experiences. However, we never seem to go anywhere or do anything very interesting. We've only ever been on a family holiday a handful of times. We've never been overseas. We haven't even been out of our state (unless you count hopping over the border to visit Canberra for the day). On a day-to-day basis, we never go anywhere more exciting than the library. We rarely meet up with friends. Actually, we all have more friends online than in real life. The last time we saw another homeschooling family was rather a long time ago.

To be honest, I haven't enough time, money, energy or even inclination to keep up with a busy and exciting lifestyle. And I wonder if I am failing my children.

"Doing things together. We're always spending time together."

Maybe it's not what we do or where we go or who we meet that's important. Perhaps the important word is 'together'.

We cook, we eat, we read, we write, we watch movies, we run, we talk, we laugh, we cry, we hug, we pray, we sing, we go to the library together. All simple things but done together with those we love.

Imogen's words warm my heart: "Doing things together. We're always spending time together."

Perhaps children don't need much more than that for a memorable childhood.

What do you think?

Is Our Unschooling Life Rich Enough?

Some unschooling families seem to live very adventurous lives that make ours look rather ordinary. And I wonder: is our life rich enough for our children? Are they getting all the opportunities they need to learn so that they grow into the kind of people who will change the world for the better?

Perhaps it's time for us to live differently. We could buy a farm, grow organic vegetables, have alpacas, spin wool, weave cloth, live in a yurt, go off-grid. Yes, we should get back to nature, step completely outside mainstream society, give our kids experiences not many people get to have. It would be good for them and good for the environment too.

But if we don't move to a farm, we could buy a campervan and then travel around Australia. See our country firsthand. Or we could sell our house, buy plane tickets, travel the world, and experience cultures different from ours.

I've read about these kinds of unschooling lives. They seem exciting and rich with experiences, and much more interesting than our family's seemingly conventional existence.

We seem to be drawn to what is different, what is novel. We dream. What would our life be like if we gave up the normal things that we're doing and set out on bigger adventures?

Years ago, I yearned to live a back-to-nature life. I dreamed about getting away from town and having a few acres where we could grow vegetables. I wanted to raise some chickens and have fresh eggs, bake bread and bottle fruit, maybe have a cow or two, a goat and a donkey. If we had space, our kids could go wild and make lots of noise because we wouldn't have any close neighbours who might complain. We could do whatever we wanted on our own patch of land.

This idea remained a dream until one day, a friend told us about a cottage that was on a 100-acre fish farm. The friend knew the owner of the farm and told us he was looking for someone to live in the cottage and feed the fish. All we'd have to do was throw some feed into the dams every evening. In return, we could live in the cottage for free. No rent whatsoever. This seemed like the answer to my dream.

I asked if we could visit the cottage before making a decision so one afternoon, my husband Andy, our children – we had five at the time – and I all piled into the car and drove quite a long way south until we arrived at the fish farm on 100 acres of Australian bush. The bush looked different from the bush that surrounds the house where we are living at the moment. With its tall gum trees and native flowers and sandy tracks, ours is very beautiful. But the fish farm bush wasn't so attractive. It looked like the poor relation with its stunted trees and low-growing vegetation. But it was still wild and untamed. It was nature. And this bush was home to a large mob of kangaroos. Who has kangaroos living on their property? It all seemed very romantic.

We had a look at the cottage, and my heart fell when I saw it because it was very rundown. No one had spent any time or money on it for years. The owner of the cottage had used it as a weekender. He had stayed there when he came to feed his fish. But the cottage hadn't been a proper home for a very long time. And it was very small. Andy, being the sensible man he is, shook his head and said, "No, Sue, we couldn't live there. We have five children. The house has only got two bedrooms. Look at the state of the place. There are holes in the walls, cracked windows and dirt. It would never make a nice place to live and to bring up children."

But the state of the cottage wasn't the biggest problem. There was also its location: "It'll take me two hours to get to work and two hours to get home again." Too many hours of travelling every single work day.

I didn't let Andy's objections stop me from thinking about the possibilities. I imagined all we could have: organic vegetables, the donkey, the chickens, the goat and the alpaca. I told Andy how much the kids would enjoy the 100 acres. They'd have lots of space to play and ride their bikes. They could wear old clothes, dig in the soil, and get as dirty as they liked because no one would see them.

"We could repair the house," I said. "We could fill in the cracks and holes, paint the walls, and replace the broken windows. Anyway, who needs a beautiful home? Wouldn't it be more adventurous to live in a rundown cottage on 100 acres of land?' I told Andy that we didn't need a pristine house like the ones in town. He wasn't convinced.

But then I suggested, if we moved, we could get a dog. We had always lived in rental homes and dogs were never allowed so when my children heard the word 'dog', they added their voices to mine: "We want to live in the cottage, Dad. Wouldn't it be fun to live on a fish farm?" Andy said he would think about it.

When we got home from the fish farm, I went to the library and borrowed every book I could find about ducks, chickens, donkeys, bottling fruit and vegetables, and everything else to do with a hobby farm. And I kept bringing up the subject of the cottage. And Andy kept saying, "It's a long way from work," and I kept replying, "Perhaps you can get another job closer to the farm. You're not happy with your present job. This could be a good opportunity for you to get a new one and for us to move and live our adventure."

And then one day, Andy said yes. We could give life on the farm a go. (I reckon he must love me very much.)

So we packed up and moved: Andy, our five children and I. At that time, our eldest child was eleven, and our youngest was one.

The first thing we wanted to do was get the promised dog. I answered an ad in the newspaper and drove back to town where I found a Collie/Kelpie cross called Rocket. She had too much energy, and she was always escaping from her owner's house. She had been picked up on the street and taken to the animal shelter one time too many, and her owner had decided that town was the wrong place for her to live. We ignored the fact that Rocket was an escapee. We thought she'd be fine living on our large property. Where could she escape to? She'd have a wonderful time on the farm. She'd be a perfect pet for our children. So I said we'd give the dog a home. Rocket's owner looked rather relieved.

And then a short while later, I realised that Rocket could easily escape from the farm because all the fences surrounding it were in a very poor condition. When our neighbour saw our dog, she came up to the fence bordering our two properties and called us over. Her first words were, "If that dog jumps over my fence, I'll shoot it." I started to worry about Rocket. What if she got out onto the road? What if she jumped over the fence? Having a dog wasn't as good as I had imagined.

The land wasn't as good as I'd hoped either. It was home to a lot of venomous snakes. I didn't think it was safe for our kids to roam free. I wanted them to stay close to the house. And although we had lots of space and we could have grown vegetables, it didn't take us long to realise that the soil was of very poor quality. That's why the trees were stunted, and the vegetation was low growing. There was another reason why they were like that: it hardly ever rained.

We had a water problem. There wasn't enough to grow vegetables. We hardly had enough for our personal needs. The water tank became the focus of my life. I spent a lot of time at the top of the ladder that stood next to the tank, checking the water level. Did we have enough to survive another week?

Regularly, we would hear a strange gurgling noise in the pipes indicating that we were almost out of water. I'd phone the carrier and hope that he could deliver some to us that same day. The water truck would arrive, and we'd go outside and watch it back up to the tank. The driver would attach a big hose to the truck and then insert the other end into our tank before turning on the pump. Always, he lost some water as he was connecting the hose. I held my breath as I watched that precious fresh water disappear into the dusty earth. But once the tank was full, I grinned. Perhaps we could have a shower or do some washing. Go wild with our water. But after a few hours, the party was over. It was time to conserve our water once again. How long could we make this tank last?

There was another aspect of country life that we didn't enjoy: sharing our home with thousands of rats and mice. During the night, we could hear them running and scratching in the cavity between the walls. I imagined them appearing through the holes, running over the floor and then up onto our bed. In the morning, all our mousetraps were occupied. But despite our trapping success, we never seemed to get the rodents under control. We adopted two cats to help with this problem, but they couldn't keep up with them either.

Andy was getting tired because of the long drive to and from work. I was also feeling exhausted. Music lessons and other activities were a long, long way from home. It took us all day to drive to town for these lessons, and do our shopping, and come home again.

Before moving to the cottage, I had said to Andy, "Just imagine being here in the summer! The kids can swim in the dams. It will be wonderful." But it wasn't. No one wanted to get into the unlined dams which were cloudy with sediment and contained all kinds of unidentified plants and creatures as well as the fish. We just weren't adventurous enough.

Although things were very different from what we had expected, we didn't at first give up. We faced each challenge as it came along. We tried hard. We had a good attitude. Yes, the experience wasn't turning out as we'd hoped, but we were learning a lot, and maybe things would get better. It might rain. Perhaps Andy would get a new job. That would make all the difference. We reminded ourselves that dreams take time. We couldn't just run back to town. We had to give things a fair go.

But one day, the owner of the farm announced that he wanted to sell it. He no longer wanted us to feed his fish, so we had to move. We talked about this as a family. Did we want to look for another farm? Or should we head back to town?

By this time, I was pregnant with our sixth child. Before we had made a decision about a new home, I had to have an ultrasound. So one afternoon, I drove from the farm and met Andy at the hospital in town. He took our children to the park while I went to see our baby for the very first time.

I entered the ultrasound room with excitement. Minutes later: “Your baby has 'an abnormality incompatible with life’.” Those words turned my excitement into fear.

Our unborn baby had a hole in his diaphragm. The doctor told me that some of our baby's organs had moved through that hole and were taking up space in the lung cavity. There was not much room for his developing lungs. The doctor predicted that by the time our baby was born, he wouldn't have enough lung tissue to survive. In other words, he was going to die.

Suddenly, our dream of living on a farm didn't seem important. I no longer cared about growing vegetables, raising animals, and spinning wool. We decided that we should move back to town. We wanted to be close to the hospital. We wanted to live in a house with town water. We wanted to be close to all the facilities. We had enough to think about without having to worry about all the little details of life. We were happy to go to the shops and buy our food, and turn a tap and see an unending stream of water appear. Yes, being self-sufficient didn't seem to matter any more.

So we found a suitable house, a conventional house, back in town. It had a good garden and beautiful surroundings, but it certainly wasn't an adventurous farm. It was just an ordinary-sized house on an ordinary-sized block of land.

Some months later, our son was born. We called him Thomas. He lived for a day, and then he died. And soon we realised that we were having experiences that nobody would ever ask for. We were learning things we didn't want to know about, such as how to arrange a funeral and what to inscribe on a headstone. We also learnt about the things that matter: what life and love are all about.

And we discovered that it's not important whether we live in a yurt or a campervan or a tumbledown cottage on a fish farm or an ordinary house in town. As long as we love. It's love that enriches our lives. It's what our kids need to experience. It's love that will change the world.

I ask my girls, "Would you like to live in a yurt?"

"A yurt? Why would we want to live in a yurt, Mum?"

"Do you want to travel the world?"

"No, we like living here at home."

Yurts and farms and campervans are perfect for some people but not for us.

We no longer live in town, but we still live in a conventional house situated on an average-sized block. It's our home. It's where we unschool. It's where we experience unconditional love.

The Extraordinary Ordinary Things of Life

I'm at Thomas' wake. I have his memory box on my knee, and I take out a few photos and pass them to a friend.

"He was a chubby baby!" she exclaims.

I reply, "He wasn't really. Those photos were taken at the funeral home. He looked different at the hospital."

I think about this. I remember how much I longed to see Thomas once more at the funeral home before his burial. He was in his coffin at the far end of the room, and I hurried towards him. And then suddenly I stopped. He didn't look like my baby. In some way, he'd changed since I'd left him at the hospital. Tears rolled down my face, and I wondered, "Did they get the babies muddled up? Is this really Thomas?"

My friend's voice interrupts my thoughts. She is asking me another question, and I open my mouth to reply. My lips move, but the words won't form. I try again, and again, I fail to say anything. I have lost control of my speech.

My friend notices my difficulties and says, 'You don't have to say anything. It's okay." But it's not okay at all. I want to tell her about my son, but I can't. I don't want her to move off and leave me alone. But she thinks she's upsetting me. She pats me on the shoulder and hurries away. And I am helpless.

Yes, I remember the day I lost control of my speech. But it wasn't just the ability to form words that I'd lost. I'd lost control of my whole life.

Life can go on the same, day in and day out. It is known and comfortable, and we feel secure. We think we are in control. Yes, we have problems to deal with, but we cope. And then one day we wake up, and life has changed forever, and we know there is absolutely nothing we can do about it.

I am very aware of how life can change so quickly. I travel through my comfortable days where I am seemingly in control, and I wonder how long it will last. What plans has God got for me? Will He allow my world to be turned upside down again? Will I once again sink into that pit of suffering?

I remember, a few days after Thomas died, going to the shopping centre and seeing two young women. As I walked past them, they continued to laugh and chat together about nothing of real importance. And I wondered why they hadn't noticed that I was no ordinary woman. Hadn't the air around them turned cold as we crossed paths? Why were they enjoying the trivial things of life while I was gripped by the arms of grief?

The trivial things of life? It's strange how unimportant some things seem when we are grieving. What if my world fell apart today? Would I continue my normal routine? Would I be interested in the little things of life? No, I don't think I would.

I think of the possibility of more suffering, and my heart skips a beat. A feeling of dread and fear overcomes me that threatens to spoil the present moment. And then I tell myself not to be silly. I say, trust. Live life to the full and don't look ahead. Be thankful for the joys of today. Don't let thoughts of possible pain-to-come spoil the present. The future is God's concern, not mine. My job is to concentrate on the little things of life.

So I get involved with the little things. I think about what I am going to wear for the day. I stand under the shower and enjoy the tingling of the hot water upon my skin. I spend time with God: I pray and read. I hang washing on the line and feel the warmth of the sun. Later, I challenge my body to a long run. Afterwards, I sit at the lunch table and devour my sandwich as I answer the girls' eager question: "How far did you run today, Mum?" We work; we share books; we chat; we laugh; we write; we discuss what we shall cook for dinner. Then my husband Andy arrives home. We hug. I pour a glass of wine, and we exchange news. Eventually, our ordinary day comes to an end.

As my children arrive one by one to say goodnight, I think about how much I love my family. I love them so much it hurts and the present moment threatens to be spoilt by the question, "What if...?" But I don't let it. I have no cause to worry.

I think about Thomas' death when I lost control over every aspect of my life, even my speech. I was sure my life was over. But here I am full of joy, surrounded by love. I still have no control over my life. I don't even want it. Yes, I am aware God could allow any kind of sorrow and suffering to touch me. But I also know He will always be there to bring me through it. For hasn't He already done that?

So I live in the present moment, and I enjoy the ordinary things of life which I suddenly realise aren't so ordinary after all. Ordinary becomes powerfully extraordinary when combined with love.

Before each child heads off to bed, I enfold her within my arms, and I hug. I hug tightly, my eyes closed, my heart overflowing with love. This is today. This is what is important. This is an extraordinary ordinary moment of my life.

Sons, Scrapes, and Love

Callum appears in the doorway. "Mum, we haven't had any mother-son time recently. How about we walk to the village for coffee? We need to catch up."

A few minutes later, I'm sitting across the table from my son. As I sip my coffee, I think about being a parent. Why do we long so much to have children when parenting isn't easy. It's true that children bring joy into our lives. But why are we prepared to endure all the pain and heart-ache that inevitably come along as well?

I look at my son, and my thoughts turn to his childhood and the day of his birth. I didn't expect Callum to be born. When I went for his 18-week ultrasound and saw his little heart beating, I couldn't believe it. "The baby is alive?" I asked. The nurse raised her eyebrows. What had I expected?

Contrary to my expectations, our baby made it through 40 weeks of pregnancy and entered the world, a beautiful, healthy child. I cradled Callum in my arms, thanking God for this gift, a blessing that seemed miraculous after four consecutive miscarriages.

Life was perfectly joyful. Just for a moment.

When Callum was a couple of weeks old, I drove to my friend Karen's home, eager to show off my baby. Karen lived at the top of a hill. I parked outside her house and got out of the car. Before I could lean through the opened rear passenger door to retrieve Callum, the vehicle started moving slowly backwards. In a split second, I saw it all: the car moving, the car gathering speed, and the car crashing at the bottom of the hill, with my baby inside it. I hurled myself back through the driver's door and pressed my foot on the brake pedal just in time. I pulled the handbrake on tightly, gathered my son into my shaking arms and headed towards Karen's house. What if I hadn't been able to stop the car? That thought went around and around my mind.

When Callum was about two years old, we visited my friend Sally who lived in the city. Imagine: two friends having an adult conversation while all our children were playing happily together. It was a perfect moment. Until the doorbell rang.

"Does this little boy belong here?" asked a man. I looked at the child standing by his side. It was Callum. "I was driving by, and I found this little fellow walking down the centre of the road."

The centre of the road? I stammered my thanks to the man while Callum grinned up at me. He seemed none the worse for his solo adventure. But I couldn't stop thinking, "What if a speeding car...?" I vowed never to let Callum out of my sight. I was going to keep him safe.

But then one day when Callum was nearly three, I lost him again. This time he disappeared down a very steep set of stairs in my sister's house. One moment he was at the top. And then he wasn't. I was sure Callum was dead. I screamed and burst into tears. How could a child survive such a fall? Then through my tears, I saw Callum pick himself up and look around. It was my turn to fly down the stairs. I gathered my son up. Callum had bounced. He didn't even have a bruise.

But Callum did get very bruised when he was thirteen. He and Charlotte were cycling around our house in different directions. All went well for a while and then there was a big crash, followed by an ear-piercing scream. I ran outside to find two mangled bikes and two children sprawled on the ground. I gathered up seven-year-old Charlotte.

"My ear! My ear! He ran right over my ear."

"Callum!" I shouted as I gathered Charlotte into my arms. "How many times have I told you not to ride in the opposite direction as your sisters?"

Without glancing in Callum's direction, I carried Charlotte into the house to examine the damage. My son must have picked himself up and followed us because after I'd determined that there wasn't much wrong with Charlotte's ear, I noticed him perched on the edge of an armchair. Callum's face was very pale. He was clutching his arm.

"I think I've broken my arm, Mum."

After spending two hours in the waiting room of the accident and emergency department of the hospital, we finally saw a doctor. I told him the story of the bike crash.

"You didn't immobilise the arm?"

"No." I hadn't thought about doing that.

"Did you put ice on your son's arm?"

"No." I hadn't thought about ice.

"Did you give him anything for the pain?"

"No." I hadn't thought about painkillers.

My face turned red. Was I the worst mother in the world?

The arm healed but one day, a few months later, Callum came hopping into the house, tears of pain in his eyes: "I was running up the back steps and stubbed my toe." It wasn't just stubbed. Callum had broken it. He hobbled about on crutches for two months.

I remember other times when Callum got himself into trouble. He almost drowned at the beach, he badly burnt the skin on his torso, he ran at break-neck speed into a head-high taut wire and narrowly escaped decapitating himself, he absorbed most of a gravel road into his legs after falling off a bike...

The other day, Callum and I were reminiscing. "You haven't broken any bones for a while," I remarked.

Callum grinned. "No, but I'm still getting myself into scrapes. They're just more grownup kind of scrapes." What kind of scrapes? That's our secret. All I can say is that Callum is still getting himself into trouble. And my heart still aches as I have to stand to one side and let him experience the trials of the adult world.

Our coffee cups are nearly empty. Callum is telling me a funny story. I look at the gorgeous smile that lights up his face. Did I really grow him from a tiny baby? Is he really mine?

I think again of the questions I am pondering. Why am I so willing to endure all the pain of being a mother? Why would I be prepared to suffer it all over again? And I know the answer. I have known it all along. The answer is love.

A Mother's Hug

I'm in bed reading. I want to turn the light off and go to sleep, but my son Callum hasn't arrived home from work yet. Now and then I glance at the clock and wonder where he is. Then just when I am about to text Callum to make sure he's okay, I hear his car pull up on the driveway. I hear the key in the lock, a bag falling to the floor, a few footsteps on the tiles outside my bedroom, and then a knock at my door.

Callum comes in and sinks onto the edge of the bed.

"I was worried about you," I say.

"Sorry, Mum, I should have texted you. So many problems..."

"Bad day?"

"It was the worse day I've ever had."

Callum's head sinks into his hands. "A man died in the car park today."

A man died in his car while waiting for his wife to finish her shopping in the supermarket where Callum works.

I crawl out of bed and wrap my arms around my son. He rests his head on my shoulder and puts his arms around me too. We hold each other tightly.

"I had to deal with the ambulance and the police and the wife. She was very distraught."

I can no longer protect my son from the pain of the world. He's grown up. He's out there on his own. And my heart aches for him.

We sit together quietly for a while. Then Callum says, "I'll be okay." I release him from our embrace, and he gets up from the bed. "I suppose I'd better go and get something to eat."

Callum stops at the door and turns around. "Thanks, Mum." He manages a small smile. "Thanks for the hug."

I can't put things right however much I want to. But I can hug. Sometimes a mother's hug makes all the difference.

"Can I have a hug, please, Mum?"

I open my arms. "Of course."

Fathers, Sons and Love

There are five cars parked on our driveway. Two of them belong to Callum. You'd think two cars would be more than enough vehicles for one young man, but Callum has plans to buy a third. Cars are his passion.

Andy sighs and says, "Callum spends all his time and money on cars."

I say, "He's young. He has passions. He has a dream."

"I was young once," says Andy. "I used to want a dream car too. But I never got one."

"You got me," I say. "You got married and had a family instead."

Andy smiles and stretches out his arm. "I'd rather have you than a car." He hugs me close.

But somewhere, hidden deep beneath his gratitude for his family, Andy still has a dream: he'd like a car that could fly along the freeway, swallowing up all the hills between home and work. His present car is small and sensible and fuel-efficient. And it grumbles when it comes face-to-face with a bump in the road. It's not very exciting at all.

Callum invites Andy to take one of his cars for a drive, his huge classic Holden Kingswood, his Green Giant. He notices Andy's eyes light up with excitement. He listens when he says, "Wow! It's huge, twice as big as my car!" He knows Andy has car dreams too. And Callum knows the kind of dream car Andy would love.

Of course, Andy doesn't want an ancient fuel-guzzling monster like the Green Giant. He dreams about something a bit newer. Less of a classic-from-days-gone-by car, and more of an exciting but reliable right-now car. And Callum has plans to make his dad's dream come true. He's just waiting for the right moment, the right opportunity.

Andy hears that our next-door-neighbour, John, is selling his car. It's a Holden Commodore, it's big, and although it's a few years old, it's practically new compared to all the ancient vehicles that are sitting on our driveway. Best of all, it's a mechanic's car, so it's in excellent condition. Andy says to Callum, "If you're set on buying another car, that one would be perfect for you. You need a reliable car to get to work in. You wouldn't have to worry every time something goes wrong with the other ones." Andy is right. Callum's cars might be classics, but usually, they are classics-in-pieces, awaiting restoration.

But Callum thinks John's car would be the perfect dream car for Andy. "What do you think, Mum? Perhaps I could pretend to buy the car for myself, and then we could give it to Dad. Imagine the look on his face when I say, 'Dad, this car's yours'!" We both smile as we picture that very special moment.

So Andy and Callum arrange to take John's car for a test drive. Callum sits in the driver's seat, and he smiles for the whole trip. "Wow! This is the best car I've ever driven. Feel that power."

Andy nods. Could he be feeling just a little bit envious? He wishes he was in a position to buy such a car. He dreams a little and then tells himself not to be so silly. He thinks it would be extravagant spending money on another car when he already has a vehicle. Yes, he's not going to allow himself to feel disappointed. He's very happy for Callum.

Callum negotiates with John, and soon they have struck a deal. John will make sure the car's in tip-top condition, and it will be ready for sale in a few days' time.

"Wow! The car was wonderful, Mum," says Callum later.

"It sounds like you'd like to have it," I observe. "Have you changed your mind about giving it to Dad?"

"Well..." he mutters.

I can understand a young man's yearnings for a car, so I say, "Think about it. If you want it, have it. We'll find another one for Dad."

But a day or so later, Callum tells me he wants Andy to have the car. "It's just perfect for him. I can make do with my cars. Dad will help me fix them. No, this is his car."

Callum tells John the car will be Andy's, but he's to keep that fact a secret. He wants the car to be a big surprise.

All week we wait while John gets the car ready. At regular intervals, Andy says, "I bet you're impatient to get your new car, Callum," and Callum replies, "Oh yes!" trying not to smile too much as he thinks about his delicious secret.

The day arrives. Callum has already arranged payment for the car. Andy and I take the girls out for the morning, and when we return, the car is waiting on the driveway. It's white and big and powerful, and it looks good!

"Do you want some coffee, Dad?" asks Callum as we enter the house. He tries not to smile too much. He tries to sound cool as if this is just another ordinary day. Soon we are all sitting in the family room with coffee mugs in our hands.

"As I've just got a new car, Dad, I thought I'd get a little present for you too." Callum hands over an envelope, which Andy tears open.

"A key?" Andy is bemused.

"Yes. A key to your new car."

Andy is dumbfounded, lost for words. "You mean... a car...? John's car? Mine... ?"

Callum, the girls and I smile. We were all in on the secret. The only person who had no idea what was going on was Andy.

"Aren't you going to have a look at your new car?" we ask. So we all troop outside, and Andy does lots of oohing and aaahing. He says, "Really? The car's mine?" a few times, while we all continue to grin. It's a magic moment.

"So I was the only one who didn't realise what was going on?" asks Andy later.

We nod. "Everybody knew, except you, Dad. John even told all his workmates about the young man next door who was buying a car for his dad."

Of course, Andy has to take the car out for a drive. He wants me to come along too. He turns the key in the ignition, and the engine roars into life. "Listen to that! Doesn't that sound good?" Soon we are sailing through the rock cutting out of the village. Andy needs petrol, but he drives right past the local service station, at the bottom of the hill, and heads towards town. He's having fun.

For the past week, Andy has been flying along the freeway each morning to school. At the end of the day, he touches his toe to the pedal, and his dream car shoots up the hills, back towards home. And Andy grins. He grins a lot. There is something really special about receiving an unexpected gift.

"Callum must love you very much," I observe to Andy. "How many sons would arrange such a surprise for their dads?"

Fathers, sons and cars. What could be better than fathers and sons sharing a passion and a dream? Unless, of course, it's fathers and sons sharing love.

Breeding Like Mice

It began with a cage, a cage Felicity dragged all the way home from town. It was large and heavy and, by the time she reached our house, one of her arms was longer than the other.

I'd already said, "No mice!"

"But the cage was such a bargain, Mum. And the boys would love a mouse. We have a cage now. We might as well get a mouse. Or two. What do you think, Mum?"

I should have said no. I should have sent the cage straight back to the St Vincent de Paul store. Some other family could have bought it and had a mouse adventure instead of us. But I looked at all the begging eyes staring at me and promised to take everyone to town to look at mice.

Of course, we couldn't buy only one mouse. No, that mouse would have been far too lonely, and that would have been very cruel. Or so I was told. So we came back with two.

Soon the little mice were running around the mouse wheel delighting everyone. "But Mum, the cage is so big. It's big enough for a few more mice." We returned to the pet shop.

The cage and six male mice took up residence in the boys' bedroom. This was a problem. The boys' bedroom is a no-go zone for girls. "We never get to see the mice, Mum," one little girl complained. "We need some mice of our own." So we went back to the pet shop where we bought an adventure playground type cage with tunnels and wheels and all sorts of interesting attachments. This time we bought two female mice, and soon they were settled in their new home in one of the girls' bedrooms.

Life ran smoothly for a while except for the occasional break out from the male mice cage, the mice being slightly smaller than the gap between the bars.

"Which side of the cage are these mice supposed to be on?" Andy would roar at regular intervals, and a boy would come running to return the escapees to the safety of their cage, away from the threat of mice traps and bait. Eventually, the mice grew big and fat, and the boys were able to relax.

Then Felicity had her bright idea. "Mum, it would be very educational if we bred mice. We could keep records, you know, of all the different traits. It would be just like a genetics experiment."

"But what would we do with all the babies?"

"Sell them to the pet shop. I saw a sign the other day: *Mice Wanted.*"

I should have said no, but I didn't. Soon we had numerous tiny hairless bundles of newborn mice life occupying the female cage with two happy mothers. The children were fascinated. They dutifully recorded all the facts and figures in scientific notebooks, and it looked like the breeding program was going to turn into a very successful learning experience.

Soon it came time to sell the baby mice and make a small pocket money fortune. "How much do you think we'll make? What shall we buy?" Felicity was sent down to the pet shop to negotiate the business deal. But *Mice Wanted* had turned into *No Mice Needed at the Moment*. Felicity came home and hardly dared tell me the unwelcome news. What would we do with all our little rodents?

The first thing we had to do was separate the males from the females. Felicity did the sorting. "Are you sure you can tell a female from a male?" I asked, but Felicity seemed confident. A while later, we realised she wasn't very good at sexing. She'd overlooked a male. Soon we were back down at the pet shop buying another cage. And then another.

It was turning into a nightmare. Our mouse population was increasing at an enormous rate. However carefully we tried to separate males from females, a male always ended up in the wrong cage. What were we going to do?

One afternoon, I sat down with the children, and we talked about the problem. None of the pet shops wanted mice. None of our friends wanted mice. And we couldn't keep them all. We'd end up with dozens of cages of mice all around the house. And they were beginning to smell really bad.

"How about we let the mice be country mice?" I suggested. We lived on the edge of a farm. Over the fence was a paddock of cows and plenty of mice. "We could take all the mice down to the paddock and let them go free. They'd much prefer to live outside than in a small cage, I'm sure."

The kids weren't so sure. "What if they come back into the house and Dad catches them in his mousetraps?"

"We'll walk right into the paddock, far from the house before we set them free."

Nobody could think of a better plan, so we put this one into action. The older children carried the cages. The younger ones took food and water: "So that they have something to eat while they learn to be country mice. They've never had to find food on their own before."

The mice were set free, and everyone trooped back to the house. We sat staring out the window looking at the paddock, and then tears started falling from the girls' eyes. Soon the slowly rolling tears turned into rivers running down little cheeks, and howls and sobs erupted. And I cried too, a big lump in my throat. I hugged little bodies close, and I felt them heave with grief.

The girls cried for their lost pets, the little mice who'd scampered up and down their arms and scurried down tunnels and who'd set wheels revolving. They cried for the loss of their dream: they never imagined it would end so sadly.

And I cried for the girls. I wouldn't miss the constant cry of "More babies! We need another cage, Mum!" And I wouldn't miss the smell. In fact, I was secretly rather glad we were once again a mouseless family. But my mother's heart was breaking because of my girls' tears.

A mother's heart? How resilient parents' hearts need to be. How many times will mine break as each child grows up: at the death of a pet, when a child gets teased or left out, when she is sick, when she fails, when she leaves home and my job is done?

Gemma-Rose was a baby at the time of the mouse adventure, and so she cannot remember those mice. She will tell me she has never had a mouse as a pet like her siblings. What will I do if she looks at me with her huge blue eyes and makes an appeal? Will I be sensible and say no? Or will I find myself at the pet shop because of love?

Am I the only parent with a too soft heart?

Because I Am a Mother

Imogen asks, "What would you like for lunch, Mum?"

"Anything will be fine. Perhaps a sandwich?"

A few minutes later: "Lunch is ready!"

We hurry to the table, and waiting for me on my plate is the last slice of the delicious three cheese pizza we had for dinner last night.

"You didn't have to give me the left-over pizza," I say. "Someone else might have liked it."

"But we wanted you to have it. Because you're the mother. You're special."

I have no choice. My daughters are very bossy. I eat my pizza, and I enjoy.

Later that day, after dinner, Sophie asks, "Can I pour you a glass of wine?"

I am about to say no, but Sophie is eager to do something for me, so I say, "Yes, please! I'd love a glass of wine."

"Take your wine and go and sit in a comfortable chair," suggests Charlotte.

"But there are lots of dishes," I protest. "I was going to help you with the washing up."

"We can do that," says Imogen.

"You're the mother. You go sit down."

"I'll forget how to work," I say. "I'll become lazy."

But the girls won't listen to me.

"You're very bossy," I observe. "You're always telling me what to do. You girls never let me do what I want."

The girls grin. They are in charge. So I take my wine and retire to a comfortable chair, and I think. I think about my daughters, who boss me about, who tell me what to do. It wasn't so long ago they were completely dependent on me, and I had to do all the looking after.

I remember all those nights when I'd have to rouse myself to feed a baby, change a nappy, take a child to the toilet, change wet bedsheets, soothe away fears. I have to admit that sometimes I hadn't wanted to do any of that. I'd yearned to stay huddled down in my warm bed and stay asleep.

I enjoyed all those baby cuddles and little child smiles, but there were times when I longed to knit or sew or go for a walk on my own, and I couldn't because I had little ones to look after.

I was so eager to be a mother. I loved my young children very much, but some days, I wanted to run away, even if only for a while. Sometimes it was just too hard. I struggled on, trying to accept the sacrifices I had to make. I was certain life would never change.

But life does change.

Gemma-Rose climbs onto my lap. She strokes my face and says, "You're tired."

"How do you know?" I ask.

"You've got your tired face on. Being a mother must be hard work."

It is hard work. It involves lots of sacrifices, especially when children are small and dependent.

"I love you, Mum. You're so special."

Yes, I am special. I'm special because I am a mother. That's a privileged role to have. I wouldn't change who I am for anything.

Would you?

Perfectly Them

Do you remember the first time you saw your child? That was a magic moment, wasn't it? I bet we all thought our newborn babies were absolutely perfect.

It's very sad that initial impressions wear off. We begin to see faults in our children. As they grow, we criticise and complain. Perhaps that's because we wonder how they're going to get on in life and fit into the world. If only they were different.

Maybe we justify our negative words. Surely it's our duty to point out our children's faults? They need to know what they have to work on, don't they?

Or maybe they don't.

I had an interesting discussion with my daughter Sophie after we'd been to a homeschool gathering. Sophie listened as a mother told everyone in earshot how lazy her daughter was. Her daughter was in earshot too.

Sophie was horrified that parents, not only criticise their kids but that they do it in public. How would adults feel if we overheard someone finding fault with us? What if they criticised us to our face?

Sophie observed two friends enjoying lunch together in a café where she worked. The women were halfway through eating their egg and bacon rolls when another woman approached their table and said, "You shouldn't eat that food. You're fat." She then pointed out that she had no problems with her weight - she was slim - because she was careful about what she ate. She thought that the two women should follow her example.

Everyone in the cafe could hear the unkind words directed at the friends. How must the women have felt? Sophie could see that their lunch together was spoiled. She cleared away their unfinished meals.

This incident makes me feel very sad. It's just not acceptable for an adult to criticise another adult, especially in such a direct and unkind and public way, is it?

But what about children? We often hear parents pointing out their 'faults': "You're too shy... lazy... clumsy... thoughtless... noisy... stubborn... unkind... selfish. You should watch what you eat and exercise more. When will you ever learn to do...?" They talk about their kids to other people. Their kids hear.

How do criticised children feel? Do they feel hurt? They know that they aren't loved and accepted just as they are. Could they be ashamed of who they are? Perhaps they feel like they are no good.

Maybe that's the whole point of criticism. If we make others feel bad, perhaps they'll do something about their 'faults'. But will they?

"Putting kids down makes them feel terrible," said Sophie. "It doesn't spur them on to do better. They just give up trying."

So what do kids need? They need to be accepted just as they are. But what if they really do have faults? Surely we can't accept our children's flaws? We can if we love. All the things we worry about might melt away under the influence of unconditional love.

"Sometimes parents complain about things that aren't faults at all," said Sophie. "These could be the things that make their children unique and special." It's a pity that we don't see that.

Years ago, I knew someone whose daughter was awkward and ungainly and not, on first impressions, as attractive and gifted as the other children. Maybe many of us might have been embarrassed if she were our daughter. Perhaps we'd wonder what other people were thinking of our child. Would we want to change her?

One day, the girl walked by with a crowd of other kids. Seeing me watching her, a friend whispered in my ear, "Her mother treats her like a princess. She feels as beautiful as the other girls."

And she was beautiful. We just weren't looking with the right eyes.

Maybe that's our problem. Our vision has become blurred. We've let other things get in the way of seeing our children clearly.

Our children don't have to fulfil other people's expectations. They don't have to be the people others think they should be. There is no reason why they should change to match our own ideas. Our children are perfectly them just the way they are. Just like they were the day they were born.

Unburying Our Love and Awe

It should have been a routine checkup, but things got a bit alarming when the obstetrician couldn't find my baby's heartbeat. Despite moving his instrument across my body to many different spots multiple times, we couldn't hear the glorious glub-dub of a 12-week old heart beating strongly.

"Sometimes it's difficult to hear the baby's heartbeat at this stage. It doesn't mean anything is wrong," said the doctor. "An ultrasound will tell us more."

So I walked across the hospital to the ultrasound department and explained the situation to the receptionist who said, "It's Friday. You won't want to spend the whole weekend not knowing one way or the other. Start drinking this water. I'll fit you in as soon as possible."

I sat in the waiting room with my jug of water, and as I sipped, I prayed that I'd have enough strength to face the words, "I'm sorry, your baby has died."

I feared the worst. After miscarrying six babies and losing our son Thomas when he was a day old, it seemed to me that this baby had also died.

An hour or so later, I was lying alongside the ultrasound screen with my eyes closed, trying to pretend I was somewhere else.

"There's your baby. Let's see if I can find the heart. Yes, it's beating beautifully!"

"My baby's alive?" I opened my eyes. Surely the technician had made a mistake? But there was no doubt. I looked at my baby. She was moving. Her heart was beating.

I floated home with a huge grin on my face. I'd been preparing myself for sorrow, but instead, I'd received joy. I couldn't quite believe it. I kept replaying the scene in the ultrasound room: "There's your baby. Let's see if I can find the heart. Yes, it's beating beautifully!"

That baby was Gemma-Rose.

When Gemma-Rose was born, I thought she was absolutely perfect. My heart overflowed with love and gratitude and joy.

Those wonderful, overwhelming feelings that we experience in the early days of parenthood don't always remain. They can appear to fade as our kids grow. I'm sure they are still there, but they get hidden under layers of worry and concern and tiredness. Perhaps we listen to other people. Maybe we think our kids have to fulfil outside expectations. Do we wonder how our children are going to fit into the world, get on with others, and earn their livings?

We try and change our children into the people we think they should be. We forget what miracles our children are and how, when we first met them, they seemed perfect just as they were.

So what do we do? Can we unbury those feelings of awe and love and gratitude? Perhaps we need to remember what's important. We have to look at our children carefully. See them as they really are. They are unique people who need us to accept and nurture and encourage them with unconditional love. They need the same love we gave them when we saw them for the very first time.

I look at Gemma-Rose. Do I have the same love for her as I did all those years ago when I held her for the first time? No. I love her even more now than I did then.

Love can grow and grow. And then when we think we can't love any more, it will grow some more. Isn't love miraculous?

Nothing is More Important Than Love

"What would you rather do, play that computer game or come and give me a hug?" I ask my daughters.

Without a moment's hesitation, Gemma-Rose says, "Hug you, of course!"

"Do you even need to ask?" says Sophie.

I am humbled. What did I do to deserve such love?

I love my children so much it hurts.

"I love you so much," I say.

My girls smile. "We know!"

Maybe my children weren't always aware of just how much I love them. I used to give them the impression I loved the good opinion of other people more. I would say such things as:

"You can't wear that! What will people say?"

"How could you embarrass me like that?"

"I haven't got time to do that with you. I have to clean the house. What if someone came to visit?"

"What's wrong with you? Kids your age can read. What will everyone think?"

I used to complain and criticise. I never appeared satisfied.

I wanted people to think I was a perfect mother with a perfect house and perfect children who were perfectly educated. But my children aren't perfect. Nor am I. One day I realised my kids love me just the way I am. They don't say, "We'd love you more if you were a better mother." Actually, their unconditional love makes me want to be the best mother in the world.

So I love my children the way they love me. They don't have to be perfect. They don't have to impress. It is enough that they are my children. My love for them overflows my heart. Yes, I love them so much it hurts.

Why does it hurt so much? Perhaps love is like a dart that wounds the heart. Maybe I imagine how I would feel if my children were no longer around. I hold my children tight, close my eyes and my heart suddenly contracts with love but also fear and pain at the thought of losing them.

I don't know what is ahead of us. I don't know how long I will have my children. At the very most I will have them here with me in our home for only a few years. So I have to make every moment count. Make each day as joyful as I can. Live life in a way that brings us together instead of pushing us apart. Live so that there are no regrets. Love until it overflows.

Nothing is more important than love. The most comprehensive curriculum, the best resources in the world, all the possible extra-curricular activities, all the experiences and opportunities I could provide, all the things I could buy: these are nothing compared to love, the unconditional kind, the kind of love with which God loves me. It is love that has the greatest power to make our children grow and develop into the people they are meant to be.

"I've come to give you your hug." Gemma-Rose climbs onto my lap. I place my cheek next to hers and drink in the sweet smell of her hair. I wrap my arms around my daughter, and I feel so very, very thankful that I have children who have taught me about love.

My Heart Skips with Love

I love how my girls will walk along the road, hand in hand, enjoying each other's company.

I also love how my kids enjoy being silly together with Andy and me. We pull funny faces at each other. We kangaroo hop up staircases. We say, "I'll race you to the next corner," and then everyone tears down the street oblivious to the stares of passers-by. Sometimes we talk in thick accents about all kinds of weird things. Very loudly. In public.

Many children might be embarrassed if their parents started hopping down the street, expecting them to follow. They'd probably cringe if their father talked very loudly using strange voices. And what about holding hands with parents and siblings? Not many kids would want to do that. It would be very uncool.

But my kids are different. They don't care what other people think. They never say, "Dad, don't do that!" while looking around to see who's watching. They don't walk along next to each other and Andy and me with their hands firmly entrenched in their pockets.

I wonder: why don't my children feel embarrassed by the things we do together? Why don't they mind expressing their love in a public way? Is it because we've never been embarrassed by them?

How easy it is to pass on the message that our kids aren't okay just as they are:

"You can't do that in public."

"Make sure you behave yourself. Don't embarrass me!"

"You can't go out looking like that. What will people think?"

Perhaps our children's attitude reflects our own.

I'm walking through the shopping centre, a girl either side of me. Their hands reach for mine. They don't care what people think. My heart skips with love.

Part VIII: Joy

The Beginning and End of Praise

Some people say that we shouldn't praise our kids. Maybe that's because kids might end up doing things only because they want to gain their parents' approval. And is there a risk a child might think she is better than everyone else if we praise her too often? We don't want our children becoming proud and obnoxious, do we?

So many parents stay well away from praise. But I don't. I think that the right kind of praise is definitely okay. Maybe it's even essential.

Praise is a natural part of our society. If I go to a concert and enjoy the performance, I applaud. If I get the chance to meet the performers or musicians, I thank them and tell them how much pleasure they gave me. If I enjoy a cup of coffee, I make a point of saying to the barista, "That was good coffee! Thank you!" I'm always looking for opportunities to tell people that I appreciate what they're doing, the effort they are making, how their talents - both the big kind and the less showy variety - are making a difference to my life and that of others.

So why shouldn't I give the same feedback and thanks to my kids?

Our children might not need our approval to motivate them to do what they love, but sometimes feedback in the form of praise is helpful. I know that when someone praises me, that praise encourages me to keep going when things get difficult. It tells me that I'm going in the right direction. I'm using my talents in the right way. Perhaps this is what I should be doing. Someone believes in me!

Of course, praise has to be sincere and specific and take into account the fact that our talents were given to us. They are a gift that we didn't have to earn. It's what we do with our talents that's important. I can't say to my daughter Imogen, "You are a fantastic singer!" That's not enough. So I say, "I enjoyed your performance immensely. Your top notes sent a shiver down my spine! You brought a lot of pleasure to the audience and me."

Or I say, "The mourners would have appreciated your singing. Your voice added beauty to the funeral." Maybe my words help my daughter see that all the hard work she puts into her music is worth it. This is what she is meant to do. By using her talents, Imogen is making a difference.

But surely all my praise makes Imogen think she is better than other people? Imogen knows that even though her musical talents may be bigger than some people's, they don't make her better than everyone else. I've always tried to pass on the attitude that our talents give us a big responsibility. We should be thankful for them. And we should use them for the good of other people.

For many years, Imogen has been the cantor and soloist at our parish church. She sits in the front row of the choir so that she has quick and easy access to the microphone at various times during the Mass. A couple of years ago, Fiona, a former cantor visited our church. Everyone was very excited to see her: "Come and sit with the choir! You can sing with us!"

I watched as all the singers in the front row shuffled up so that Fiona could sit with them. Would there be enough room for everyone in the pew? And then I saw Imogen give up her seat. She took her music and, without a fuss, made her way to the last row of the choir. She was willing to take a backseat where no one could see her. "I can sing just as well from the back as the front, Mum."

Isn't the willingness to put others ahead of ourselves worth more than the most extraordinary talent?

Often we look at praise from the perspective of our children. Is it good for them? Or maybe it's bad? But do we ever consider how praising affects us? When we praise properly, we are forced to look carefully. We can't praise without first appreciating our kids' talents and accepting who they are. Praise gives us a sense of awe: these are our kids! It leads to gratitude.

Perhaps we need to praise our kids (and other people), not only for their sakes but for ours as well.

We praise because we love. And the fruit of praise is joy both for the receiver and the giver.

So praise starts with love, and it ends with joy. What can be wrong with that?

Sometimes We Don't Need a Good Reason

Gemma-Rose (8) is playing by herself in the family room. The floor has disappeared under a sea of Barbie dolls, clothes, and accessories. My youngest daughter is absorbed in a huge game. I watch as she lines up all the Barbies and Kens. And then I notice something very strange.

"Why are the Ken dolls wearing dresses?" I ask.

"They don't have anything else to wear," Gemma-Rose replies. "All the trousers are worn out."

She shows me a garment that was once a sparkly prince's suit. The pants are split in a dozen places. "They can't wear these," Gemma-Rose giggles. "That wouldn't be modest. And the Kens can't go around wearing nothing at all. That would be even worse." She pretends to avert her eyes, and she giggles again.

Naked Kens? No, we can't have that. Something has got to be done.

"I'll have to buy them new clothes," I decide, and Gemma-Rose's eyes light up. I hardly ever buy her toys because she's inherited a mountain of them from her four older sisters. She also has things that used to belong to her brothers.

I take a trip to town to search for new Ken clothes. Sophie comes with me, but we leave Gemma-Rose at home. She is still absorbed in her huge Barbie game. There is only one shop in town that sells toys, so I head straight there. I look along the shelves. There are plenty of Barbie clothes but not a single Ken outfit.

"What do they expect Ken to wear?" I ask. Sophie shrugs her shoulders, not knowing the answer. "Barbie dresses?"

What am I to do? I can't go home empty-handed and watch the light fade from Gemma-Rose's eyes. But then I see something. Sophie sees it too.

"Wow! Look, Mum! Merida from the movie *Brave*! Isn't she pretty?"

"Do you think Gemma-Rose would like a Merida doll?"

"Oh, yes!"

Should I buy it? Or shouldn't I?

Gemma-Rose would love this doll.

It's a lot of money.

But it's so pretty.

I was only going to buy a set of Ken clothes, not a doll. Gemma-Rose has plenty of dolls. Look at all the ones she has inherited from the older girls.

But those dolls are looking old, and their clothes are wearing out, and it is so special owning something that was chosen just for you.

Buying the doll wouldn't be sensible.

But I won't have a little girl who wants to play with dolls, for much longer. Soon I won't have anyone to buy dolls for.

But there is no one to pass the doll onto when Gemma-Rose no longer wants to play with it. It would be a waste of money.

Think of her smile if I came home with a doll.

It's not her birthday. She'll get spoilt.

Or maybe she won't.

I come to the conclusion that Gemma-Rose doesn't need another doll. There's no good reason why I should buy it. But I don't listen to reason.

Go on. Buy the doll.

So I buy the doll, a pale-skinned Merida doll. There is a delightful sprinkling of freckles on her nose and cheeks, and she has long red hair that falls in curls over her shoulders. Gemma-Rose is going to adore her.

I walk through the front door and call, "Gemma-Rose! I have a present for you!"

Gemma-Rose runs towards me, and I hold out the plastic shopping bag. She reaches in and draws out the doll in a box, and her eyes open wide. She can hardly speak: "For me? Merida! Is it mine?"

I assure Gemma-Rose that she is not dreaming. The doll belongs to her. She thrusts her arms around my waist, and I am well and truly hugged.

"I couldn't find any Ken clothes," I say apologetically. But Gemma-Rose no longer cares about Ken clothes. The male dolls can continue wearing dresses. She has a Merida doll. An unexpected Merida doll. A new doll that I chose just for her. She grins widely.

And then I realise that life is not always about making sensible decisions. Sometimes doing things for no good reason at all is very important.

I bask in all Gemma-Rose's radiating joy, and I grin too.

Trying to Be a Fun Mum

When my first two children were very small, I had a best friend called Mellie. We got on extremely well despite being very different.

I was an always-in-control type of person. As well as liking an organised and spotless house, I loved my children clean and tidy and always presentable. Hair ribbons were good too. I encouraged my children to sleep and eat at regular times, and I approved of empty plates.

In contrast, Mellie was a very relaxed and comfortable-with-herself kind of person. Her children ate what they liked when they liked. They wore whatever they liked too. Mellie never shouted, "Where's your jumper? It's too cold to run around in just a T-shirt." She trusted her children were the best judges of their own needs. Mellie's house was never organised. It was a children's adventure playground from one end to the other. Mellie's kids didn't need to worry about damaging the carpets or making a mess. They could spread their games all over the house. They had fun.

Fun? Yes, sometimes I wondered what Mellie thought of me. Did she think I was too restrictive, too bound up in unnecessary rules and regulations? Did she think I wasn't a very fun mother at all? Now Mellie didn't say anything. I just looked at her ways and compared them to mine, and I wondered.

Several times a week, Mellie dropped off her small son Jack at our house. And I looked after him while she worked. One day Jack arrived with a bag of toys. Soon he was sharing the contents with my daughter Felicity. Out came a toy car, a big stone, a pencil, a bear and a lipstick.

My first thought was, "Oh, no! Lipstick! That'll make a lot of mess." I was just about to demand Jack hand that pink stick over when I stopped. I thought, "If Mellie thinks it's okay for children to play with lipstick then perhaps I should let them keep it. I shall be a fun mum for once. We can clean off the mess later."

So I sat back and watched the two four-year-olds playing together. Jack drew all over Felicity's face, and she drew over his. "It'll wash off," I reminded myself as I itched to grab the stick. They giggled as they drew patterns on their arms and legs. I suggested some paper, and they filled a pile of sheets with swirls and crosses. Both children's eyes were bright with enjoyment. They had huge grins on their faces. They were having a fantastic time. And I was absolutely certain that I was an incredibly fun mum.

When Mellie arrived to pick up Jack, she looked at her lipstick-decorated son, but she didn't say a word. I ignored the mess too. "See you on Thursday!" she called out as she left. The lipstick was never ever mentioned.

We moved house, and Mellie and I drifted apart. Now and then, we'd exchange a letter, but it was a long time before we had the opportunity to meet up in person. Then a couple of years ago, Mellie and her husband Evan came to visit.

Soon Mellie and I were sharing memories. "Do you remember this...?" and "Do you remember that...?"

"Do you remember how I liked to be in control of everything?" I asked Mellie, laughing but also wincing a bit at the memory. "I always wondered what you thought of me. We were so different. I always admired your relaxed mothering style and wished I could be like you."

Mellie laughed. "Oh, I think I was too relaxed at times," she admitted.

"But you were fun. Do you remember when you let Jack bring that lipstick to our house? I wanted to take it off him, but I decided I was going to be a fun mum like you."

Mellie opened her eyes wide, was silent for a moment, and then a huge laugh spilt from deep within her. "I didn't let Jack bring along that lipstick. I didn't even know he had it."

"You didn't?"

"When I saw Jack covered with lipstick, I was horrified. I wondered why you hadn't confiscated it. I thought you were a very irresponsible mother. But I didn't want to tell you."

So I hadn't been a fun mother after all. I'd been irresponsible. Twenty years later, it didn't matter. I laughed too.

A fun mum? What makes someone fun? Is it letting everyone do as they like, or is it just letting go of the things that aren't really important?

I ask my children – my children who no longer have to empty their plates or wear matching clothes (though I still like ribbons!) - "Do you think I'm a fun mum?"

"Oh, yes!" they all say.

I think back to the day of the lipstick disaster all those years ago. I remember Felicity's and Jack's bright eyes and the sound of their giggles. Irresponsible? No. Despite Mellie's opinion, I am still absolutely certain, on that particular day, I was an incredibly fun mum. I think Felicity and Jack would agree.

The Splat

The women's race is about to begin.

"Are you ladies going to run?" I ask, looking at the row of mothers sitting on the sidelines. They all cross their arms, shake their heads emphatically and remain firmly attached to their chairs.

"What about you? You could have a go," one woman challenges back.

"But I'm the oldest here," I protest. "You're all much younger than me." I know my excuse is poor. I'm not exactly a fragile old woman. I'm fit and healthy.

Then Imogen appears. "Come on, Mum. The race is about to start. You are going to run, aren't you?"

My old age excuse won't convince Imogen, so I say, "I'm not dressed for running." I look down at my long skirt and boots. "I can't run in these clothes."

Or can I? Suddenly, a wild thought comes into my head. Shall I do the usual mother thing and stay safely on the sidelines? Or shall I be daring? Should I throw caution to the wind and do the unexpected? I imagine flying through the air, my children cheering me on. I shall feel wonderful as I cross the finish line.

I have made my decision. Imogen smiles as I take my place with all the other daring mums. Yes, I can do it. Probably no one knows I can run. I'm going to surprise them all. I will be spectacular.

Ready. Set. Go.

We are off. I can feel the breeze on my face as I race through the air. I am moving beautifully. My arms are pumping. For a full ten metres, I am poetry in motion. And then my feet slip from underneath me. I am doing the unexpected. I am flying towards the ground. I hit it in one huge, spectacular, surprising splat.

I lie still, and my friend Michele abandons the race and comes to my aid. "Sue! Are you okay?" I think for a few seconds: am I okay? No, something is wrong. I don't feel quite right.

Then I realise that what I'm feeling is not pain but embarrassment. I look up at the anxious faces around me, and then I smile, and I jump up quickly. "I'm fine. It was my boots. They're not designed for running. I should have run barefoot." I am anxious to explain that it was the boots, not me. Everyone looks relieved, and although no one laughs, I feel a bit foolish.

Dirts covers me from head to foot. Someone kindly dusts me down. Imogen insists on examining me for injuries but finds only two gravel rash hands.

"I told you I wasn't dressed for running," I say again feeling very silly.

Later, as we are travelling home, we talk about the athletics carnival.

Sophie: "I came first in the cross country race and third in the sprints."

Imogen: "I came second in my race."

Charlotte: "Our relay team came dead last, but at least we tried!"

Gemma-Rose: "I ran two laps."

Andy: "I don't know where I came in the fathers' race, but I beat Uncle Ath, and that's all that matters."

Me: "I went splat! No one else went splat like me!"

I sit quietly thinking. I wanted to surprise everyone by doing something spectacular. I'd imagined flying across the finish line in triumph. Instead, I'd ended up flat on the ground covered in dirt. Perhaps I should have just stayed safely on the sidelines with the sensible mothers. I wouldn't have ended up feeling so embarrassed after performing my unexpected splat.

Why do we get so embarrassed when we fail? Do we really look as silly as we feel? And how much fun are we missing out on as we sit safely on the sidelines, too afraid to get involved?

"Are you going to try again next year, Mum?" Sophie asks. "Will you race again?"

I am silent for a few moments. Will I play it safe, or will I take a risk?

"Next year, I'm not going to run in boots. I am going to wear proper running shoes."

The girls smile at me. "You'll be spectacular, Mum!"

I grin back at them. And I decide that from now on I'm going to be daring and adventurous. I'm going to have fun!

A Thrilling Experience

We are going on holiday. We have booked a cottage by the lake, not far from the beach, and we are excited. It will be our first going-away-holiday for a few years. We are taking the girls but not the boys. They will stay at home because they have to go to work. They will also look after the cats. Poor them! Poor cats! Will the boys remember to clean the kitty litter?

In the shed of our dream cottage-by-the-lake, there are six bikes, and I have been thinking: could I become a bike rider at my not-so-young age? Could I be daring? Will I fall off?

I can ride an exercise bike. I perch up there on the saddle, my legs pumping up and down, and never once have I toppled off. I turn the tension knob and struggle up make-believe hills. Then I fly down the other side before challenging myself to a flat terrain sprint. My legs are a blur. And even then, I don't fall off.

But a real bike?

I didn't learn to ride a two-wheeler bike as a child. I never had the opportunity. Our house sat halfway down a steep hill. Maybe my mother pictured me flying down that road, pigtails streaming behind me, voice screaming as I sped out of control before landing in a heap, arms and legs everywhere. Did she imagine herself picking up the pieces? All I know is that I never had a bike. Child protection, I guess.

Andy is a cyclist. More precisely, he is a cyclist when he has a bike to ride. Quite often he goes to the garage all primed for exercise only to discover his bike is missing a seat, a wheel, or a chain. Someone, who shall be nameless, has once again transplanted bits of Andy's bike to his own. Need a new tyre? No problem! Just exchange a wheel with Dad's bike, the spare parts bike. He won't mind. Or will he? Bike bits litter the garage floor and rarely is there a bike complete and ready for action.

Years ago, Andy and I went youth hostelling in Bath, England. We discovered a bike hire shop, and Andy's eyes lit up as he imagined cycling around the town. It would be far more fun than sight-seeing on foot. We could cover more distance, whip in and out of the traffic, experience the thrill of flying along in the breeze.

So we hired a couple of bikes and adjusted their seats. I mounted eager for that thrilling experience. Soon I would be flying along effortlessly, with the wind lifting my hair, passing all the poor tourists on foot. I smiled. For a while, all went exceedingly well. I could pedal. I could balance. I didn't fall off. I was enjoying myself.

With confidence rising, I headed out into the main street traffic. And then when I least expected it, that thrilling experience became far more thrilling than I ever anticipated. I tried to change lanes. For the first time ever, I removed one hand from the bike and stretched it out, indicating I was moving right. And then I wobbled. The front wheel went one way, the back the other, and I just knew I was going to fly through the air and land right under the bus that was fast approaching. I was going to die. I'd never get to marry Andy. My mother was right. Bikes are a danger.

But I didn't end up on the road in pieces. I don't know what happened. It's all a blur. All I remember is being back on the footpath, safe but shaking all over. I told Andy I was never going to ride a bike again. When I'd calmed down, I remembered that the best thing to do after a fall from a bike is to get right back up on the saddle. Or was that after a fall from a horse? And did I actually fall? It didn't matter. There was another reason I had to try again: we'd hired the bikes for the whole day, and we couldn't waste our money.

So I climbed back on the bike, but I didn't head onto the road. Instead, we found a park where I could practice balancing and riding one-handed while indicating. We spent hours cycling up and down the paths, and I very politely thrust out my arm now and then to tell all the pedestrians that I'd be circling the fountain or heading right just before the statue. It turned out to be a fantastic day. And it was also the last time I rode a real bike.

So shall I be adventurous? Shall I join Andy and the girls when they set off for a cycle around the lake, when we go away on holiday?

The answer is yes. I really have no choice. I have a reputation to uphold: I am a daring mother. I am the sort of mother who has the courage to enter races when sensible mothers refuse to take part. I am a mother who runs and falls splat on her face and still gets up and vows to do it all over again.

But for just one moment I think: what if my bike wobbles out of control and deposits me splash in the lake? It could be very embarrassing. I may end up with my hair plastered close to my head. But will that kill me? No. I am willing to take the risk.

We are going on holiday, our first away-from-home holiday in years. I have booked a cottage by the lake, not far from the sea. In the shed of our dream cottage, there are six bikes, and we are going cycling: Andy, the girls and me.

Hold on Tight

Every Tuesday morning, my daughters and I pile into the car and head off to town. While Charlotte and Sophie are enjoying their piano lessons, Gemma-Rose and I have a mission to accomplish. Can we do all our shopping, and then drive back to the music teacher's house before the older girls reappear? It's always a race.

Last Tuesday we must have run up and down the supermarket aisles much quicker than normal because, before we knew it, we were back at the car, stowing our shopping in the boot, with minutes to spare.

"It's a pity you're not little anymore," I said to Gemma-Rose. "We could have stopped off at the park for a few minutes on the way back. You could have swung on the swings."

"Nobody gets too old for the swings, Mum," Gemma-Rose smiled. "Even Imogen likes to swing, and she's 20!"

"So you want to go to the park?"

My eleven-year-old daughter nodded her head.

Soon we were at the park. Gemma-Rose hoisted herself onto the swing, thrust her legs backwards and forwards and swung towards the sky. As I watched her, my heart yearned for years gone by when I regularly stopped at the park with my troop of young children. "Push me higher, Mum!" little people would urge. "Catch me, Mum!" they'd cry as they slid down the slippery dip. "Watch me, Mum! I can climb high!" Yes, I miss those days when a simple trip to the park was a pure delight for everyone.

"Do you want to have a go, Mum?" Gemma-Rose called, as she put down her feet and brought the swing to a halt.

Me? On the swings? "Why not?!"

"Do you need a push, Mum?"

"No, I remember what to do!"

Soon I was swinging higher and higher. I began to feel like Auntie Jenny from my children's novel, *The Angels of Abbey Creek.*

Auntie Jenny is a lot of fun. She doesn't just push the swing. She sits on the swing and has a go herself. The children watch as she swings higher and higher. "Will she swing right over the top in a circle?" Lizzie wonders.

Would I swing over the top too? I began to feel a little bit dizzy, as the ground rushed up to meet me and then raced away again. I wondered why the council hadn't banned swings. Surely swings aren't safe? What if a mother fell off?

"What if I fall off?" I shouted.

"Just hold on tight, Mum!"

So that's what I did. I held on tight.

I held on tight to the swing. I held on tight to the moment. I savoured it completely before it disappeared forever.

"Not many mums swing on the swings," observed Gemma-Rose, as we left the park.

I don't suppose they do. But they should.

Do you?

Speed Angel Joy

I am sitting by the lake watching four girls scooting along the path. They are the Speed Angel Sisters, and they are fast! Now and then, the girls veer off onto the grass and come to a sudden halt: a pedestrian is approaching. When the speedway is clear again, strong legs start pushing, wheels revolve, hair flies back, and sounds of laughter drift towards me.

Four tired girls drag themselves back to the picnic table. They are breathless and red-faced, but joy pours out of them.

"Wow! That was fun," Sophie (10) exclaims as she plops herself down next to me.

"Thirsty? Hungry?" I ask, and four heads nod emphatically. I pass out drinks and slices of cake, and for a few minutes, there is not a sound except for the screeching of the sulphur-crested cockatoos which are flying overhead. Other birds catch our attention. We name all the ones we can see. Then a black and white bird on long thin legs struts by, and we wonder what it is. I open the bird book, and soon we've identified it. It's a magpie lark.

Talk turns to autumn and deciduous trees. Then the girls take a walk around the lake gathering leaves and noticing the different tree shapes. They take photos of birds and leaves and the lake and each other. They are thinking of scrapbooks and stories. When they return to the picnic table, they unpack their sketchbooks and pencils. A minute later, four girls are busy drawing, and while they are working, we continue to talk.

Why were all the non-native ducks ejected from the lake? Where did they go? Didn't they have a right to live at the lake? Weren't they born there? And if you are born somewhere, doesn't that give you the right to call a place home? What about all the non-indigenous Australians? But also, what about the indigenous peoples? How did they feel when outsiders invaded their homeland? How do they feel today?

The girls have rested. It's now time for more lake-side scooting. After tossing their pencils and sketchbooks into the basket, the girls grab their scooters. They run down to the path and begin flying along.

I sit and watch my daughters, and my heart overflows with joy. Here I am with four of my children enjoying the autumn sun on a Thursday morning. I look at the blue, blue sky, and the sun shimmering off the water, the coloured leaves, the birds, and the beautiful smiles on the faces of my daughters. It is a perfect moment, a moment I want to remember forever. Surely I must be the most blessed mother ever?

I wonder about joy. What is it, and where does it come from? What is this feeling that's flooding my heart? Could it be love? Could it be God?

I remember some words from the book *I Believe in Love* by Fr d'Elbee:

Do you think you are a joy for Jesus?... is it not a matter of elementary logic that a father and his child should be a joy for one another? Jesus, You are my joy, and I, too, am Your joy. Is it not written that "His delight is to be with the children of men"?

I think about how my children love me. I think about their trust, their delight and enjoyment of life, their joy. And I wonder: am I like a child? Do I trust? Am I a joy and delight for God like my children are for me?

The morning is over. We are driving home. I reflect on what I have learnt today. What have my children added to my education? I think about the number of birds and trees I can now identify and how I can explain how photosynthesis works and why leaves change colour in autumn. Then there are the sketches and the photos, and the scrapbooks I might help make. I recall the dilemma of being a non-indigenous duck. I could have learnt about the fun of scooting. I could have been a Speed Angel Mother flying along with the wind in her hair. Yes, it has been an education-packed morning.

But there is one more thing I have learnt, something much more important than identifying birds or trees or taking good photos.

I have learnt about joy, about a mother and her children being a joy for each other. And how important it is to slow down and spend time together learning and sharing, loving and enjoying one other. How many times do I say, "I'd like to do that with my children... one day... when I get time"? But time moves so fast. My four scooting Speed Angel Sisters will grow up before I know it. And will I look back and wish I'd spent more time just enjoying my children, delighting in them, experiencing the pure joy of being their mother?

And will I have been God's little child scooting along through life with trust and confidence, delight and abandonment? Will I have taken joy in Him who takes joy in me? Will I have tried to love as He loves me?

Part IX: Forgiveness

When We Fail

"I didn't feel right from the moment I woke up," says Amina. "I knew it was going to be a bad day."

My friend pauses to sip her coffee before continuing: "Do you ever have those days when you feel tired and out of sorts? It's so hard to communicate properly. You say the wrong thing. It feels like no one's listening." I nod.

"We'd been invited to Sandy and Matthew's party. But yesterday, I just didn't want to go. I moaned, and Jake told me that I'd been the one to accept the invitation, not him. And then we got into a huge argument. I said I wasn't going. Jake said it was too late to back out. And then I told him to go without me. And he said not to be silly. I couldn't stay home by myself. He insisted we'd have a good time once we got there. Anyway, the kids were looking forward to the party. I suppose they were until we started arguing. At that moment, they were hiding away, probably wishing I'd cheer up and things would get back to normal."

"So, what happened?" I ask.

"I refused to go to the party, and Jake kept trying to change my mind. The minutes ticked by. Then Jake said, 'We're going to be late,' and I felt even worse because I knew he was going to give up and go without me."

"But you didn't want to go."

"But I didn't want to stay at home either. I was all churned up inside. What if everyone went to the party and enjoyed themselves and I was left alone to wallow in my misery?"

"So you went?"

"Yes. At the very last minute, I ran out of the house, slamming the door behind me and got in the car. Jake smiled, but I refused to smile back. I sat in stony silence the whole way to the party. When Sandy greeted me at the door, I had to pretend everything was okay. Have you ever had to slap a smile on your stiff face and hope no one notices you're in a rotten mood?" I nod.

"The kids went off in search of their friends and Jake helped himself to a beer. He asked me if I'd like a glass of wine. I wanted to say yes, but I said no. I was determined not to have a good time. But Jake looked like he was enjoying himself. This really annoyed me. How could he smile and make small talk when I felt so miserable? It didn't seem right."

"What happened?"

"A few people talked to me, and I tried not to show them that something was wrong, and then that got too hard, so I retreated to the far corner of the garden by myself. I had my camera with me, so I took some photos and tried to look busy and normal."

Amina stares out the cafe window for a long moment. And then she looks at me and says, "I felt so bad inside." A tear slides down her cheek. "I just wanted to leave the party. Get in the car and drive away. Keep driving and never return. I thought I'd be doing Jake and the kids a favour. Surely they didn't want to be with me? I didn't even want to be with me. So I went in search of Jake and asked for the car keys and told him I was leaving. He didn't want me to go. He said he needed me. I refused to believe that and kept demanding the keys. Eventually, Jake gave them to me, and I walked to the car."

"Did you drive away?"

"No. I didn't really want to leave."

"What did you want?"

"I wanted things to be normal again. I wanted to put things right. But I didn't know how to do that.

"I walked down the street and then came back and sat on the bench that's in Sandy's front garden. I stared at my feet, trying not to cry. And then I heard someone coming through the garden gate. I took a deep breath. It was Pia. She sat down next to me. I don't know how she knew I was in the front garden by myself. I thought she was with all the other teenagers.

We sat quietly together for a couple of minutes and then Pia reached out for my hand. I looked up, and she was smiling. It was such a gentle, warm, loving smile. It was as if she was saying, 'I love you, Mum. It's okay.' Pia pulled me close. And all those miserable feelings melted away. I felt so loved. I'd failed, but it didn't matter. I was loved, regardless."

"So everything was alright?"

"Yes. I had wanted to put things right, but I couldn't do it alone. I was in too deep. Pia recognised that. She wanted to help me. When she reached for my hand, instantly, everything was okay."

Amina finishes her coffee and then she says, "Do you know how it feels when you fail, but no one criticises you? What it feels like when they don't hold your actions against you but just want to help? How it feels when other people are more concerned about you than what you have done to them?"

"You feel like you want to be the best person in the whole world."

Amina raises her eyebrows in surprise. "You understand!"

"You want to be worthy of all that love? You want to be the best wife and mother you can possibly be?" Amina nods.

My pretend friend reaches for my hand. And I whisper, "Oh yes, I understand perfectly. Every word. Your story could be mine."

Damaged Flowers

We entered the florist shop. Crammed into its tiny space were pink and blue teddy bears sitting on shelves awaiting newborn babies, bobbing helium balloons, racks of greeting cards, potted plants with hothouse flowers, and hanging bamboo wind chimes. And on the floor, there were numerous silver metal buckets, overflowing with the most exquisite flowers with a thousand different scents.

I was at the counter, digging about in my bag for some money when I heard: "Well, it's your flower now. It's no good to me. I can't sell a broken flower. You may as well have it."

I turned my head to see a woman thrusting a bright yellow lily at Gemma-Rose. My seven-year-old daughter took the bloom and then bowed her head towards the floor.

"Children ought to be taught not to touch!" the shop assistant said, looking directly at me.

"I'm sorry," I apologised. "I'll pay for the whole lily stalk and the broken flower."

"No, that's okay," the woman said gruffly. "But I can't have everyone coming in here and touching. Even adults do it. The flowers are delicate. If people damage them, I can't sell them."

I hastily agreed as I handed over my money for the greetings card I'd selected. I then decided it would be prudent to get away from the annoyed woman as fast as we could.

"You know you shouldn't touch," I reminded Gemma-Rose as we headed out the door, and then looking at her subdued face, I added, "Was it just so beautiful you had to feel it?"

Gemma-Rose's little face bobbed up and down, and tears welled in her eyes. By the time we reached the van, a river was streaming down her face. She was sobbing; her little heart was breaking. My heart cracked and felt broken too. I bent down and enclosed Gemma-Rose's heaving shoulders in a big hug. I wanted to put things right for her, to get rid of all those awful feelings that were consuming her, to see her eyes light up again. The sun had disappeared from her day. And from mine as well.

"If I went back to the shop and bought that damaged lily stalk for you, would that make you feel better?"

Gemma-Rose nodded, so I took her hand and led her back up the road and into the florist shop.

The shop assistant: "You're back?"

"Yes, we want to buy the flower my daughter broke. She broke it so I should buy it and then everything will be put right."

The woman reached into the bucket of lily stalks searching for the one with a ragged section where a flower was missing. After a few seconds, I could see she couldn't decide which stalk was the damaged one.

"This might be the one," she said finally.

"I'll have another stalk too, please. The flowers will look pretty on the table, won't they, Gemma-Rose?"

She nodded and smiled as I pulled out my purse. I handed over some money, and then I said, "All fixed."

"The flowers are delicate, you know," persisted the shop assistant. "Children have to be taught..."

I interrupted, "But it's all fixed now! The flower now belongs to us." And we left the shop, with Gemma-Rose carrying her bouquet, knowing we wouldn't be back.

I can understand the woman's frustration. She is a business woman. The flowers are her livelihood. But I also know mistakes sometimes happen. It's how we handle other people's mistakes that is important.

I think about mistakes in general, how you can't go back and unmake them. But we can choose how we deal with them. We can make someone suffer when they have made a mistake. We can make them feel very miserable. We can make them pay. Or we can turn that mistake into something good, an unexpected gift.

Just imagine:

"Oh, the flower is broken. I bet you didn't realise it was so delicate. Never mind. Would you like me to show you the flowers and then you won't have to worry about damaging them? You can have the lily. Isn't it beautiful? Take it home and enjoy it!"

Gemma-Rose's eyes would have lit up with pleasure. The broken flower would have been transformed from a mistake into an unexpected gift, making a little girl happy.

And she would have known not to touch the flowers the next time we went into the florist shop.

It sounds like I've got it all worked out, doesn't it? No doubt, I always handle other people's mistakes in the right way. Or perhaps I don't.

I think about the time when Andy threw his red t-shirt into the washing machine with all the white clothes, including my new skirt. I remember how someone else knocked my favourite framed picture to the floor shattering the glass. And what about the time my precious Aberystwyth mug from my university days ended up on the floor in a hundred pieces?

I turn red thinking of how I reacted. And suddenly, the florist's actions no longer annoy me. I'm feeling guilty about telling you her story. I could easily have found an example of my own to share.

I think about the mistakes I'm always making. Does God shout, "How many times have I told you...? How could you...? When are you going to learn...?" No. God forgives me and uses my mistakes for good. He turns my damaged flowers into beautiful, unimaginable gifts.

So why can't I do the same for someone else?

The Lost Head

We love to visit Athanasius and Edith and their children who all live in the city. But we do not love the city. We can't understand why Ath and his wife Edie prefer to live in this crowded, noisy, busy place when they could live down the road from us enjoying the bush, the clean air, the peace and quiet, and our company. And also a long trip to work.

Ath has invited us to lunch. We travel up the freeway, gathering more and more traffic, the closer we get to the city. Cars weave in and out and whiz by at dangerous speeds. I shut my eyes, but I can still feel the sudden braking as yet another crazy driver forces his way into the lane ahead of us. Finally, we are there. I sigh with relief.

Ath opens his front door, his children pour out onto the driveway, and we receive a huge welcome. I bend down, and little arms fling themselves around my neck and hold me close. Children pull us inside. We sit down. We feel a bit hot and bothered after our long trip. But not for long. Edie places cups of freshly brewed coffee into our hands, and dishes of nuts and biscuits appear by our sides. I look around, feasting my eyes. There are fresh lilies in a sparkling vase on the coffee table, soft plumped up cushions behind our backs, a thick rug under our toes. I lean back and gently put the rocking chair into motion. I feel special. I feel pampered. This is wonderful.

Ath and Edie have a gallery of photographs on their living room wall. There are beautiful images of exquisite newborn babies, cheeky toddlers, a grinning young boy. I leave my comfortable chair and walk around the room, paying careful attention to each of the displayed pictures. Suddenly I stop. "That's Pope John Paul II. He's in your wedding photo!" I exclaim. Ath explains how he and Edie travelled to Rome for a papal marriage blessing. Edie looks so beautiful in her bridal dress; Ath is a very proud husband; Pope John Paul II smiles gently upon the newlywed couple.

Talk turns to honeymoons. Ath and Edie spent part of their honeymoon in Ars. How I would love to go to Ars! St John Vianney is one of my favourite saints. I want to hear all about the village, the church, the saint.

"We bought a statue of the Cure of Ars, but it got damaged. His head has broken off," Ath says. "I guess we could fix it with a bit of glue."

"Give it to me," I insist. I know a man who is an expert at fixing statues. Len restored the two large statues at the entrance to our parish church. He could easily fix the head of the precious honeymoon saint.

"Sounds great," says Ath. "Perhaps Len could fix my Infant of Prague statue at the same time?"

"And my Sacred Heart one," I add.

I take the two statues and St John Vianney's head, and I wrap everything very carefully in tissue paper. As soon as I arrive home, I transfer all the pieces to my 'safe place', the top drawer of my chest.

A few days later, knowing I am likely to see Len at Mass, I go to my drawer to retrieve the statues. I pull out the chipped Infant of Prague and St John Vianney's body. But where is his head? I tip everything out of my drawer, and then I replace it all. No head. I empty the drawer again and have another look. Still no head. I search a third time. Where can it be? I cannot believe that I have lost the head of a saint. I have lost the head of Ath and Edie's precious honeymoon statue. My heart sinks. What will they say?

I sit down at the computer to make my confession.

Dear Ath,

I am so sorry. I have been careless. I have lost the Cure of Ars' head. I know the statue is so precious to you."

I feel awful. How can I have done such a thing?

Soon a message arrives in my inbox. It's from Ath. I hardly dare read it.

"Dear Sue,

It's only a statue. Please don't upset yourself over it. People are more important than things. Edie and I now have a good excuse to return to Ars. Please don't think about it anymore."

I feel relieved. What a good friend Ath is!

I still have the Infant of Prague, so I take it, and my Sacred Heart, to Len. He says he will be delighted to fix them.

A few weeks pass and a few more. Ath doesn't ask about his statue, and I don't mention it. Several months go by. Then one morning, I catch up with Len after Mass.

"Sue, I am so sorry. My wife Anne usually does all the detailed work on the statues. But she hasn't been well. Her hands have been shaking a lot. The other day she picked up all the statues. And then she dropped them. They shattered into dozens of pieces. I wasn't able to save anything. I'm so sorry."

"Don't worry, Len," I say. "They were only statues, only things. It doesn't matter."

As I arrive home, I think of Ath. I still have to tell him about the Infant of Prague. I sit down at the computer:

"Dear Ath,

I saw Len this morning at Mass. He had unfortunate news. I'm very sorry..."

The reply comes back:

"Dear Sue,

It doesn't matter at all. The statues were only things. Poor Anne. I will pray for her."

The next time I see Ath, I beg him, "Please do not give me anything precious of yours again. I cannot be trusted. I will only worry." But then I remember it's too late. Ath has already entrusted me with something priceless, someone infinitely precious: his daughter, Augusta. How glad I am to have my beautiful Goddaughter. I wonder if Ath will ever let her come to stay overnight. Or will he worry I might lose her?

I'm in the living room, reading a book. Suddenly there's a loud crash and someone shouts, "Oh no! What have you done?"

I hear Andy running towards the kitchen. "What did you break?" he asks.

A little solemn-faced girl looks up at him, but before she can say a word, someone pipes up, "It's only a thing, Dad. Things can be replaced. People are more important!"

And Andy agrees and hurries off for a broom while the worried look on the little girl's face disappears.

Yes, people are much more important than things. A great lesson taught to us by the lost head of a favourite saint and the wisdom of a very forgiving friend.

Part X: Babies and Toddlers

Babies and Toddlers and Unschooling

When we were homeschooling rather than unschooling, and we had babies or toddlers in our family, life sometimes got very stressful. Keeping up with the older children's learning and, at the same time, seeing to the needs of our little ones sometimes seemed almost impossible.

I once wrote:

There were days when I'd crack: "If you don't do your school work... if you don't learn this... or that... if you don't try... I will send you to school. I can't take any more." I'd rush out the back door and sit on the garden wall, my head pounding, my heart racing. I'd kept my children home so we could enjoy each other so that I could give the best to my children. And some days we didn't enjoy anything at all: the baby would cry, the toddler was demanding, and I didn't have the energy to encourage the older ones along, to make them do the work I thought they should be doing. I didn't enjoy feeling so tired and helpless and frustrated. I felt I was failing both as a mother and a homeschooling parent. Was it worth it? Should I carry out my threat and send my children to school? But I couldn't quite do it. I knew this job of raising and educating my children was mine alone, and I had to find a way that worked.

Of course, I did find a way that worked. Over time, we made changes and eventually arrived at unschooling.

And that might be the end of the story because babies and unschooling are perfectly suited to each other. All we have to do is go with the flow. Forget about what we normally do and accept the new situation. Learning will continue whether we're looking after babies or doing what we used to do before they were born. Actually, the baby seasons of our lives are unique and very rich learning experiences.

I could write all that and then move on. But maybe that's not enough. Although we know in theory that everything in life is a learning experience, we might still worry. We feel pulled in multiple directions. We want to fulfil the needs of our older kids as well as the younger ones. Even if we're not directing our children's learning, they still might want our help. What about strewing and getting involved with all their projects and working on our interests? Will our children become resentful and complain if we haven't got time to take them places or find resources or offer our help? Will their learning be adversely affected if we can't be involved? And what about our own needs?

We could fight to keep life the same. We might try to make the baby fit into the family so that life can carry on as usual. Or we could accept and adjust. But what will help us do this? What do we need to hear so that we can put aside our concerns, relax and enjoy this very special family time with our little ones?

Do we need to change how we're looking at the situation, think more about what we learn during baby times, do some creative thinking about other possibilities, ponder love and self-sacrifice, consider what's most important and what being a family really means, and recognise that this is a time when we need to trust?

The Baby Season of Life

"Sue, how did you cope when you had babies in your family? How did they fit into your unschooling way of life?"

I've been asked these questions a number of times. Here's what I reply: "We didn't fit our babies into our life. We adjusted our life to fit around them."

Babies and toddlers are such precious little people. Maybe we don't always appreciate this when we're tired, and we have lots of things pulling us in many different directions. Babies are a real blessing, and their needs are just as important as the educational needs of our older children.

The baby times of our lives don't last for very long even though some days we imagine they will. Needy babies grow into curious toddlers. And toddlers turn into little independent people. One day, we suddenly realise our child is no longer following us around. Her world has expanded. She's outside playing with her siblings. And we look back and wonder how we got here so fast. And maybe we wish we'd enjoyed our little ones more instead of letting stress chase away the unique delights of this special time of life.

We should put the needs of our babies and toddlers first. That's easy to say. But can we do it? How do we feel about putting aside all our usual activities for a time? Peaceful? Accepting? Or do we feel guilty if we're not able to do all we used to do? Our older children also have needs. They want us to help them with their activities. They'd like to go places and do things with us. And how can we help them as well as look after ourselves and the younger members of the family? Because if we don't keep up with everything, won't our older children get 'behind'? Or maybe they'll complain. And the last thing we need is resentful and unhappy children to deal with.

The problem is that even if we want to, we can't keep up with everything we'd like to do. That's impossible. But it's also okay because our kids won't get behind and maybe they won't get resentful either.

The baby seasons of our lives are full of wonderful learning experiences if we just look with the right eyes. Of course, everyone can learn about changing nappies and putting babies to sleep. Children will soon know all about the development of babies: when they crawl and walk and talk and start to eat solid food.

But older siblings will also learn about self-sacrifice and love.

Our children watch us carefully. They see us putting others ahead of ourselves. We emerge out of deep sleep in the middle of the night to feed babies. We make dinner for hungry toddlers at the end of the day when we'd rather collapse into an armchair. We wash mountains of clothes. And, hopefully, we also make time for smiles and hugs and kisses. Yes, our kids notice what we do. They learn that we make sacrifices because we love them. In their turn, I'm sure our children also learn to put others ahead of themselves.

Maybe some people imagine that unschooled kids are self-centred. Life revolves around them and their interests. Perhaps they expect their parents always to be on hand to assist with whatever they're doing. And if they don't get the time and attention they feel they deserve, they'll complain and become resentful. But it's not like that at all. Instead, unschooled kids are considerate and caring. They're willing to help out so that everyone gets their needs met in the best way during these busy times of life.

My kids also used to get on and do things by themselves. Be independent. I didn't feel guilty because I wasn't always at their sides, helping them. Kids have to assume responsibility for their learning, don't they? Baby times give them the opportunity to pursue their learning in an active way.

And it wasn't all work. My children loved having a baby or toddler to carry around. When people exclaimed over the sweetness of baby smiles or stroked chubby baby cheeks, they grinned. This was their little sibling! They felt special by association.

So my older children carried babies and changed nappies and played baby games, giving up their time willingly while they waited for life to return to normal (with smiles on their faces). Is that all they did? No. We did lots of other things as well.

The baby season of life is a perfect opportunity for some creative thinking. We might not have been able to do everything we wanted to do, but we found lots of other enjoyable ways to spend our time.

In one of my very first blog posts, I wrote:

I am reading to the older children who have sprawled themselves on the floor at my feet. Gemma-Rose is on my lap feeding. Soon she will sink into a deep sleep, and I know if I don't move, we can enjoy quite a few chapters of our book before she wakes up and needs my attention.

We are walking around the garden centre. Sophie looks gorgeous with her white hat jammed onto her head. She is quite content to sit in the moving stroller as we look at all the plants, comparing the different species, trying to decide what we'll buy to take home.

We have taken our books outside, and we are sitting under the crab-apple tree reading. Sophie is sitting in the sandpit next to us. Now and then, someone buries her feet in the sand, and she giggles.

Our living room is a mess. There are toys strewn from one end to the other and Imogen is sitting right in the middle. She thinks the other children are playing with her. She doesn't realise that we are engrossed in an interesting discussion.

The boys are outside with Gemma-Rose. They push her on the swing and chat together. Inside, the girls and I are sewing.

I am helping Imogen with some writing while I sway from side to side. There is a baby in the sling who will stay asleep as long as I keep moving.

We are visiting the museum or park or walking down a bush track. Our baby is asleep in the sling. Two of my older kids bounce our toddler while we amble along. The slow pace gives us a chance to talk about what we can see.

My children are outside having a fabulous adventure. They're building cubby houses under the pine trees. They have a pile of dress-up clothes. Someone says, "Let's pretend." The game will last all day.

The older kids are involved with their projects. If they need help, they are content to wait. I am asleep on the bed with the baby.

So how do we get through the baby season of life? We look for the delights. We help each other. We think creatively. We recognise that these times give us unique learning experiences. We trust.

And we relax knowing that we are meeting everyone's needs even if life looks different from normal.

Seeing to the Needs of Our Babies

My first child was a perfect baby. She ate and played and smiled, and then when she was tired, she put herself to sleep. She even slept through the night. I thought I was a perfect mother. (What was everyone else doing wrong?) But my second child wasn't quite so obliging. Cracks began to appear in my perfect mother image. My third child? When he joined our family, if I'd still had any high opinions of myself, they'd have fallen into a heap. He had no routine whatsoever. It's just as well that by that time, we'd discovered attachment parenting.

Yes, my ideas about parenting had changed. I'd realised that fulfilling a child's needs, however much work that involves, is much more important than getting her into a routine and being able to boast, "I have a perfect child. She even sleeps through the night!"

When we had babies, I breastfed them around the clock, whenever they were hungry or needed to suckle.

I slept with our babies snuggled up next to me.

I carried our babies in a sling. When they were tired, I didn't put them in a cot to sleep. I left them snuggled up in front of me. They went where I went. They were always in the middle of the action of family life.

There were times when I got overtired. Then I yearned for a full night's sleep. In a bed by myself. I wanted my space back. I also wanted my arms free so that I could do a few things for myself.

At these times, I envied my friends who had their children in a routine, who put their babies in cots and then walked off to do things of their own. I wanted to be like the old Sue, whose babies slept through the night because she was a perfect mother. But even if my babies had been obliging, I couldn't return to those early days of mothering. I wasn't that person any more. I'd realised that parenting isn't about me. It's about my kids. Whatever it takes, I'm willing to see to their needs.

Sometimes people would say such things as:

"If you sleep with your child, you'll never get her out of your bed."

"Put your baby down. You don't need to carry her all the time. She'll never learn to walk."

"Don't feed her so often. She doesn't need all that milk."

"You're important too, you know. Your child has to learn that."

"You're going to end up with spoilt children."

But I didn't listen. I kept feeding and sharing my bed and carrying my babies. I accepted that I would make sacrifices for the first few years of each of our children's lives. That time was for them. My time would return eventually.

So what happened? Do I regret all that time and attention I gave my children?

I have no regrets whatsoever. I am glad that I gave my kids what they needed. None of those dire predictions came true. My kids didn't end up becoming spoilt.

And I wonder why. Why doesn't attachment parenting lead to self-centred children? Surely if we see to all our children's needs, they'll soon learn that all they have to do is demand something and someone will come running to give them whatever they want? All that well-meaning advice does sound sensible, doesn't it?

Maybe when we meet our children's needs, they feel right inside. In some way, we're filling them up with something good. Could it be love? Is this the most fundamental of anyone's needs? Our kids feel connected with us, and we feel connected with them.

A mother once left a beautiful comment on my blog telling me how she enjoys feeding her baby with her older children snuggled up, one on each side of her. Her older children are patient. They wait for the baby to finish feeding. They know the baby's needs come first. And I think that comes from being loved themselves. They know they are loved. They have been in the same position as the baby, and now they are quite content for the baby to have his turn. They don't need to be jealous or fight for attention. Their love buckets are full and overflowing. They can be generous and love in their turn.

Seeing to the needs of our babies and toddlers has nothing to do with spoiling them. What we're doing is ensuring our children feel right inside. We're giving our kids a wonderful start in life so that they can, in their turn, pass on to others what they've received themselves.

How to Have Demanding Children Who Rule the House

Things people sometimes say:

"You're not feeding that baby again, are you?"

"If you feed your baby to sleep, she'll never learn to go to sleep on her own. It won't hurt her to cry."

"Are you giving into her again?"

"If you carry your baby around all the time, she'll never want to be put down."

"You're still feeding during the night? It's time you got that child into a routine. She might cry for a few nights, but it'll be worth it."

"When are you going to wean that child? It's not as if she needs your milk, you know."

"I wouldn't sleep with your baby if I were you. You'll never get her out of your bed."

"You're spoiling her!"

"You're making a rod for your own back."

"Show her who's boss."

"You're in charge."

"She'll end up ruling the house, you know."

"She'll turn into a demanding child."

I breastfed my babies whenever they needed it, all the way around the clock most times. I carried my children everywhere, in my arms or a sling, and later in a backpack. I slept with my little ones snuggled up next to me in bed.

Some days I wanted my space back and yearned to have my arms free. Some nights I got fed up of being woken yet again by a hungry child who took up too much of the bed. I didn't always want to find a child at my breast every time I lowered myself into a chair. Sometimes I cried and wanted to run away.

But I breastfed, carried and slept with my children anyway.

What happened? Did I end up with demanding kids who rule the house?

Yes, I did.

I slip through the back door, trying not to make a sound, but moments later, my daughters appear.

"Mum! Why didn't you tell us you were hanging the washing on the line? You're not allowed to do it by yourself. We want to help."

I find an onion, a chopping board and a knife. But before I have removed the onion skin, I hear a voice. "Mum! What do you think you're doing? I'm making dinner tonight. Go and rest."

As soon as we have eaten dinner, I head towards the sink and turn on the tap.

"Mum! That's my job. Someone pour Mum a glass of wine and make her sit down."

"I'm not allowed to do anything," I complain. "Who's in charge around here?"

"We are!" my children shout with big grins.

Yes, my children rule the house.

"Mum, I need a hug," says Gemma-Rose, as she climbs onto my lap

"Can I have a hug?" asks Imogen, opening her arms.

Callum comes home from work. "I need a hug, Mum!"

Small bodies wriggle inside the shelter of my arms. Bigger bodies enfold me inside theirs. It's never-ending. I lose count of the number of hugs I have to give my children each day.

Yes, my children are very demanding.

So how do we have demanding kids who rule the house?

Love them. Love them some more. See to their needs. All of them, whatever it costs.

And ignore all those things some people might say.

When Does Unschooling Begin?

Children are curious people. They're wired to learn from the moment they're born. And parents seem to have a natural desire to help and encourage them.

When we had babies in our family, I always surrounded them with interesting things. I bought bright toys for them to look at, feel, listen to, and even taste. I brought them household items like wooden spoons and pots and pans. I named things again and again, without ever tiring of it. I sang to them in my tuneless voice and also introduced them to proper music. I took our children on outings and showed them leaves and flowers, waves and sand, shops and people. I let them feel the sunshine on their skin and the wind in their hair. I played games, talked to them, read books, pulled funny faces and laughed with them. We had quiet times, rocking and snuggling. I carried our babies in a sling or popped them into a chair where they could see me while I worked. I included our children in all aspects of our lives. By doing this, I surrounded them with a rich environment.

While our children were absorbed with all these experiences, I observed them and listened to them. I got to know them and their particular needs. I developed empathy. I became connected with my children.

As our kids grew, I recognised that some things interested them more than others. They pretended to be pirates or princesses or firemen or superheroes. I found them toys and books that reflected these interests. I provided materials for them to experiment with. I listened as our kids told me about the things that were important to them. I answered their never-ending questions.

I did what parents are naturally drawn to doing. Perhaps you did all these things too?

So what happens when we expose our young children to a rich environment and encourage them to explore it? They grow and develop. They learn to walk and talk and jump and dance.

They draw and scribble and create. They accumulate all kinds of facts which delight and interest them. Of course, with each little development, we smile and encourage. We cheer our children on. We are proud parents taking great enjoyment in the development of a unique little person.

Then one day, our children are old enough to go to school. It's time to make some decisions and move onto a new phase in our child's life.

But what if we didn't even think about this new stage? What if life just carried on as normal? We'd continue taking our children out into our amazing world and bringing that world to them. We'd continue encouraging, helping, listening and interacting with them.

Would our children keep learning? Yes. They'd continue to learn in a natural way. They'd be unschooling.

Unschooled children explore the world, learning from everything that happens in their lives. They follow their interests. They use and develop their talents. They observe, ask questions, ponder answers, read books, watch TV, search online for information, discuss, play games, experiment, maybe even enrol in a course. They don't follow someone else's plan for their learning. They have the freedom to learn what is important to them.

I used to think of the first few years of my children's lives as the attachment parenting ones. Then once my kids turned five, they began unschooling. Perhaps unschooling follows attachment parenting. It's a natural progression.

Or does unschooling begin at the beginning of life? When parents say to me, “My child is only three, but we’re going to unschool,” should I say, “But you’re already unschooling!”

I think I should.

Saying No

I wonder why we get so afraid of saying yes to our kids. Perhaps we think they will get spoilt if we respond to their requests in a positive way. Children won't appreciate the special things of life if they experience them too often. Maybe we ought to ration them out.

Every evening my youngest daughter Gemma-Rose asks if she can play a computer game after dinner.

"Do you think I should let you rot your brain with more computer games?" I ask.

"Oh, yes!" she grins.

Of course, I always say yes. I don't really know why Gemma-Rose bothers asking me. "Why do you ask me when you already know my answer?" I say, and she replies, "It's the polite thing to do."

So Gemma-Rose plays computer games after dinner. One day she might decide to do something else. And even if she doesn't, her brain isn't in any danger. That's just our joke. She knows I'll say yes when other people might count the number of computer hours consumed and then say no.

So I say yes. I say it a lot. But this doesn't mean that there aren't times when I say no.

A few years ago:

A friend says, "We're having a party on Saturday evening. Will you come?"

Should we say yes? Our closest friends will be there. It would be lovely to see them. We'll have a good time. But it'll be a late night. Our baby and toddler will get overtired. So will I. And we have to get up early on Sunday morning to go to Mass. I'll get grumpy. So will my children. Sunday will be a difficult day. A survival day. A lost day.

I know a lot about lost days. So many of our days have fallen into the black hole of our life. All because I put other people's expectations ahead of the needs of our family.

It's hard to say no, isn't it? What if our refusal offends? People might think we're unfriendly. Often we don't want to appear impolite, so we cave in and say yes when we want to say no. And then later, we have to deal with the consequences.

My friend is waiting for an answer.

"Thank you for your kind invitation," I say with a smile. "I'm sorry we're unable to come. We hope your party is a huge success."

A polite refusal without a long and involved explanation.

Kids grow. Life changes. One day a no will turn into a yes.

Part XI: Teenagers and Young Adults

Not For Sale

There are many negative memes about teenagers like this one:

Teenager for sale. Fully equipped with rolling eyes, deep sighs, and sarcastic comments. Plays video games and texts 200 wpm. No reasonable offer will be refused.

Perhaps if we didn't assume teenagers were going to be trouble but instead, listened to them, treated them with respect, and trusted them, they wouldn't roll their eyes and we'd discover they are delightful people.

I once left a protesting comment on a negative teenager meme that I found in a social media feed. The friend who had posted it told me not to get so upset. It was only a bit of fun. Where was my sense of humour?

But is it fun? Or are these kinds of memes, where parents laugh at their teenagers and commiserate with each other, unhelpful? Could they be more than not helpful? Are they disrespectful? They could end up damaging the relationship between parent and child.

My teenagers aren't for sale. Probably yours aren't either.

Teenagers Are People Too

At Mass on Sunday, during the Prayers of the Faithful, we were asked to pray for sullen teenagers.

When we returned home, Imogen was most indignant. "Why does everyone automatically think teenagers are sullen? Charlotte and I are teenagers, and we're not that way."

"It's the typical teenage stereotype," said Charlotte. "It's not necessarily true."

I think my teenage girls are quite right. Society tends to think of teenagers in a certain negative way. Parents expect trouble when their children hit these years.

"She'll be a teenager in a few months," says a mother, rolling her eyes. Yes, she's not looking forward to it at all. She's sure the next few years are going to be very difficult.

But is it inevitable that our eager-to-please and easy-to-love children will suddenly turn into difficult-to-live-with teenagers?

My teenagers are delightful people: well-balanced, lots of fun, interesting, and loving. Are they unusual? I don't think so. There are many wonderful teenagers around. But maybe you are thinking, "I know many sullen teenagers."

Could it be that these teenagers:

- Have to live with lots of rules and regulations?
- Don't have enough privacy?
- Are criticised for their choices in such things as clothing and music?
- Are ridiculed or put down when they share their ideas and dreams?

- Are expected to be difficult just because they are teenagers?

Perhaps teenagers become sullen and hard to live with because they are not trusted and treated with respect.

I want to keep my teenagers safe. Of course, I don't want them to fall into bad company or do wrong things. My heart will ache if they give up our family's values and beliefs, and I'd like to prevent them from making mistakes that they will regret. So should I hang on tightly to my teenagers so that they don't get into trouble? Or should I trust them to do what is right?

"Should I trust you?" I ask Imogen.

"Mum, of course, you should!" It's my daughter's turn to roll her eyes.

She's right. And I do.

But what if my teenagers make mistakes? Will I wish I'd kept control over every aspect of their lives? Is that the responsible thing to do? No. I think there's less chance of my teenagers getting into trouble if I trust them than if I controlled their lives with a long list of rules and regulations. Rules can be broken. They encourage rebellion. Connection is a much safer option.

Trusted or not, all teenagers are capable of making mistakes. But so are adults. I make them all the time. Mistakes are how we learn. But I'm confident that if my teenagers ever get into trouble, they will come and talk to me and we can sort things out. They trust me, maybe because I trust them.

"I wrote a story about teenagers," I say to my daughters. "I'm putting the record straight. Not all teenagers are sullen. Teenagers are wonderful people." Then I add, "I need a title for the story."

Teenagers Are People Too," says Charlotte, without hesitating.

Some people do say such things as:

"You'd think teenagers were a different species."

"Sometimes, teenagers act as if they've come from another planet."

"I can't wait for my teenager to become human again."

Teenagers are people too. They're not aliens. Yes, Charlotte's suggestion is perfect. Teenagers are delightful people who can be trusted. That's a better description of teenagers than sullen. Wouldn't you agree?

Keeping Teenagers Safe

I settle myself into a comfortable chair in the living room and open a book. But before I can read more than a page or two, the rest of my family appears.

"What are you doing, Mum?"

"Is it coffee time?"

"Shall I fill the kettle?"

Soon we are drinking coffee and talking together, and my book is forgotten. The conversation turns to a podcast that I made about reading, writing and coarse language.

"I've been thinking about what I said in that episode. Do you think I was wrong to say that parents should trust their kids when it comes to choosing such things as books and movies?" I ask my children. "Should I look at all books before letting you read them? Is it wrong to trust you? Perhaps I'm an irresponsible mother. Maybe I'm not keeping you safe from the dangers of the world."

Opinions fly back and forth across the living room. Everyone has something to say.

"It would be really good if I could record some of this conversation," I say. "You all have some very interesting things to say. How about I interview a couple of you for this week's podcast?"

So that's what I do. I interview Imogen (20) and Charlotte (17) and ask them for their opinions on keeping children safe from the dangers of the world, including inappropriate books, the Internet, movies, and emails.

"Is the world a dangerous place?" I ask my daughters, and they reply, "Yes, it is. There are dangerous things out there in the world, and it's a parent's responsibility to protect a child from them."

"I've been doing some googling to find out what other parents do to keep their kids safe," I say, "because most people are doing something very different from us. I was interested to see if other methods are working.

"It seems to me that most parents are keeping a very close eye on what their kids are watching and reading, and they supervise their time on the Internet very closely. Everyone is saying, *Do not let children have unsupervised time on the computer. Make sure the computer is in a place where parents can see the screen at all times.* So most parents are being very diligent about policing their children's activities in potentially dangerous areas.

"Many parents would, I imagine, read books and watch movies before they offer them to their children to make sure that they are safe. I guess parents have to be very fast readers to keep up. Children can be prolific readers!

"In my travels, I came across a website that offers spyware. Parents can use it to spy on their children's computer activities so that they don't have to look over their shoulders constantly. There is a record of the activities that they can access later on. They can also use the spyware to check their kids' phone messages and emails. What do you think about this? Is spying on children necessary? Should it be allowed?"

"I don't think it should be allowed," says Imogen. "I've heard of children whose parents have used spyware, and they think it's a great, great invasion of their privacy. They don't want anyone constantly looking over their shoulders. They want their parents to trust them."

"So you think spying on children breaks down the trust between a parent and a child and will ultimately damage the relationship between them?"

"Yes, I do."

"Some parents say that this is a big issue. It doesn't matter how the child feels. Parents are just doing what is necessary to keep them safe. Eventually, the child will recognise that the parents only spied because they cared."

"I see where they're coming from," says Imogen, "but I don't think a teenager would see it that way."

"Some parents say, *We have to do unpopular things because we're the parents. We're not interested in being friends with our teenagers. That's not our role. Being a parent means keeping our kids safe regardless of what we have to do."*

"Yes, parents need to keep their children safe," says Imogen, "but there is another way to do that. Parents don't have to act like the police."

"The problem is that some parents think there isn't another way," I say. "But there is, isn't there? But before we talk about that, perhaps we can look at the downside of spying. If our relationships were damaged, but in the process, our children were kept safe, we might say it was all worthwhile. But do you think policing children's activities does actually work?"

"No."

"Parents are damaging their relationships for nothing?"

"Yes. If a parent spies on their children's computers, the children will use someone else's computer to do whatever it is that they want to keep private. If they ban their children from reading certain books, children will read those books in another place. Spying and policing will only result in children doing things secretly. It's not going to stop them."

"So it's going to make teenagers deceitful? There's always a way around these things, isn't there?"

"Teenagers can go places. Parents can't police them when they're not at home."

"The only way to be sure they're not doing what parents don't want them to do is to keep them at home?"

"Exactly."

"Parents can't follow their teenagers around. They can't be sure of where they're going and what they're doing. But parents could be suspicious. They could find themselves checking up on them: *Where have you been? What have you been doing?* And that doesn't do a relationship any good, does it?

"Let's talk about that other way of keeping kids safe," I say. "When we police children's activities, control is coming from the parent. It's coming from outside the child. So the child is safe only as long as the parent is there making sure she isn't doing anything wrong. Once the parent has gone, the child is free to do whatever she likes and could get into all sorts of trouble.

"But with the method of keeping teenagers safe that we're talking about, control comes from within the child. A child chooses not to engage in certain dangerous activities. She knows what is right and what is wrong, what is appropriate, and what isn't. And she can be trusted whether a parent is there or not.

"This sounds good, but a parent might object: *A child cannot make a distinction between what is right and what is wrong. She can't be trusted to make the right choices.* Imogen, do you think teenagers can be trusted?"

"Yes, I do."

"So if we believe a child can tell the difference between right and wrong when she goes to the library and looks at the books, she can make the right choices for herself.

"Yes."

"How can we get to the situation where a child does know the difference between right and wrong? Does a parent just say, *Go and read what you like, listen to what you like, and watch what you like? I trust you will make the right decisions.* Is it that easy?"

"No, it's not," says Imogen. "It's all about the relationship a parent has with a child. There needs to be trust and respect and the ability to have a conversation. That's what's important. Parents need to have the right relationship with their child, one where they can share the values they believe in, one in which they can help her develop her sense of right and wrong.

"And then once a child shares a parent's values, she can go out and use those values when reading books or when she's on the Internet. She might say, *This book doesn't feel right to me. It doesn't fit the values that I have picked up. I'm not going to read this.* But before a child can do that, parents need to build up a relationship of respect and trust. It has to be a relationship where a parent can have conversations and pass on the right values to her child."

"Some people might say, *Why should children listen to their parents rather than to others from outside the family, their friends and other people in the community?* Do you think it's all to do with the relationship parents have built up with their children?" I ask.

"Yes, that's right."

"So it's not as easy as it sounds. It does take a lot of effort and time to build up a close relationship.

"Some people say that they're not unschooling, but they still have a good relationship with their children. What do you think are the essential things that make a difference?" I ask.

Imogen says, "The parent and the child need to trust and respect each other. Everyone agrees that children need to trust their parents. They need to respect what they say. But the same is true for parents. Parents need to trust and respect their children. When you become a teenager, you want to be treated as an adult. You can think and reason and make decisions, and you want your parents to acknowledge that. So it's not just a child-parent relationship that teenagers want. They want an adult-adult relationship. They want to be able to talk to their parents, to have discussions, to be allowed to have opinions instead of being put down as if they were children: *You don't know anything. You're not old enough."*

"Parents can be very good at lecturing their children. They say, *This is what I think is wrong with this book and this is why I don't want you to read it.* But there's no dialogue, is there?" I say. "It's just the parent laying down the law. Should a parent allow a teenager to have her opinions and listen to them? Because many parents say, *I've told my child what's wrong with it,* and maybe they think that's enough. The parent has spoken, and that's all that matters."

"It's much better to have a conversation about it, discuss it, listen to a child's opinion, give feedback to each other," says Imogen. "You listen to what they think, and they listen to what you think. Talk it out together. Because if you tell teenagers something, they will think, *She's laying down the law again.* But if you talk with them, they'll feel like they're being respected and what they have to say is valued. They're more likely to listen to what you have to say because you're listening to what they have to say."

"Let's talk about what happens in our family," I say. "You read a lot of books. If I tried to keep up with them all I wouldn't do much else, would I? So tell me what happens when we go to the library."

Charlotte joins the conversation: "Imogen and I usually collect some books together. We look at each cover and glance inside. If the book looks interesting and there's nothing obviously wrong with it, we'll borrow it."

"Then we take the books home," continues Imogen, " and we start reading them. Generally, in the first few chapters, we can tell whether it will be an appropriate book for us to read or not."

"And if it isn't," says Charlotte, "We put it back in the basket to be returned to the library, and we try something else."

"You've learnt to pick up the subtle messages of the book?" I ask. "Because some things don't jump out at you on the first page, do they?"

Imogen: "Yes, it's not always easy to tell from the first page, whether it's a good book or not. You've got to read some of it. And sometimes it's not a particular thing; it's a feeling: *This book doesn't feel right.* If it feels that way, we won't read it."

"It's better to be able to pick up the subtle messages rather than just say, *This is a vampire book, so I'm not going to read it. This book has bad language on the first page, so I'm not going to read it,*" I say. "You have to make decisions about the book as you're reading it. Writers can influence a reader in subtle ways. The danger isn't always immediately obvious.

"Tell me about the standards you and Charlotte have for books."

"We have an easy way to tell whether a book is appropriate or not," says Imogen. "I think, *Could I take this to Mum? Could I show this to her?* If I feel there's something in the book that doesn't allow me to do that, I won't read it. Not because I'm afraid of what you might say or because I think you'll be angry with me. I do that because I trust you know what is right. And if you don't think it's right, I trust it's not right for me."

"So you wouldn't be tempted to read that book privately?" I ask.

"No."

"I can trust you?"

"Yes, you can."

"Some people have asked, *How do you know what your children are reading?* Even if I trust you, I don't know what you're reading. How do I find out?

"Ask us," Charlotte says.

"You'll give me an honest answer?"

"Yes. Why should I hide what I'm reading?"

"I don't have to spy? I don't have to police what you're reading? You will tell me?"

"Yes."

It's as easy as that.

When It's Unnecessary to Make Rules for Teens

If parents fail to make rules that their teenagers must abide by, are they irresponsible? Perhaps children need to be told such things as:

"You can't go to that late night party."

"You can't wear that immodest dress."

"Alcohol? Drugs? No way!"

"I don't want you associating with those teenagers. They're a bad influence."

"You can't play that computer game. It's too violent."

"You can't smoke."

"No, you can't read that book. It's full of coarse language."

Because is it really okay if a child does any of these things?

Should we make strict rules to protect our children? Perhaps we should explain our reasons but say an emphatic no.

We could think:

"Sometimes we have to be tough because we love."

"We have to lay down the law even if our children protest. Parenting isn't about being popular, you know."

"We can't side-step our parenting duty."

"We might be in for some battles, but we have to expect that. It's part of keeping our kids safe."

"It's just what we have to do."

Or is it?

What if our kids don't want to do any of the above things in the first place? Then there wouldn't be any need for rules, would there?

Is it possible to bring up children so that we can trust them to make the right choices, without us telling them what they can and cannot do? I think it is.

Some people might object: "Teenagers can't be trusted. They're too young to make their own decisions. They are easily swayed by the opinions of others."

Maybe the objectors would be right if trusting is all about letting children go their own way and accepting whatever they do no matter what that may be: "Do what you like!" But that's not responsible parenting.

In order to trust our children, we have to be so connected to them that they will accept what we believe is right and what is wrong.

So how do we do this? I think it's all to do with treating our children with respect and unconditional love so that they will trust us, respect our opinions, and be willing to follow our example. This isn't easy. But then again, policing rules isn't easy either.

"Hey, girls, what would you say if said I won't let you go to an all-night party, you can't smoke, and you'd better not even think about dressing immodestly? And if you want to go to see an X-rated movie or read an unsuitable book, well, you're not going to be allowed to." My voice dies away. My girls are giggling.

"Are you serious, Mum? You don't have to tell us we can't do those things. We don't want to do them."

If teenagers don't want to do all the things that we are worried about why make rules?

A while back, my girls were talking with some of our friends about rules.

"Rules are necessary!" someone said. "How else will children do what is right and avoid what is wrong? How else can parents keep them safe? You can't bring up kids properly without rules."

Instead of protesting, Charlotte asked, "Do you think I turned out okay?" Everyone nodded before she added, "I was brought up without rules. Mum never makes rules for any of us."

Wouldn't it be nice if this was the end of the story? Unfortunately, it's not. Because even when people have the evidence right before their eyes, they are still reluctant to accept it. Oh, yes, they make the right sounds. They look like they are agreeing. But deep down, those old ideas refuse to shift.

And I'm not talking only about parents. Teenagers also have trouble rejecting redundant ideas even when they've experienced their negative effects. Why is this? What was good enough for them will be good enough for their own kids? Or are they just not used to thinking for themselves?

That's not a problem I have with my kids. Unschooled kids think about things all the time. They don't just follow the crowd. And so they don't need rules.

When Teenagers Don't Know Who They Are

"Teenagers often act differently in front of their parents than they do when they're with their friends," observes my daughter Sophie (16). "I've watched my friends. They act one way when they're away from their parents. But then as soon as their parents appear, their language changes. They talk about different things. They become different people."

"Are there two Sophies?" I ask. "Perhaps you change when Dad and I aren't around."

"I'm the same person when I'm with you, when I'm with my friends, and when I'm with both you and my friends," says Sophie.

"So it doesn't matter who you're with, you talk using the same language?" Sophie nods. "You have the same opinions?" Another nod.

"So you don't have to pretend to be someone you're not when you're with family. And you don't have to act cool and try to be different in front of your friends?"

"No, I have the confidence to be me," says Sophie. "You have let me voice my opinions and develop my personality. I'm myself at home because you don't shout me down. You say, 'Tell me what you think.' You're interested in my thoughts. You let me be myself at home so that when I go out into the world, I have the confidence to be myself around other people.

"But this is often not the case with other families because they say, 'You have to think the same as we do. You have to talk like us.' Yes, they set down the rules. The children have to be duplicates of their parents and adopt their way of thinking.

"And so when kids go out into the world, they don't know who they are. They think that it's not cool to be their parents, so they copy their friends. They end up doing and saying things that parents might not necessarily agree with."

Sophie continues, "Most teenagers don't have the confidence to be themselves. Parents have prevented them from discovering who they are. So they copy the people they're with and pretend to be just like them."

"You said that kids could end up doing and saying things that parents might not necessarily agree with," I say. "That sounds dangerous."

"Yes, they might do what is wrong instead of what is right."

"So it's dangerous for parents to insist that their kids have the same opinions as them?"

"Yes." And then Sophie adds, "You know what's funny, Mum? You let me have my own opinions and be myself and guess what's happening? I'm turning into a mini-mum!" She laughs, and so do I.

Despite what Sophie says, she isn't really a mini version of me. She's a person in her own right. Different to me in many ways. But I know what she means. We're the same at our cores. And when we're connected like that, our differences are okay. They're necessary. They're what makes us special.

Teenagers, Parents and Differing Opinions

Why do some parents want to impose their opinions on their children? Do they do this because they care? Perhaps they want their teenagers to benefit from their experience. Prevent their children from going down wrong pathways and making mistakes, ones they might have made when they were younger. Maybe it feels safer to force their teenagers to adopt the ideas they think are right rather than let them develop their opinions for themselves.

Sometimes it can look like teenagers have accepted their parents' opinions. But do they really agree or have they learnt that it's best to keep what they think to themselves? Perhaps kids feel their parents don't value what they have to say. When they share their thoughts or ideas or opinions, their parents might cut them off: *Where did you get that idea from? That's ridiculous! This is what you should be thinking*. The parent is communicating: *I'm the adult, and you're the child. Listen to my opinion because it's right*. And this is frustrating for children. They learn not to share anything with their parents because they don't want to be lectured every time they open their mouths.

Deep in their hearts, parents know when their teenagers haven't taken on board their beliefs or opinions. It's impossible for them to relax and say: *They know what they're doing so I don't have to worry*. They realise that their children don't own the opinions: they don't really belong to them. So parents can't relax. They have to keep checking. Find ways to determine whether their kids still have the same opinions and beliefs as them. Keep repeating what they believe to be right.

So how do we deal with any differences in opinion? Well, we can't say, "You're wrong!" That's not the way to get our kids to listen and accept what we have to say. Instead, we can talk together. Share our point of view with a light hand. Listen with interest to theirs. Perhaps our teenagers just need an opportunity to explore and develop their opinions. With time, they might end up agreeing with us.

But what if our teenagers continue to hold opinions contrary to ours? Then we have to accept this. If we think they are way off track, then we should trust – because we are closely connected to them – that they will eventually come to realise that they are wrong. With our love and respect and support, they will get to the right place in their own time.

Of course, teenagers sometimes have very good opinions of their own. Adults aren't always right.

Sheep, Surgery and Confident Sons

Callum and I are having some mother-son time at our local café. As we sip coffee, I ask about his work, and he tells me he isn't feeling very confident. I am surprised. Callum is a very outgoing young man. He always looks like he has everything under control.

"I worry about doing something wrong and upsetting my boss. And now we've been told we have to check customers' bags as they come through the check-out. What if they don't like it? What if they get upset with me too? If I don't do it, I'll get into trouble."

What can I say? Should I give Callum some of my motherly advice? I decide to share a story.

"I never had much confidence when I started working," I admit. My son's ears prick up. It's been a long time since I last talked about my working days. Does Callum even remember I used to work in the veterinary physiology department of a university?

"Professor G was the head of our department. He was a tall forbidding-looking man with absolutely no people skills. He related much better to all the animals he dealt with than to human beings. We were all rather terrified of Prof, especially us younger people.

"Now and then Prof would come into the staff room and announce that he'd be performing surgery the next day. 'I need someone to set up for surgery and assist me,' he'd say. All the junior employees, including me, would look anywhere but at Prof. We all wanted the floor to swallow us up, but as that never happened, we tried to look as inconspicuous as possible. Who would he choose? Who would be the unlucky person who'd have to set up everything perfectly to Prof's high standards? Who would have to obey his constant barking orders the next day, without making a single mistake?

"I lived in fear that Prof would choose me to be his assistant. It was a terrible feeling. Then one day, I decided I hated being frightened. I could no longer live like that, and I was going to do something about it. I was going to learn how to set up surgery and assist so well that if chosen, I would do such a good job, there would be no need for me to quiver and shake and worry I'd make a mistake.

"I also decided that, despite his fierce appearance, Prof was just another person like me. I had no reason to be scared of him.

"I started asking questions about things I wasn't sure about instead of pretending I knew what I was doing. I listened carefully, and soon I was so good at setting up for surgery I could have done it with my eyes closed. I still needed to keep my eyes open when I was assisting, though! It wasn't long before surgery became fascinating rather than scary. I asked intelligent questions while we worked because I was interested, and Prof started chatting to me instead of barking at me. And my confidence grew.

"Soon I noticed Prof stopped choosing a random victim to help him. He'd come into our room and say, 'Sue, can you set up for surgery and assist me tomorrow?' I'd got so good at doing this job that Prof always wanted my help instead of someone else's. I am sure my colleagues were rather relieved. Me? I felt pleased. I'd learnt a new skill, conquered a fear, and my work was appreciated."

Callum is listening carefully. I can tell he is thinking about my story. "Thanks, Mum!"

We finish our coffee. Callum heads off to work, and I return home.

Months pass, and then one day I say, "Callum, do you remember that conversation we had in the café last year, the one where I told you how I used to set up for surgery, the one about my confidence problem? Did you solve your own problem?"

Callum smiles in his charming way. "I decided to talk to my boss about all the things I wasn't sure about. He was willing to help me when he realised I was having trouble. I listened and learnt."

"What about the bags and the customers?"

"I thought I would chat with everyone as they came through the check-out. Be friendly and interested in them. When it came time to ask people if I could look in their bags, no one minded because they liked me. I just became good at customer relations!"

So Callum is now a confident employee who is good at his job. He has become so good he has been offered a job as a store manager.

Sometimes a mother has a story to tell. And sometimes a son will listen.

I think about what my friend Beate once said. We were talking about all the different things we did before we found the job God intended for us. Beate remarked that all these experiences are good. Nothing is ever wasted.

Working in the veterinary physiology department was definitely not my vocation. But I did learn things I have carried forward with me. Gaining those surgery skills taught me not to be afraid to ask questions and to listen carefully and learn. They gave me the confidence to tackle anything.

Operate on a sheep? Would you have guessed I have such skills? They're not very useful skills for a mother to have, I admit. But they provided me with a great story to share.

And Callum now realises if his mother can learn how to set up and assist during surgery, then he can do anything.

Are Your Young Adult Kids Still Living at Home?

It's my daughter Imogen's birthday. We're having a breakfast picnic at the lake to celebrate. As we're enjoying our bowls of muesli and yoghurt and munching on our hash browns, I look around the picnic table at my three young adults and two teenagers.

Three young adults? Yes, and they all live at home.

"Are you still living at home?" My older kids get asked this question quite a lot.

"When people ask me if I'm still at home," says Imogen, "I get the feeling that they think I should have moved out by now."

Maybe the word 'still' implies that my young adult children should be living independent lives. Somehow I've failed. Because isn't it a parent's job to prepare her kids for the outside world as quickly as possible? Shouldn't we open the door and encourage them to leave? We've done our bit. We've given them all they need. Isn't it time for them to move on? If they're still living with us, something must be wrong.

Except I think there's something very right about having adult children who aren't in a hurry to leave us.

I am glad my still-at-home adult kids aren't saying, "I can't wait to leave home! I want to be free to live my own life. Be who I really am." There's no need for them to say such things because they're already free. Free to have their own opinions. Free to do what they think is right. Free to be who they are, not just in front of their friends but at home with us as well. My kids don't have to escape home in order to be themselves.

So some of my young adult children are still living at home. Maybe some people think that they don't want to leave because they're living an easy life with us. Why move out when you can live in a place where someone else is paying the bills and doing all the work? Except it isn't like that.

My kids help with the expenses of running a big household. (Sometimes I wonder how we'd manage without their contributions.) They also do much of the work. They share the housework and the driving. They even share their talents by doing such things as teaching their younger sisters how to play the piano.

Everyone in our family works together to help and support each other as we follow our dreams and fulfil our missions. We're all encouraging each other to become the people we are intended to be. Nobody ever gets too old to be part of this team.

A day will come when my at-home young adults will feel it's the right time to move away from us, just like their older siblings did before them. But until then, they're welcome to stay where we can help them, and they can help us. Regardless of age, they'll always have a place in our home.

Sometimes we talk about the future when Andy and I are old. "I don't want to live in an old people's home," I say.

"You won't have to, Mum," my kids say. "We'll look after you."

Yes, a day will arrive when our kids will look after Andy and me instead of us looking after them. They'll welcome us into their homes. Not because it's their duty. Not because they have to. But because they'll want us to be part of their lives.

Just like we want our kids to be part of our lives. For however long they need us. There are no time limits.

I take another look at all my big kids seated around the picnic table. My heart flows over with love for them. Why would I want to push them out the door before they're ready to go?

I suddenly know what I'm going to say next time someone asks, "Are your kids still living at home?"

"Oh yes, isn't that amazing? I'm so glad they like living with us. I love having adult kids who want to live at home."

What to Do When Kids Reach the Teenage Years

It's the Monday before Christmas. I'm sitting in a cafe with my daughter Imogen. While we sip coffee, we chat about our plans for next year. Will I continue to blog about unschooling?

"There are lots of good unschooling blogs written by younger mothers," I tell Imogen. "I sometimes wonder if I should move onto something else."

I describe how these bloggers are well informed and passionate. They write about unschooling and gentle parenting, sharing all the ideas they're putting into action with their children. They have built up big communities around their blogs. Other mothers relate to their posts.

Sometimes I'm envious of these bloggers. They seem to have very clear ideas about parenting and education. When I was at their stage of life, I spent a lot of time experimenting and failing and starting again. I certainly didn't have any ideas worth sharing with others. I wouldn't have been a good role model for other mothers, unlike the younger unschooling bloggers who are coming along behind me. Yes, they're doing a great job spreading the word about unschooling. So perhaps it's time for me to move onto something else.

Or maybe it's not.

"Yesterday, I received a lovely message from someone who has just discovered my blog," I say to Imogen. "She was delighted to discover it because there aren't that many bloggers writing about teenage and young adult unschoolers."

So why is there a shortage of older unschooling bloggers?

"I'm fortunate," I say to Imogen. "Many bloggers stop writing about their kids when they become teenagers. Their children no longer want their lives to be out there in public. But you don't mind me writing about you. You even let me interview you. I can post photos. Without you, I wouldn't have much of a blog."

Yes, maybe many unschooling bloggers stop writing when their children reach the teenage years because of privacy issues. But could there be another reason as well?

"I bet some unschoolers stop blogging because they stop unschooling," suggests Imogen. "It's fairly easy unschooling when kids are small. There seems to be a lot of time ahead. Why not relax and enjoy life? Then when a child becomes a teenager, things become serious. Parents start thinking about the future. Will their kids get into university, get a job, have a successful life? They begin to put pressure on their kids to make up their minds about what they want to do. They are no longer happy for them to follow their interests in a relaxed way."

"I suppose parents might also worry about their kids getting into trouble," I add. "Mistakes suddenly seem more serious. What if their kids want to do all the things that parents are worried about? Could it be time to take away their teenagers' freedom? Should they make some rules to keep them safe?"

"One day, everything is okay. And then suddenly, just because their children reach a certain age, things change," says Imogen.

"Did I put pressure on you when you became a teenager?" I ask.

"Oh, no! Life just continued on as normal."

"There was no need to change? Unschooling prepares everyone for the future?"

"Yes."

"Parents shouldn't worry about their kids getting into trouble?"

"No."

"So what would you say to a parent who wants to know what she should do now her child has reached the teenage years?"

Imogen says, "Allow your kids to keep exploring their interests, thoughts, ideas and opinions. They need lots of time to discover their strengths and talents, try out their ideas and find out who they are and what they believe. Don't throw away the foundation you've been building up for many years. Teenagers and parents need those strong connections. Those bonds will keep them safe."

Day by day, gradually and naturally, our kids are growing into the people they are meant to be. They will get there. All we have to do is live one day at a time. Keep trusting.

And don't stop unschooling.

Part XII: Chores

The Right Question

A lot of parents are looking for the magic answer to the question: how do we get kids to do the chores? But what if that's the wrong question to ask? Could this be a better one:

How do we bring up our kids so that they freely choose to help other people?

We could search for a method that encourages our kids to do chores because it benefits them: a reward for helping, a punishment for failing to help, a fun way of doing what has to be done. But wouldn't it be better if our kids chose to help because they are generous people who love and care about others? We want their decision to join in with the work of the family to come from within them and not be imposed by a parent.

Does this sound impossible? Or maybe you understand what I'm trying to say because you've also experienced the generosity of kids who work hard for the sake of those they love.

Getting Kids to Help with the Chores

It took me years to work out how to encourage my children to help with the chores. Before that happened, I tried all the usual methods.

I designed rosters with jobs for each child for each day of the week. I wrote out lists of chores and let my children choose: first in, first choice. I tried a lucky dip system. I disguised chores as games. I let my children experience the consequences of undone chores. By turn, I wheedled and threatened, pleaded and demanded, praised and complained. And yes, the chores got done, and we lived in a clean and tidy house. But my children only worked because I prodded them along. They never learnt to offer their help gladly.

I knew there must be a better way, but for a long time, I was too busy and tired to want to discover it. With a baby crying in my arms, and mess everywhere, I just wanted the jobs done NOW and quickly: "I've asked you for help. Please do it!"

Then one day, I stopped and thought about how I reacted when my children asked me for help.

"Can you help me with this please, Mum?" one of them would say.

I'd sigh and say, "In a minute." Quite often, that minute turned into hours. Sometimes I forgot altogether. I didn't exactly give my children the impression that I was eager to help them. Admittedly, there were times when it wasn't possible to help my children straight-away. Babies and toddlers are rather time-consuming and unpredictable, and so it wasn't always possible to do things for my older kids when asked. But I got into a bad habit of never getting around to helping, even when nothing was stopping me. Didn't I already do a lot for my children, without helping them with all the unexpected little extras they wanted me to assist with?

One day I decided to try something new.

"Can you help me with this please, Mum?" asked Charlotte.

I didn't say, "Maybe later," or "Can you ask someone else?" or "In a minute," as usual.

"Of course, I can," I replied, putting down my work immediately. I remembered to smile at the same time. It wasn't easy at first. But old habits can be changed. And I found out that children really do appreciate my help.

"Thank you for taking us to our piano lessons," says Imogen.

"It was my pleasure," I say. Even though there are lots of other things I'd rather do than spend a morning driving to and from town, it *is* a pleasure. It's a pleasure doing things for those we love. Although helping isn't always convenient or what we want to do, especially when we are tired, we can still choose to do it. And that's what I had to model for my children.

Regularly throughout the day, Gemma-Rose comes to me and asks, "Can I do anything for you, Mum?" She makes me a cup of coffee. She arranges some flowers in a vase and places them in my bedroom. She smiles and says, "I like cleaning your bathroom. Don't you love cleaning toilets?" (I can't say I do!) She sneaks out and brings in the washing off the line when no one is looking. I tried doing that once.

I came inside lugging the heavy washing basket, and Imogen said, "Mum! How did you manage to sneak outside without us knowing? You should have told us you were bringing in the washing!"

"I didn't want to disturb you," I replied. "I managed on my own."

"But we like helping you."

Children who like to help? Isn't that what we all want? And I have discovered I like to help them too, especially when it's not expected.

"Was it you who swept the kitchen, Mum?" asks Gemma-Rose. "I was about to do that."

"I thought I'd help," I smile.

My youngest daughter gives me a hug. "Thank you!" Then she asks, "What can I do to help you?"

Helpfulness begets helpfulness.

Getting kids to help with chores? I discovered it all had to start with me.

More About Chores

How can we encourage our kids to help with the chores? The answer is simple. If we want our kids to help us, we must be willing to help them.

Whenever I share this idea, some parents tell me it won't work: "Sue, that all sounds good, but I've tried being a good example for my kids. It doesn't make any difference. They're quite happy to let me do all the work. Maybe you've got a special kind of child." I don't agree. So what's the problem?

Could I have given you a false picture of what helping looks like in our family?

Maybe you think that my kids instantly respond when they see I need help. Perhaps I never have to ask them to do anything. Could they be so in tune with the needs of the family that no one ever has to ask for help?

It is true that we do have a good idea about the needs of everyone in our family. We do lots of talking as well as observing. For example, we all know what standard of housework we need to achieve to keep everyone happy.

But there are times when I do ask for my kids' help, just like they ask me for mine. We might retreat into our own worlds and become oblivious to what's going on around us. We fail to see someone needs help. We might not realise there's a chore that needs doing immediately. For example, the washing might need taking off the line before the sun sinks too low and the clothes become cold. If no one has noticed, I do say, "Could you please help me with this?"

And there are times when I fail to ask for help when I should. Sometimes I think I can do things on my own. When my kids find out that I worked alone, they say, "I would have helped you if you'd asked me." It's good to ask for help, especially if we do need it. We can't expect kids to always notice what needs doing without us mentioning it.

So I sometimes ask for help. But do my kids always respond to my requests instantly? No, there are times when they don't. But this is okay. Even though I try and help as soon as I am asked - because otherwise I might get distracted and minutes might turn into hours, and I could even forget - I know that it's sometimes very difficult to drop what we're doing. We might lose some valuable work if we're interrupted. So if a chore can wait, I wait. That's the respectful thing to do. I know that my kids will help when they get a free and convenient moment.

But what if our kids aren't willing to help even if we ask them, and even if we're willing to wait?

My first thought is that we can't help our kids only because we want them to help us. Even though we hope they will follow our good example, this can't be our reason for helping them. We can't have an ulterior motive. We have to give our help freely. We have to continue to help even if our kids fail to reciprocate because this is the right thing to do. Kids are clever. They know when we're only doing things because we want a response from them. They need to be able to trust us. We have to want to help them genuinely.

Sometimes parents tell me that they can't respond to every request for help from their kids. It's not a matter of waiting until a more convenient time. They just can't take on anything extra. They are already busy enough. Maybe they have babies or toddlers as well as older children. Perhaps they aren't in good health.

Yes, helping isn't always easy. But even if we can't physically help our kids, perhaps we can cultivate a helpful attitude. Helping isn't only about sweeping floors and finding lost shoes and driving children places. It's also about being willing to listen and chat, find solutions to problems, read books and play games. We have to be willing to give our kids our time and attention in whatever way we can.

Kids are very perceptive. They know when we're making excuses to avoid helping them. They also know when we're genuinely unable to help. When I'm unwell or overtired or genuinely short of time, my kids not only accept that they can't have my help, they want to give me theirs. Instead of saying, "Can you please help me, Mum?" they'll say, "What can I do to help you?" They'll take over and do all the chores and much more to make my life easier.

Have you ever noticed how little kids love helping us? We don't have to persuade them. They like working hard. But then a day might arrive when they start to grumble. And they decide doing chores isn't so good after all. I wonder why they change their minds. Could it have something to do with us?

Perhaps we don't encourage our kids to help. We're not patient with them. Or we complain about how they're tackling a job. We want to take over and tell them how we want it done. And could little kids hear us moaning about the chores, how we hate to do them? Even if we don't like doing chores, perhaps we need to make sure our kids hear that we do like helping those we love. So kids who start off wanting to help pick up the message that chores are hard work and no one likes to do them.

Could I have gone overboard with this discussion about chores? Perhaps chores aren't worth worrying about. In the whole scheme of things, they're not very important. Could we be spending too much time and energy trying to persuade everyone to do them when it would be better to say, "If that dirty floor bothers you, do something about it"? If it doesn't bother anyone, no one has to clean it. The chore belongs to whoever who would like it completed. Which is okay. This might work. But is this the right thing to do?

What happens if a dirty house does bother someone? Even if we don't care about the mess, shouldn't we care about the person who feels unhappy because the chores are undone? Shouldn't we be willing to help, not necessarily because we like a clean house, but because we want to put things right for the person we love? Someone has a need and we can fulfil it.

So maybe when we're trying to encourage our kids to help with the chores, there are a few things we could ponder:

Can our kids trust us? Do they think we're only helping them because we want them to help us?

Do chores only become important when they fulfil a need within someone?

And should we choose to do chores, because we love the person who has the need?

Perhaps the chores problem isn't really about washing dishes and cleaning bathrooms. Could it be about trust, fulfilling needs and love?

A Generous Attitude

I need to be a good example if I want my children to help me get our house organised each morning. I have to jump out of bed prepared to dive into the chores. Because if I am willing to help my kids, then they'll be willing to help me.

Sometimes there are piles of dirty dishes waiting on the kitchen bench, and I don't want to wash them. I think: *somebody else will come along and do that job in a minute.* And someone probably would. I have to fight the temptation to ignore the dishes and instead do what I'd prefer to do. I could get away with that because I'm the mother.

Sophie once said to me that sometimes she gets the feeling that parents think they're better than children. Many kids have to do the dirty and uninteresting work of the family. They do the chores while the parents make the decisions. Sophie said that she's glad that Andy and I help. We're all part of the team. And Sophie is thankful for that because she doesn't mind working when she knows everyone else is willing to work as well. We're all in this together. We support each other.

And working together has great benefits. It draws us together. Even though we might not like the work, it does strengthen family bonds.

It took me a very long time to work out how to encourage kids to do chores. Like many families, I organised the chore list, and I expected my kids to do everything on it. I used to think that this was okay. I was always shouting such things as: "You haven't done your chores. Come on; you're lazy. When are you going to get them done? You're letting the family down." And then when the chore list method didn't work, I tried bribery. Maybe a reward system would be more effective. Or how about punishing my kids for not doing what I asked? I tried lots of different approaches before I worked out exactly how to get everybody to cooperate.

As I said, I have to be a good example. I have to help others if I want them to help me. It's a very, very simple idea, but it's not so easy to carry out because all of us are tempted to be lazy. Sometimes I get fed up of being a good example. I just want to sit still and do nothing. Let someone else do the work.

Recently, I had a moment when I didn't want to be that good example for my children. And I didn't even realise it at first. It was lunchtime. My daughter Imogen had decided she wanted to go shopping after we'd eaten and she invited Gemma-Rose to go with her. Now Gemma-Rose was drying dishes and Imogen was impatient: "Hurry up and get those dishes done because I want to go out. You're holding me up."

And I told Imogen that instead of nagging her sister to dry the dishes more quickly, why didn't she pick up a tea towel and help her? The dishes would get done a lot faster, and it would be much more pleasant. There was some truth in what I said, but what I should have done was get up off the sofa and say, "You want to go out shopping? You go. I'll finish those dishes for you." That would have been the better thing to have done because I ended up nagging in my turn.

Now, Imogen, because she's a good person, didn't complain. She just grabbed a tea towel and dried those dishes with Gemma-Rose, but I felt bad later. I thought, *If I'm not willing to step in and do something above and beyond what I'm expected to do, how can I expect my children to be generous?* Yes, we want our children to do, not only what has to be done but to go beyond that, and be generous.

There was another occasion when I failed to do what was right. Every Saturday morning, Imogen has a singing lesson. She leaves the house just before 9.30. The rest of the family has a slow morning. We might get up a little bit later than we do in the week, shower, and then potter around doing the morning chores. Of course, chores still have to be done even on the weekends, but we do them at a more leisurely rate.

Anyway, Imogen dashed out of her bedroom. As she was thrusting on her shoes and pulling on her coat, I said to her, "What chores have you done this morning?" And she said, "I haven't had time to do any." And I said, "You should have got up a bit earlier to get some chores done to help the family."

Imogen didn't say anything. She just hurried off to her singing lesson. But later, I thought, *No, that wasn't very nice.* What I should have said was, "Don't worry about the chores. I will do them for you." I didn't need to tell Imogen that she should have got up earlier. She was very aware of that. Maybe she was feeling bad about having to race out of the house without helping the family. I'm sure Imogen would have felt very grateful if I'd offered to do her chores. And my action would have inspired her to step in and help somebody else in a similar situation another time.

Maybe we worry too much about fairness. We try to divide up the chores in an even way. But this encourages everyone to do their share and no more. Wouldn't it be better to be generous? We have to be willing to go beyond what is expected and help each other with love. Parents as well as kids. Even when we don't feel like it. It's the right thing to do.

The Radical Chore Roster

I once wrote a blog post about encouraging kids to do chores. People flocked to read it. But most left feeling very disappointed. "That won't work," they said. Perhaps they thought my solution was too simple. But my fellow radical unschoolers understood what I was saying. A few of them were eager to share their own stories on this topic.

One mother told me about her children, who are always generous with their help. She said, "And never a chore chart in their lives. They are just nice and generous because they have been treated with generosity."

When I replied to this commenter, I ignored her words about chore rosters. I didn't want to reveal that we do, in fact, have a roster.

I thought about the ideas in my blog post. How can they work together with a chore roster? Surely kids aren't free to choose whether they do the chores or not if there's a roster on the wall telling them what they need to achieve? And if that's true, maybe we aren't radical unschoolers after all. What if somebody came along and said, "Yes, I can see that you're unschooling, but you're not radically unschooling."

I wondered if the no-chore-roster radical unschoolers had discovered something I'd missed. Perhaps there were real benefits to not having a roster, even one that had been written by my children and seemed to be working. And so I decided I should get rid of ours. Get rid of it quickly before somebody discovered we were using it. We'd become *real* radical unschoolers, and then no one could tell us we were doing things wrong.

So one day I took our chore roster off the fridge door, screwed it up and threw it away. Then I told my kids what I'd done. When they saw the roster in the bin, they opened their eyes wide, and someone said, "Why did you do that, Mum? What's wrong with our roster?"

I had to search for the right words. I couldn't just say, "Radical unschoolers don't use chore rosters." What does it matter what other people do? I had to work out why radical unschooling and rosters are incompatible.

A moment of thinking and then I said, "I think rosters don't encourage anyone to do more than their fair share. You do your jobs on the roster, and then you go off without worrying about anyone else. You are only willing to give so much. I would rather you look around and say, 'Hey, that job needs doing. I'm willing to do it.' Help each other more."

My children looked at each other and then at me and said, "Mum, we already do that." They explained that, yes, they have a roster and there are assigned jobs on it, but quite often they do each others' chores. They help each other out. If somebody isn't home, their chores get taken over by the others in the family. No one sticks to her chores and refuses to do more. My children were already doing what I wanted them to do. I just hadn't seen it.

Why would my kids be willing to do more than was expected? I realised that they were following my example. Yes, it had all started with me. Each morning, I do my chores. I vacuum my bedroom and bathroom, and then I move on to the living room. And then instead of rolling up the cord and putting the vacuum cleaner away, I continue down the hall and vacuum the kitchen and family room as well, even though this is somebody else's job on the roster. When my kids find out I've done some of their chores, they always say, "Thank you, Mum. Thank you for doing my job." And I always reply, "You're welcome. I enjoyed doing it for you."

I guess we have been helping each other generously for a long time. And when I realised this, there wasn't any real reason to throw away the roster, was there? I could have replaced it on the fridge door. But I didn't. I still couldn't get past the thought that radical unschoolers don't use chore rosters. I was worried about what people might think of us. Maybe I wouldn't have cared about other people's opinions if we'd been living a quiet life. But I'm a blogger. We share our lives with anyone interested. I knew someone could stop by and tell me I had no right to write about radical unschooling because I was doing it all wrong. And I didn't like this thought. So the roster remained in the bin.

The days went by, and the chores seemed to be getting done just the same as ever. Nothing much had changed. Everybody was considerate and helpful, and I smiled. We didn't need the chore roster. Things were working perfectly without it. But then one day, I found the roster in the cupboard. Somebody had rescued it from the bin and smoothed out its wrinkles.

I gathered my children together and said, "I just found the roster. What's it doing in the cupboard?" And someone said, "Mum, we need the roster. We use it to check things off. We want to make sure we've done everything before we get on to the other work of the day." Someone else added, "We can't always remember what needs doing on what day."

Yes, we need to do certain chores on particular days. For example, the roster helps everyone to remember that we have to place the garbage bins on the footpath on Monday because they are emptied early on Tuesday morning.

My children convinced me the roster was useful. They wanted to use it. So I put it back on the fridge, and I thought, *We will be radical unschoolers who use a chore roster.* I no longer consider rosters incompatible with a radical unschooling way of life. It just depends on how we use them.

I think the problem is that most people use chore rosters in an attempt to get their children to work. The parents draw them up and hand out the jobs to the children, and then they expect them to do them. It's a family rule. I know all about this because we used to do this when our children were little. I used to tick off the chores as my children completed them. "Have you done all your jobs on the roster?" I'd ask. And if they hadn't, I'd say, "You can't have your morning tea until you've done everything. And if you don't hurry up, morning tea time will be over."

Looking back, I am not happy with how I handled things. I cringe as I read my words. They were cruel. That wasn't the right way to treat my children. I used the roster in the wrong way.

These days, the roster belongs to my kids. They choose to use it. They write it. They modify it. They can choose to ignore it. The roster is a tool. It's not a rule.

Maybe we listen to other people's ideas because we want to do things properly. And this can be good because we can all learn a lot from one other. As long as we don't get side-tracked by our need for approval, our need to belong, our concerns about what other people might think of us, and our lack of confidence. Sometimes we might be wrong, and it might be beneficial to listen to other people. But then again, sometimes 'wrong' is actually right. Like a chore roster. A radical chore roster might be exactly what a family needs.

My need for other people's approval forced my kids to do what was right in secret. They had to hide their roster from me. Isn't that sad?

The Weekly Chores that Don't Always Get Done

We have a list of chores that only need doing once a week such as cleaning showers, dusting the house, mopping the family room floor, and polishing the piano. We all discussed who could do what and when and put together a mutually acceptable once-a-week roster.

So we all know what needs doing and who's doing what. We're organised. And we're all willing helpers. So every Saturday we get to enjoy clean showers, a shiny piano, sparkling floors, and a dust-free house. Or do we?

Some weeks no one does their weekly chores. We all get busy, and we'd rather spend our time doing other things, so we ignore the roster. All of us.

Sometimes I think it would be good if we completed the weekly chores each week. I wish everyone wouldn't ignore them. So I think about how I could encourage my family to do everything on the roster. Should I complain that no one is doing the chores even though everyone agreed that they would? Or should I start by doing my chores without fail? I can't expect anyone to do what I'm not prepared to do, can I? And then what? Next, I could do the other chores on the list. I could disregard who agreed to do what, and get out the cleaning equipment and do the jobs myself. With good grace, and not because I want to make anyone feel bad.

Do you know what would happen if I did that? My children would see me working and say, "Mum! I should be doing that." They'd take the cleaning cloths and sprays from my hands and start work themselves. They wouldn't want to see me doing what they have agreed to do. That wouldn't be right. My kids aren't lazy or selfish. They just get distracted by other things. Just like me. Sometimes weekly chores don't seem very important at all.

My kids are willing to do whatever it takes to fulfil my needs. If I need a clean bathroom and shower, they will give it to me. But first, I have to show them that I need that clean bathroom. It's something I want each week. How can I convey the message to my family that the weekly chores are important when I fail to do my share?

Clean showers and a dust-free house are nice. But not essential. Unless, of course, we haven't experienced them for quite some time.

"Hey, girls," I say, "have you noticed how grimy the showers are? Perhaps it's time we did our weekly chores."

We gather the cleaning equipment. We work hard. Soon our house is gleaming. We've solved the problem until the next time we surface from our computers and all the other things that take us away from the lesser things of life. Then someone might say, "Have you seen all the dust on top of the piano? Perhaps I should do some dusting." Then we all decide it's again time to do our weekly chores.

Weekly? That’s not quite right, is it? I think we need a new name for these occasional chores.

Fairness

When I married Andy, I had very definite ideas about what our life together would look like. We were going to be equal partners (with me in charge). I was prickly and defensive and very opinionated. There was no way Andy was going to take advantage of me - he didn't intend to - just because I was now his wife. I decided I was going to do no more for my husband than what an equal partnership demanded.

"You'll have to iron your own shirts," I announced. "And I'm not going to do all the cooking."

Why did I marry Andy? I married him because I love him. It took me a very long time to see that when we love, we give of ourselves freely. We are willing to serve. Marriage is not about taking from a spouse or remaining stubbornly independent. It's not a mutually agreed upon partnership where every give and take is noted, added up and balanced equally.

I was afraid to look after the man I love. I wonder why. Maybe I was afraid I'd end up doing all the giving, and my husband would just lap it up without reciprocating. But that's not what happened. The more I give, the more Andy gives to me.

I love. And I am loved.

And now we love our kids.

Isn't it wonderful when everyone gives of themselves without worrying about fairness?

"I'll make your lunch for you."

"I'll clean your bathroom."

"I'll iron your shirt."

"I love helping you."

Part XIII: Food

A Fussy Eater

This morning when I got out of bed and went into the kitchen, I discovered Charlotte ladling porridge into bowls. She slid two bowls onto a tray, together with two mugs of tea, and then handed everything to me: "For you and Dad!" I hurried back to bed to enjoy my breakfast, tucked up under the warm quilt. The porridge was creamy and had brown sugar sprinkled over the top. It was delicious, and I scraped the bowl clean.

I remember an older friend telling me about the porridge he used to eat as a child. His mother made it with water and salt, and I doubt he scraped his spoon around the bowl, trying to capture every last morsel. He probably didn't lick his lips with satisfaction when he finally laid down his spoon. But he was expected to eat all that porridge up, regardless of whether he liked the taste or not. Was it my friend's father who insisted that uneaten food be served up for the next meal... and the next... until it was eaten? I forget exactly who did that. Someone did.

We all like the taste of porridge (made with milk), but there are some foods we disagree about. Andy hates coconut, and I will not touch pears or fennel. Each of our children has one or two pet disliked foods too, but Gemma-Rose has a long list of things she will not let past her lips. I won't say she dislikes the taste of all these things, for many of them she hasn't even tried.

I don't insist Gemma-Rose eat foods she thinks she won't like. But it was different for my older kids. Charlotte says, "When we were younger, you made us eat everything, whether we liked it or not. I had to eat pumpkin soup." She grimaces as she remembers. "I soon learnt pumpkin soup tastes even worse cold than it does when it's hot."

Did I really make my children sit at the table until their food went cold? I suppose I did.

I used to say, "Just eat one mouthful. How do you know you don't like it if you won't even try it?" But I could never persuade my children to taste anything that they'd decided they didn't like the look of. They'd sit at the table with their mouths firmly clamped closed.

"If you just eat a little, you can have dessert." I wasn't above bribery. Surely the promise of a treat would persuade them? Just a taste. That wasn't asking too much, was it? However, not even the thought of chocolate cake or ice cream could open my children's mouths.

But I wouldn't give up. No, it was a real battle of wills. Why wouldn't they eat the food I'd carefully prepared? Didn't they know how much time I'd spent cooking it for them? It tasted good. I liked it. Why didn't they?

I must have won a few of the battles. Charlotte now eats pumpkin soup even though she doesn't like it. But what a price I must have paid to have my way.

Then one day I'd had enough. Dinner times were too stressful. I decided, as long as it wasn't inconveniencing the rest of the family, everyone could choose to eat what they wanted. It also occurred to me that I wouldn't like it if anyone forced me to eat fennel or pears. And so I gave in. Was I too soft? Or perhaps I became wiser with experience?

Every day we cook a meal that most of us like. Usually, it's only Gemma-Rose who screws up her nose when she sees what's for dinner. "You can have just the rice," I say. So I ladle out the rice into bowls and add curry to seven. I sprinkle a handful of cheese and a few nuts into the eighth bowl and say, "That one's Gemma-Rose's." She smiles. She doesn't mind rice and cheese and nuts.

And some days I cook what Gemma-Rose likes to eat for all of us because everyone deserves to have their favourite meals added to the weekly family menu.

Sometimes I say, "One day Gemma-Rose will decide to try new foods for herself. She won't always be a fussy eater." But I've been saying this for years. My youngest daughter is eight years old, and she still isn't showing any signs of developing more adventurous tastes. Should I take action? Does everyone think I am spoiling her?

I think of the possible battles ahead if I decide Gemma-Rose has to start eating exactly what the rest of us are having for dinner. I wonder whether forcing a particular food upon her will only increase her resistance to it. And I think: if they aren't inconveniencing anyone and health is not an issue, doesn't everyone have the right to make their own food choices, even children?

Andy has made a delicious ragout as well as a potato casserole for dinner. He is about to serve them up.

"Give Gemma-Rose just the potato casserole," I say. "More ragout for us."

Gemma-Rose is happy. We're happy. Is there really a problem?

Love and Food

Years ago, I used to battle with my kids over food. Whenever I placed something in front of them that they didn't like the look of, I'd say, "There's nothing wrong with it. It tastes fine. Eat it!" They were never convinced. Their mouths remained firmly closed.

I'd then say, "How do you know you don't like it? Just taste it." I'd wave one forkful or spoonful in front of their faces. "Eat one mouthful," I'd wheedle. But one mouthful was one mouthful too many.

Next, I'd resort to bribes: "If you eat your dinner, you can have ice cream for dessert."

And then when I couldn't tempt my kids with ice cream, I'd threaten them with some kind of punishment: "You can sit there all night until you eat your dinner." My kids were prepared to wait as long as it took.

None of my techniques worked. I was rarely successful when it came to forcing my kids to eat.

I wonder why I persisted. Did I think it was my duty to bring up kids who weren't fussy, who'd eat whatever I placed in front of them? Maybe I was concerned about what other people might think of my children. What if we were invited out to dinner and my child wouldn't eat what was on her plate? Would my friend raise her eyebrows? Would I feel embarrassed?

Maybe it was a matter of convenience and cost. I wanted cooking to be as easy as possible. I was prepared to cook one meal only.

Did I want kids who would obey me? "I'm the mother, and you're the child. Do as I say."

Perhaps I wanted my kids to appreciate my cooking efforts: "I spent a long time cooking that meal for you."

Eventually, I came to my senses. I stopped forcing my kids to eat. Instead, I thought about how we could see to everyone's needs in a practical and cost-effective way.

These days, we plan our meals together, making sure we include each person's favourite dinner sometime during the week.

We modify meals to make sure no one has to eat anything they don't like. And sometimes, if we can't modify a meal, the cook is prepared to make a special meal just for one.

We'd been doing all this for a long time. It had been working very well. It was just the way we did things. But then something happened which made me think further about the whole issue of food.

My daughter Sophie developed an intolerance to dairy foods. Fortunately, I didn't say, "You used to eat cheese and milk. I can't see why you've suddenly decided you can't." I knew why Sophie couldn't eat these foods. I could see it. They made her feel sick.

So for the past few years, we've been modifying our meals for Sophie, replacing the dairy components with other foods. Or we've been cooking her something different from the rest of the family.

When there's a health issue, we do whatever is needed, don't we, regardless of the work involved? So, in theory, it's possible to do the same if it's a taste issue. But do we? Do we take aversions to certain foods seriously enough? Are we willing to accommodate different tastes?

I discovered that the work involved in seeing to everyone's needs isn't as great as I used to think. And it doesn't have to be expensive. It just needs a bit of thought and planning.

Everyone is important. It's not too much trouble to make each person a meal they can eat. We're willing to do what is needed because we love one another.

Love: isn't that what cooking family meals is all about?

Encouraging Kids to Eat a Healthier Diet

A few years ago, I was pondering healthy eating. Was I eating a good enough diet? At the time, sugar was a hot topic. Lots of bloggers were writing about their experiences of giving up this food. I skimmed through these posts and, yes, there did seem to be good reasons for not eating sugar. I could see why people were eliminating it from their diets and encouraging others to do the same. But I didn't want to do this myself. I couldn't. I wasn't in a position to give up sugar.

What would we do if our hosts offered us sugar while visiting their homes? I couldn't say, "I'm very sorry, but we don't eat sugar." That would seem impolite.

Maybe my kids would protest if I refused to buy sugar. Andy might protest too. We can't force our ideas on our family, can we?

And what would we do when birthday time came around? What's a birthday without a cake baked with sugar and iced with sweet frosting?

Finally, could I actually live without sugar? It's rather delicious. It's one of the simple pleasures of life.

So I pushed the idea of giving up sugar to the back of my mind. But rather inconveniently, it refused to disappear. It hung around, hoping to catch my attention. And one day the no sugar idea did exactly that. When it pushed its way to the forefront of my mind, instead of thrusting it instantly away, I pondered it properly. I examined it from all angles. I asked myself, "Are my reasons for not adopting this way of eating just excuses?"

Perhaps if our hosts offered us food containing sugar when we went visiting, we could eat it without saying anything. We didn't have to be fanatical about it, did we? A little bit of sugar wouldn't hurt us. And we could solve the birthday cake problem by looking for delicious alternatives. We could celebrate birthdays without a traditional sugar-laden cake. And I might not miss the sugary pleasures of life if I found other foods to replace them. Healthy doesn't necessarily mean bland.

But what about my family? Would they be open to the idea of giving up sugar with me? For, of course, I couldn't just announce, "We're all giving up sugar!" and then expect everyone to fall in with my plan. I knew this would not be a respectful way to encourage my kids to eat more healthily. I also knew this approach wouldn't work. Yes, I discovered a long time ago that we can't force kids to eat everything we put in front of them.

So what did I do? Well, for a while, I did nothing. Then one day - Sophie tells me it was a couple of days before her birthday- when I was out shopping with the girls, we saw a stack of *I Quit Sugar* books on a table by the checkout. While we waited our turn to be served, we flipped through the pages of this very attractive book.

"What do you think about sugar?" I asked my girls. "Do you think it's bad for us?"

"Well, we could buy the book and read it and find out," suggested Imogen.

So I bought the book. We took it home. And then I said, "Why don't you read the book and let me know what you think?"

Imogen and Charlotte disappeared into their bedroom with the new book. They read the information. They looked at the recipes. They visited the *I Quit Sugar* website. Then they reported back to tell me what they'd found out.

"We should give up sugar, Mum." That was their verdict.

We called Sophie and Gemma-Rose so that they could be part of the discussion. They also needed to be included in any decision we were going to make. Imogen explained all the ins and outs of the issue. She told the younger girls what giving up sugar would entail. And then everyone agreed that we'd become a sugar-free family.

By this time, it was Sophie's birthday. Imogen had made her a traditional sweet cake: a delicious white chocolate mud cake dripping with frosting. As we cut it, Sophie said, "I wonder how much sugar is in each slice," and Imogen replied, "Don't think about that today. Just enjoy it."

But the next day, we did think about the sugar content of everything we were in the habit of eating. We started reading labels and comparing foods. We used up the sugar stored in our pantry and decided not to buy any more. We searched the supermarket for natural sweeteners. We googled 'sugar-free recipes'. It was all rather interesting.

Sophie once said, "When we went running, the other girls and I stayed together in a pack. This way, we could talk about giving up sugar as we ran. I remember how passionate we were about this topic. It was exciting. Who would think that quitting something that most people think is good could be so much fun?"

Giving up sugar wasn't as hard as I'd anticipated. Our diet became more varied. We bought better quality foods that were tasty. Best of all, we enjoyed discussing the issue and working together to put our decision into action. And it felt good too. We were doing something that would improve our health.

"How do we encourage kids to eat a more healthy diet?" I ask Sophie.

"Parents can't just announce that they're changing the family diet: *This is what we're going to do, and this is why.* If you'd have done this, we might have felt hostile to the whole idea. We might have thought, *Oh no, we can't eat sugar anymore.* It would have felt like you were taking something away from us. We might have been afraid that we'd miss out on the things we enjoyed.

"It's good to get kids involved. Let them do the research. Discuss things. Ask kids what they think. Give them a choice. When parents do this, kids are more open to new ideas. They could even feel excited about changing their diet."

"Should all families give up sugar?" I ask Sophie. "What if that sounds like too big a step?"

"All families should decide for themselves what they want to eat. And then make changes slowly. Let everyone adjust gradually. Little changes make a big difference over time."

And don't be fanatical. Having a less than healthy treat now and then won't hurt.

Treats? Now I'm thinking about finger buns. I love finger buns covered with pink icing and lots of sprinkles. I could buy some for morning tea. But do I really want a sweet bun? Perhaps I'd prefer some nuts or some berries. How about some yoghurt? Something sugar-free?

It's funny how tastes can change.

Part XIV: Being Different

A Silent Thrill

When my first child was a baby, I read all the parenting books I could get my hands on, including one with a title something like *Your Child Can Be a Genius*. I read the book and then thought about its message very carefully. And quickly. If I wanted to have an exceedingly clever child, I had no time to lose. Wait too long, and my chance would be gone. Everything happens in the first few years of a child's life. Or so the author said.

I wasn't sure I wanted my child to be a genius. Wouldn't that make her different from everyone else? And then wouldn't her pathway through life be more difficult? Perhaps happiness results from being part of the crowd. Maybe we have to fit in. No, I wanted my children to be 'normal'. But they haven't ended up normal at all.

Somewhere along the way, I stopped worrying about who I wanted my children to be, and I started encouraging them to be who they are. I realised every child is unique and special. She or he doesn't have to be like anyone else.

Happiness doesn't result from being part of the crowd because, despite appearances, the crowd isn't made up of kids who are all alike. They're just pretending to be the same so that they'll be accepted. They're too afraid to be themselves. Unlike my kids.

My daughter Sophie once said, "Sometimes people think I'm normal. They assume I'm just like them. But then they start talking to me and suddenly realise that I'm different."

"Do you like being different?" I ask.

"Oh, yes!" My teenage daughter smiles. "Being different gives me a silent thrill!"

Different But Okay

I received a letter from the education department:

If you want to reregister your children as homeschoolers, fill in the appropriate forms. If you don't, please send details of the school your children will be attending.

School? What if my girls went to school? Would they cope? How would life change?

These were idle thoughts. I know I can't send my girls to school. It wouldn't be fair to them. They'd soon realise they are different from everyone else. The other kids would realise this too.

Are my children different because they have been unschooled? Or is different who they are? Has unschooling just given them the freedom to be themselves?

I went to school. I was different. I didn't fit in. I felt like I wasn't worth knowing. I wasn't popular. I wasn't pretty. I wasn't particularly clever. I ended up being a disappointment, never matching up to other people's expectations. I didn't make anything of my life. Or so I was led to believe.

But I now realise that I'm not the person I thought I was. I am not a disappointment. I've done lots of worthy things. This might not be the right thing to say. Maybe I can think it, but it's wrong to tell other people. I shall say it anyway: I *am* clever.

Yes, I'm different, but that doesn't mean I'm not okay.

My whole family is different. How are we not like most other people? I ask my daughter Sophie if she feels different from other kids her age.

"Oh, yes! I'm definitely different."

"In what way?"

"I think differently, especially when it comes to learning. Most teenagers look at learning very negatively. It's something they have to do. It's boring. But I find everything potentially interesting. School kids and even many homeschoolers regard life and learning as two different things. They get their work out of the way, and then they get on with life. But for us, the real stuff of life is learning. Learning and life are interchangeable.

"Many kids my age don't have any opinions. They copy other people. They try to say the right things, dress the right way, behave in a way that's acceptable to the group so that they are popular. They want to be liked and accepted."

Sophie tells me that she's comfortable being herself. She doesn't feel like she has to follow the crowd. She's confident and self-motivated. I can see that she doesn't need other people's praise or approval.

"Do you feel any pressure to be like everyone else?"

"No."

"Is that freeing?"

"Yes, I know I don't have to fit in. I don't have to pretend to be someone I'm not."

Yes, Sophie is happy being who she is. She doesn't mind being different.

But would school change all that? Would it give Sophie the message that different is wrong? Would school be a miserable experience for her just like it was for me? We'll never know because I sent off the necessary forms to the education department. I reregistered my children as homeschoolers. School is not an option.

I want my kids to know that even though they are different, they're okay. Just like me.

Making Friends and Being Different

It's Saturday afternoon. I'm at home, settled in front of the heater, thinking about socialisation. Am I feeling sociable at the moment? No. I'm quite capable of socialising, but I'm happy sitting here alone with my computer. Actually, I often feel like staying home and not seeing people. And my girls feel the same way. I suppose part of this has to do with the fact we're introverts. But some of it is due to the fact we're isolated unschoolers.

Now we've all heard people criticising homeschoolers for keeping their kids home: "But what about socialisation?" This is ridiculous because our kids have more opportunities to get out into the real world to meet all kinds of people than do school kids. I tend to ignore the socialisation issue. For us, it's an old debate.

But there's another aspect of socialisation that does affect us. I've had homeschoolers tell me that I need to provide more opportunities for my girls to meet other children, especially those of their own ages. "Come along to our homeschool group. You need to make an effort for your kids' sakes."

For a long time, I smiled politely and ignored this advice. Then one day, the words 'you need to make an effort' took hold of my mind. Perhaps other people were right. So I consulted my daughters. "Do you think we should go to a homeschool group? We might make some new friends. Should we give it a go?" We decided we would.

Everyone in the group was welcoming and friendly. There was just one problem: we were the only unschooling family. The girls didn't like how everyone expected them to join in with organised activities that they weren't interested in. That's not the way we do things. Conversations weren't very relevant to us. Kids talked about what year of school they were in and what assignments they had to do. Parents chatted about curricula and planning and how to make kids do their school work. And that was okay because they needed to talk about such things. But we didn't have anything to say on these topics.

One day, after we'd been going to the meetings for nine months or so, we looked at each other and said, "Do we really want to go today? Or should we stay at home?" We stayed home. And that was the end of that.

We'd tried going to a homeschool group. We'd given it a fair go. We couldn't see the point of continuing. Other people might criticise us, but we were happy.

Why do we worry about socialisation? Are we afraid our kids won't be able to talk to people? Maybe they won't be able to make friends. And they need lots of friends. Or do they?

As introverts, I don't think we need crowds of friends. A few kindred spirit ones are enough. To be honest, we haven't found any of these locally. Unschooling has made us different from those around us. No, that's not quite true. Unschooling has allowed us to be who we are: different. But maybe one day we might meet other people just like us. As Sophie once said, "I can't be the only weird person in the world!" In the meantime, we do connect up with like-minded unschoolers online.

Despite the fact my girls are weird, they can talk to people, any people, not just unschoolers. They have good communication skills. And this is something not all kids have.

"They don't know how to talk properly," observes Sophie referring to some school kids she knows. "They have no idea how to have proper conversations where everyone is included. They talk about themselves all the time. They're not interested in hearing what other people have to say. They don't really want to know about me."

And this can be hard. How do you become part of the conversation when no one is willing to listen? When no one is interested in what you might have to say? When they don't even realise you'd like to be included? Often, my girls give up. As they say, sometimes it's the people who are always speaking who have a problem. Just because someone has no shortage of words doesn't mean she knows how to talk.

Getting together regularly with other people doesn't necessarily teach us how to communicate and get on with others. That's the conclusion I've come to. So I've stopped worrying about such things as homeschool groups and organised field trips. As long as our kids are capable of being sociable, it doesn't matter if they choose to stay home.

Of course, my girls have each other. We're a crowd on our own. What would I do if I had an only child? I don't know. I've never experienced that. Have you?

The Real Problem with Being Different

I'm sitting at my friend Amina's kitchen table enjoying a cup of coffee when Harry appears in the doorway.

After greeting me, he says, "I'm going to the library, Mum. See you later."

I like Amina's son very much. He's generous and hard-working and always very polite. "There's something very special about Harry," I say.

"Yes, there is," smiles Amina, "but would you believe there was a time when I wanted to change him?" She leans towards me as she says, "Harry has always been different. From a very early age, he had a mind of his own and was never interested in conforming to the group. And this caused me a lot of stress.

"He'd be invited to a birthday party and refuse to join in with the games. He didn't want to do as he was told or play by the rules. He had other ideas. While the rest of the children followed instructions and did as expected, Harry would wander around exploring on his own.

"Years ago, we were invited to a weekly drama class with several other families. We met in someone's home. Harry refused to sit in the circle and pretend. He wouldn't be a dragon, an old woman, an upper-class gentleman. Instead, he roamed our friend's house exploring and playing his own games, and there was nothing I could do about it. I tried glaring, frowning, bribing, cajoling, and pleading, but Harry wouldn't listen to me. He wouldn't come and join in with the other children.

"The other mothers would look at me with pitying eyes. Maybe they thought I was a hopeless mother, a mother who had no control over her son. They probably got fed up with Harry and me."

Amina lowers her voice. "I don't like to admit this, but one day I said, 'Harry, can't you do as I want for once? Can't you be nice to me just for one day?' Harry looked confused. Be nice to me? I don't think he deliberately tried to upset me. He was just being himself. Wasn't that okay?

"It was probably just as well we homeschooled Harry and didn't send him off to school. I can imagine: 'Mrs Bell, we need to talk about your son. He refuses to do anything we say. He won't sit at his desk. He wants to roam around and explore, and that's not allowed.'"

Amina is quiet for a moment. She sips her coffee and then says, "I might have done a disservice to Harry. I've mentioned the things that frustrated me enormously. But it wasn't all bad. As you can see, he grew into a very hard-working, reliable, caring child. He might not have wanted to join in with all the activities the other kids were involved with, but he was willing to spend hours jiggling babies and making up games for toddlers so that I could have a break. He may have his own way of doing things, but he has never failed to help with the household chores - hanging out washing or cleaning or doing dishes.

"I've always been very proud of Harry despite his differences. But I do wonder about the future. He isn't exactly outgoing. And he has his quirks. What will happen when he leaves home and goes off into the world? Will he fit in? Will he find his place?

"A few years ago, I thought I should try and change Harry. Make him more like everyone else. If he were part of the crowd, if he did things in the same way as everyone else, I wouldn't have to worry about him. I started saying things like, 'Harry, perhaps you should try hanging out the washing without worrying about whether the pegs match. Harry, I know you like your routines and hate change, but maybe you should make yourself do things differently now and then. Harry, it wouldn't hurt to join in with a soccer game occasionally. It's a friendly thing to do. And maybe you should practise starting conversations. You need to be more outgoing.'"

"What happened?" I asked.

"Well, Harry was eager to please me. He was willing to do everything I suggested. He tried to become the person he thought I'd prefer him to be. And that almost broke my heart. In the end, I decided to let Harry be who he is. His differences are what make him special."

"Being different isn't bad," I say.

"No," agrees Amina. "Different is actually good. There's absolutely nothing wrong with Harry. The problem doesn't lie with him at all. It lies with other people."

Yes, most people aren't good at accepting those who seem different from them.

"Wouldn't it be good if differences were accepted?" I say. "Imagine if society didn't expect us all to be the same. We'd all be valued for our unique gifts. They'd be a place in the world for everyone."

"Even though I wouldn't change Harry," says Amina, "I still have odd moments when I worry about him." She drains her cup and places it on the table, and then she adds, "But that's my problem, not his. When I begin to worry, I know I'm failing to trust. Sometimes I don't even want to trust. I just want things to be different. For my sake."

I know how my pretend friend Amina feels. I understand her story. I've had problems trusting as well. Sometimes I've wanted my kids to be more 'normal', to be part of the crowd. Such children would be much easier to parent. I wouldn't have to worry about them. They'd be no need to trust.

Trust: that's the real problem, isn't it? There's nothing wrong with being different. Different is okay.

Who We Really Are

There's nothing like death to make us realise what's important in life. I discovered this when our son Thomas died. Suddenly all our usual worries dissolved away. We no longer cared about other people's opinions of us. We had no energy for pretending to be who we're not so that we'd be accepted.

I suppose when I revealed who I truly was, some people might have said, "She's not herself, poor thing. She's just lost a baby." They probably made excuses for me. With time, I'd heal, and the 'real' Sue would return. Except she didn't. The real Sue remained as she was.

It's strange how we sometimes feel we have to hide who we are and what we believe. Do we do this because we think no one will like the real us? Perhaps we've been told we have to be a certain way to be accepted.

But I've heard that in trying to please everyone, we end up pleasing no one, especially ourselves and our families. So we might as well be who we are. We don't have to pretend. Who we are is who we are meant to be. And there's nothing wrong with that.

Part XV: Parents

Letting Our Kids See the Real Us

Years ago, I used to swap between the homeschooling methods frequently as I tried to find the perfect method of educating my kids. My children must have felt very unsettled, never knowing what to expect from me. They couldn't trust me from one day to the next.

A similar thing might happen when parents start unschooling. Do our kids believe us when we say such things as "You can use the computer for as long as you like"? Perhaps they detect the reluctance beneath our words and don't trust us.

I asked my teenage daughter Sophie about trust. How can a parent build up a relationship of trust with a child? She said we can't trust someone if we don't know them very well. So we need to let our kids get to know us properly. Perhaps we never think about this and just assume that parents and children know each other naturally.

It's important for us to share what we're interested in, and what's important to us. Have real conversations with our kids and not interrogations. Share our dreams and our hopes. Admit our mistakes. Let our children see the real us. Allow them to help us. Let them get close.

Sometimes we're so concerned about being good parents and seeing to the needs of our kids that we hide who we really are.

Accepting Ourselves and Our Kids

One day, many years ago, when I was in the supermarket with several of my children, I met a mother with a girl of about seven. As I reached past the woman to get a packet off the shelf, she looked at my youngest child and said, "Your baby might be beautiful now, but just you wait!" She then turned towards her daughter and said, "She's a little poisonous bunch-back'd toad! I'll be glad when she goes back to school."

The mother was stressed out, and although I felt sorry for her daughter, I also felt sorry for her. What had gone wrong? The daughter who'd started life as a perfect princess had turned into a poisonous toad, at least in the eyes of her parent.

Now we might not tell strangers our children are toads, but I'm sure most of us have sighed loudly, at one time or another, and complained about them to our friends.

"If only she were more outgoing or adventurous. She won't try anything new."

"If only he were less boisterous or impulsive. I can't keep up with him. He's driving me crazy."

"If only she weren't such a daydreamer. She wastes her time instead of getting on with her work."

"If only he weren't so stubborn. He won't listen to me or do anything I say."

"If only he weren't so reserved. He doesn't want to join in. People think he's very unfriendly."

Somehow our perfect babies turned into imperfect children. Or maybe we just got picky. Could we have had our own ideas about how our kids were going to grow and develop? Do we feel disappointed? Or maybe we just worry about our kids. If only they were different, their pathways through life would be easier. Our job would be easier too.

Of course, we have to accept our kids exactly as they are, even if we think they have faults. We may be right about those faults. But then again, we may be wrong. Faults or no faults, it doesn't matter. It's not our job to criticise and pull our kids down.

So how do we get back to appreciating who our children are? How do we put aside all our silly preferences and worries and accept the wonderful unique beings we are privileged to have as part of our families? Maybe part of the answer is wrapped up in ourselves.

Yesterday, I bought a new pair of running shorts. When I got home from the shops, I drew them out of my bag and waved them in front of my family saying, "Look! I found some longer shorts that will cover my old legs. They'll hide my wrinkly skin."

One of my girls said, "But Mum, you haven't got wrinkly legs."

I sighed and disagreed.

I'm always moaning about some part of me that's not quite right. I often complain about my appearance. I'm getting older, I don't look like I used to, and I'm not happy about that.

My latest lament: "Quinn's wrinkly face is very cute. I wish my wrinkles were considered attractive." (Quinn is our Shar Pei/Great Dane dog.)

My body's heading downhill at a furious rate. Or at least that's what I think. And I'm finding that hard to accept. Maybe that's because I can still hear the voices from my childhood telling me I'm just not good enough the way I am.

But this morning, as I ran around the park with two grinning dogs at my side, I wasn't worried about my wrinkly old legs. Instead, I was thinking, "I'm glad I have strong legs that can run." And maybe that's the answer to my problem: I should concentrate on what I am grateful for, the good bits about being me, and ignore the bits that make me feel unsettled and unhappy. It may turn out that all the things I moan about are insignificant. Maybe I've been giving them more space in my head than they deserve.

And perhaps we shouldn't allow any negative thoughts about our kids to enter our heads either. We certainly shouldn't voice them out loud to other people. Instead, we can go looking for all the wonderful qualities that our children have. Concentrate on these and ignore the things that niggle us because it might turn out that we're not looking properly. We're focusing our attention in the wrong direction. All those faults and flaws that we think are so important might dissolve quietly away under the influence of unconditional love.

So how can we more easily accept our kids? Perhaps we can start by accepting ourselves. Our kids are wonderfully unique people. And so are we.

Of course, my appearance is a very superficial problem. Probably it would have been better to have shared a story about one of my many character faults. But I think my ageing problem illustrates the point I want to make even if it's not very important.

Just in case you're wondering, the woman in the supermarket didn't really call her daughter a poisonous bunch-back'd toad. I used this Shakespearean insult because I didn't want to repeat the woman's unkind word.

The Shaming Things People Say

She was so fat she couldn't fit into a telephone box. How could anyone be that big? It didn't seem possible. But it was. It was common knowledge. How did she feel? Was there anything wrong with her? Unfortunately, we didn't wonder. Instead, we felt sorry for her daughter. Who wants to have a mother so big everyone talks about her?

People talked about my mother too. But not because she was fat because she wasn't. She was beautiful. People said, "Surely, she can't be your mother?" It didn't seem possible. She looked more like my sister.

There was another mother. She wasn't fat either. She had the opposite problem. She couldn't put on weight. She ate and ate to prevent herself from disappearing. She could eat donuts by the boxful. My friends and I wished we could eat as many cakes as we liked. Well, I suppose we could have. As long as we didn't mind not fitting into a telephone box.

The skinny mother belonged to the tennis club. So did mine. (I don't think the larger mother did.) During the school holidays, I went to the tennis club too. I'd sit quietly in the corner listening to the women chatting in between games. They often talked about their weight and other people's. "Did you hear about the woman who lost a lot of weight? She and her husband are getting a divorce. He says she's changed, become a different person." A better person? A worse one? I don't know.

All my life, the issue of weight has been at the back of my mind. Am I too fat? (Never too thin.) Can I afford to eat a helping of this? Yes? No? Perhaps not.

I come from a less-than-average family. We're not tall. We're not wide. We were made to be small. Small is who I am. Sometimes I imagine what it would be like if I put on lots of weight. Would I become someone else? What would people think if I became round and wobbly? Would they talk about me: "What happened? She used to be so small. Why did she let herself get that way?"

Yes, people might talk. I couldn't bear that, so I watch what I eat. I also run. But even though I do all that, I still weigh more than I should. Not much. Not so you'd notice at first glance. But if you look closely, you might see that I'm not quite what I used to be. I'm not happy about that. How did it happen? A lack of self-control? I feel ashamed.

I'm ashamed of quite a few things. My strong legs carry me up steep hills, but you should see my arms and my soft pillow middle. If I weren't so lazy, I'd lift some weights, do some Pilates, tone up this body of mine. Perhaps some exercise would send everything back to where it belongs. Or could it be too late? I could tighten up all my muscles, but what about my skin?

My skin is sliding down my face. There's a nice pool of it under my chin. Why didn't I buy the necessary lotions that would have kept me looking young? The anti-ageing ads warned me. But I didn't listen, so it's my fault that I'm looking old. I feel ashamed.

Of course, I don't feel ashamed all the time. I'm not that wrapped up in myself. I know there are more important things in life than what we look like. But still, feelings of shame lurk at the back of my mind. They're always there waiting, hoping to spoil a happy moment. If I'm not careful, they can control how I feel.

Have you ever thought about how shame controls?

Shame is used all the time in schools to make kids work: "If you don't pass your exam, you'll be at the bottom of the class. What will your parents say?"

Parents use it to control their children's behaviour:

"Don't ever do anything that will bring shame to the family."

"How could you have done that? You should be ashamed of yourself."

Or sometimes parents don't have to say a word. It's all in the look. We don't even have to open our mouths.

I hate feeling ashamed. I don't want my kids to feel this way. I don't want them to live with this burden. So I watch what I say. And I thought I was doing okay until the other day.

Sophie and I took a trip to Sydney together. As soon as we arrived, we bought coffee from a kiosk in the park outside the art gallery. As we sat sipping, we took photos of each other. And we soaked up the happy moment.

When we got home, Sophie showed her photos to me: "Aren't these great, Mum? You look so beautiful!"

I looked. And instead of smiling and accepting the compliment, I said, "Oh no, look at the wrinkles around my jaw! I look old." The happy moment we'd captured turned sour.

I often say, "I look so old!" and "I feel so fat!" With those words, I'm passing on old mother and fat mother stories to my children. This time, the stories aren't about telephone boxes and donuts and someone else's mothers. These ones are about me.

Passing on the stories. Passing on the shame.

Will my kids' happiness be controlled by their weight, their age, their appearances? Or can I do something to prevent that? Perhaps I need to accept myself just as I am. Like my kids do. They think I'm beautiful. Maybe I am.

So I have a new story. I don't mind if it's passed around. It goes like this:

I'm Sue Elvis. I'm not as young as I used to be. I have wrinkles and crinkles and skin that's sliding south. My muscles are soft, and my middle is a bit like a pillow. But that's okay because however old I am, whatever I look like, I'm still me. And that's who I'm happy to be.

Yes, I don't want to be anyone else.

"I look better when I smile," I say to Sophie as I scroll through her photos. Yes, a huge smile lifts my skin high, putting everything almost back in place.

I think I'll keep smiling. This won't be difficult to do. You see, I've got a lot to smile about. Have you?

How Unschooling Is About Both Parent and Child

We can't make anyone become the person we'd like them to be. We can't say, "If you only did this or that you'd be a better spouse or friend or child." We can't change people. But we can change ourselves. We can try and become the person we'd like those closest to us to be. We can treat others the way we want them to treat us. We can be a good example. And who knows? Other people may reciprocate. They might start treating us the way we're treating them.

But what if they don't? What if we try to be a better spouse, for example, and nothing happens. What if our husband or wife continues relating to us as normal? They don't seem to notice the extra effort we're making. Maybe we feel they're taking advantage of us without offering anything in return. Do we say, "I tried hard to be a better spouse, but it didn't work? He could have met me halfway, but he didn't. I'm not going to bother trying anymore. He doesn't deserve it." Do we give up?

I think we often give up when we're trying to improve our relationships with our children. We might decide we're going to become a better parent. Perhaps we're going to watch what we say, be more patient and gentle, stop yelling, help instead of nagging, listen more instead of lecturing, be a calmer and kinder mother or father. So we try hard to be a good example, to be the people we'd like our kids to be. But we only give our children a certain amount of time to respond to us. If they don't start copying our behaviour, we give up and resume our old relationship with them. We say, "Whoever said we have to be a good example is wrong. Their children must be different from ours because it doesn't work in our family."

I really do think that the way we treat others affects the way they treat us. Sometimes we just have to give people more time to respond. But what if we put in a lot of effort over a long period with no result? Should we throw our hands in the air and say, "I can't be bothered anymore? I tried, and I'm not going to try any longer." No, I think we have to be a good example, whether we like it or not, whether it has the desired result or not. We have to do it because it's the right thing to do.

We have to become the best people that we can be. Become who we are meant to be. Not just for our children's sakes or for our spouse's sake or anyone's sake. No, we have to do it for ourselves.

Unschooling is just as much about the parent as it is about the child. We might decide to unschool because we think it's the best way to bring up our children or educate them, to help them become better people. But the longer we unschool, the more I realise that it is me who is changing. And it has to be that way if I want unschooling to be effective for our children, for our family.

For how can we expect our kids to become the people they are designed to be if we're not prepared to do the same ourselves?

An Unexpected Opportunity

Andy and I got married straight out of university. Two people with two degrees and no jobs started a new life together. But we weren't without an income for very long because Andy applied for all kinds of jobs and he accepted the first offer that was made to him. He found himself a safe and secure but unexciting job in business, and that's where he remained for 25 years.

Then one day, Andy rang me from work to say, "Sue, I've been made redundant. I'm finishing work today. I have to give back my company car so could you please meet me at the station?"

Safe and secure jobs aren't always safe and secure.

A few hours later, I drove to the station, parked the car and waited for the train to arrive. Soon, I saw him. Andy was ambling along the platform, swinging his empty briefcase, one man among the many women shoppers returning from the city. And even though he had a smile on his face when he greeted me, I felt very sad for Andy. He had worked so hard and then one day, he was cast aside with no thanks, no farewells, no speeches or gifts.

Andy hadn't particularly enjoyed his job, but he'd always given his best to it. He'd been willing to do it because it allowed him to support our children and me. And now that job had disappeared.

At first, Andy felt very strange, not going off to work each morning. All the other men had somewhere to go each day and something to do. Andy was the only husband we knew who was at home without a job. It was as if he'd lost his place in society.

There is no doubt that initially, this was a worrying and anxious time for us. Would Andy get another job? Would we survive financially? What did the future hold?

But slowly we began to appreciate the fact that, for the first time in years, Andy had lots of time to spend at home with our family. He could get involved with what our kids were doing; he could join in with morning prayers instead of rushing out the door before everyone was up; he and I could take leisurely walks to the village at odd times of the day; he could linger around the lunch table enjoying a conversation. How many fathers ever have this opportunity? The only downside was money.

Andy knew he had to do something about his situation, so he applied for some marketing manager jobs that he was more than qualified to do. But I could see his heart wasn't really in it. I asked him what he'd like to do if he could start all over again.

"Be a school teacher," said Andy.

"You could go back to uni and do your Master’s of Teaching," I said.

"What about money? What about our family?"

"You've always looked after us. Now it's your turn to do something for yourself," I insisted. "Let's talk to the kids."

I called a family meeting, and I said, "What do you think about Dad going back to uni? We'd have to live frugally for a long time, but I think it's Dad's turn to follow his dreams."

And all our kids said, "Yes, you've got to do that, Dad!"

So Andy applied to do a Master’s of Teaching. He was accepted on the course, and before long, he was attending lectures and working on assignments.

One day, Andy had to pick up a book from the university campus. "Why don't you come with me? I could show you around," he said. A couple of hours later, we walked through the campus gates. I looked at the students. Some were hurrying to lectures. Others were relaxing outside in the shade of the trees. Probably no one noticed me walking beside Andy. But I imagined them looking at me and wondering: "What's that woman doing here? Surely she's not a student? She doesn't look like she belongs."

After collecting the book, Andy and I went to the coffee shop. As we sipped our drinks, Andy exchanged words with a few people who walked past. Unlike me, he felt relaxed. He fitted in. I thought about how difficult it must have been to go back to university as a mature-aged student. But Andy made it look easy. He'd made friends. He'd adapted to new ways of learning. He'd found his place.

Andy completed his degree course, and then one day, a letter arrived from the university. Andy opened it and then said, "Hey! Guess what? I finished my degree in the top 10% of my year. I'm on the Dean's list."

"Dean's list? What's that?"

"I've no idea, but it must be something good otherwise they wouldn't have bothered sending me a letter."

Andy looked at me, and I looked at him. "Top 10%? Do you think they made a mistake? The letter has my name on it, but perhaps they've got me mixed up with someone else." Andy threw the letter onto a pile of paperwork on his desk and then forgot about it.

A few weeks later, another letter arrived. Andy opened it and said, "Hey! Guess what? I finished my degree in the top 2% of my year. I'm going to get a Dean's medal."

"A Dean's medal? What's that?"

"I've no idea, but it must be something good otherwise they wouldn't have sent me a letter." Andy grinned and added, "I think this time, they must definitely have mixed me up with someone else." He threw the letter on top of the pile of paperwork on his desk and soon forgot about it.

It wasn't long before a third letter arrived.

"Perhaps they're going to make you chancellor of the university," I teased Andy.

"It's the details of the awards ceremony. In a couple of weeks, I'm going to be presented with my Dean's medal. I'll probably turn up, and they'll say, 'We're so sorry, Mr Elvis, but we've made a mistake. The Dean's medal was meant for someone else'."

"We'd better go anyway. Just in case."

So on the night of the awards ceremony, Andy and I returned to the university. We walked through the door and up to the reception desk, where a woman was handing out name tags to all the graduates. Would there be one for Andy? There was an anxious moment as the woman sorted through the badges spread out on the desk in front of her. But there it was. I smothered a giggle and Andy tried not to look at me as he accepted his name tag, seat number and program while listening to the directions of where he had to sit. But once we were in the auditorium, he laughed too.

"It looks like you're going to get a medal!"

"We'll see. I haven't been presented with it yet. There's still time for someone to find out that I'm an imposter."

The minutes ticked by. The presentation of the Dean's medals was the last item on the awards program. Finally, Andy was standing in line.

"Dean's medallist for the Master's of Teaching degree... Andrew Elvis!"

I tried to clap and take a photo and absorb this very special moment all at once, and failed to do any of this properly. It was all over far too quickly. All I remember is Andy's happy face and a very proud feeling that swept through me.

Later, Andy showed me his medal. He opened the blue velvet-lined presentation box to reveal a large solid disc bearing his name. Yes, the medal is his. There was no mistake. He'd earned it. It was meant for him.

Receiving a medal was very exciting, but the lessons we learnt from Andy's university experience were far more important than a circle of metal.

We learnt that:

- Even though parents would like to help their kids get a job that sets them up for life, this might not be realistic. Some people have more than one career in a lifetime out of necessity or choice.

- A love of learning is more important than a secure and safe job. Jobs can disappear. Employees can be made redundant. But if we know how to learn and find life interesting, we will be able to change direction if necessary.

- A secure and safe job shouldn't be our priority. We shouldn't be afraid to follow our dreams and do what we want to do. Who knows? We might be successful.

- It's never too late to learn. When we need knowledge, we can learn it.

- We learn best when we're passionate about our subject. Andy graduated in the top 2% of his class, not because he was lured on by the thought of the Dean's medal - he didn't know it existed - but because he was very interested in the Master's course that he'd chosen to do.

- We all respond to encouragement. We encouraged Andy to follow his dream. And Andy's achievement certainly encourages our children to follow theirs.

Yes, Andy gave our children a vision. He showed them that anything is possible.

Our life changed a lot during the two years that Andy was studying. Because we didn't have an income, we had to live very simply. We didn't have money for treats or holidays or elaborate gifts. But we didn't care about those things. We had something much better.

For two years, we had a unique opportunity to spend lots of time together. We had a house full of learners. We'd all get up each morning, and talk about our plans for the day. What would we learn? How could we help and encourage each other? This experience drew us close together. It taught us a lot about family and learning and life.

Sometimes the difficult times of life turn out to be unexpected opportunities. If we look at them carefully, we might discover a gift.

Part XVI: Difficult Days

An Unschooling Imposter

I once wrote these words in a social media post:

Do you ever have times when you fall apart? You just can't cope? You question everything you're doing? I felt like this last week. You see, we're not a perfect family. In particular, I'm far from the perfect mother I'd like to be. I've wondered if I'm on the wrong pathway. What if I'm leading others astray by sharing my stories?

Yes, I've had a difficult time recently. There have been too many problems for my soft mother's heart to deal with. I've wondered: why do my kids have problems? Have I failed in my parenting? Or is it unschooling that has let them down? Perhaps I'm just not a good unschooling mother?

Whatever the reason, I decided I could no longer write about unschooling. How can I expect other parents to follow my poor example? I felt like an unschooling imposter. And so I wanted to delete everything I've ever created. Remove all evidence of my family, my unschooling stories and me from the Internet.

But when the time arrived to press 'delete blog', I couldn't quite bring myself to do it. Instead, I found a plugin that makes blogs private. But even then, I hesitated. I didn't end up activating it. I decided to think about things for a while.

While I was thinking, several unschooling blog articles appeared in my email inbox. They were written by younger mothers who seem to have things all worked out. They're proper unschooling mothers, not imposters like me. They're doing a fantastic job of not only unschooling their kids but also spreading the unschooling message. Perhaps they're doing things far, far better than me. Yes, that might be true.

But I also wondered: does *anyone* have everything worked out perfectly? Or do we all have times when we feel like we're failing? Maybe some people never share their low times. But does this mean they never have them?

Low times don't mean we aren't unschooling properly. They don't indicate that unschooling doesn't work. Low times, when we struggle to get through our days as we deal with various problems, are a natural part of life.

When life isn't going as well as we'd like, we might be tempted to look around at what other people are doing. Maybe it's time to leave unschooling. The critics are probably right. Moving on is the sensible thing to do. Except I could never do this.

I am an unschooler for life. Nothing will change that. Why? Because I know it's right to respect kids, to accept them as they are, to forgive their mistakes, to trust them, and to love them unconditionally. It would be wrong to grab hold of control, insist my children do what I tell them, try and turn them into the people *I* think they should be, and withdraw my love whenever they make a mistake so that they remember to behave better in the future.

My post continued:

Yes, I've had a low week. But this morning, I woke up and one of the first things I thought about was how, the other day, when I wasn't coping, when I no longer wanted to be a mother, my girls wrapped their arms around me and held me tight. They didn't criticise and condemn me. They just loved me as I was. All the pain and hurt came flooding out with my tears. It was okay. Unconditional love. That's what it's all about. We don't have to be perfect. As long as we love and forgive and help each other. And that's what I'd like to share with you today.

It's all very well loving each other when our days are perfect. That's easy. But when things aren't so good, can we continue loving each other? For example, can we choose not to take offence when someone treats us unfairly but instead try to understand and be forgiving? Can we pull each other up again when we fall? Can we help each other become the people we are meant to be? If we can then, even if everything is not looking and feeling as we'd like, we'll be unschooling perfectly.

So even though I'm far from perfect, I don't think I'm an unschooling imposter. There isn't any real reason for me to stop writing and disappear. I'm not going to do that. Instead, I want to stay and continue encouraging you to unschool. Keep trusting.

Unschooling is the perfect way of life, especially when life seems far from perfect.

Memories of an Inexperienced Mother

When our first child was five days old, I was discharged from the hospital. A nurse carried our brand new daughter to the door, where my husband Andy was waiting to drive me home. The nurse turned to me and gently placed our baby in my arms before smiling and wishing us well. And I thought: *She is going to let me walk out the door with this baby. She is going to let me, a mother with absolutely no experience, take a baby home. Surely I need some kind of qualification before I'm allowed to be in charge of such a precious child?* The nurse said goodbye. Andy and I passed through the door. And no one stopped us.

It suddenly struck me: I was a mother with full responsibility for a child. Andy and I were about to begin our parenting adventure, and we realised we didn't know much about babies at all. Oh, we'd read a few books and shared ideas with some other parents-to-be, but theory is totally different from reality. We knew we'd have to be quick learners if we were all to survive.

Everything went reasonably well for a few hours. We were excited. Our baby was going to have her first bath at home. We gathered the baby bath and the stand, a soft fluffy towel and a soft face washer, the baby soap, the baby shampoo, the baby bubbles and the baby powder, the rubber duck, a clean soft pink singlet, a tiny pink baby Bonds suit, a hand-knitted cardigan, a nappy, a baby brush, the camera... and finally, the baby.

While I carefully peeled off Felicity's clothing, Andy, just as carefully filled the bath with water warmed to the perfect temperature. Then I nervously slid our baby into the bath, making sure to rest her head on my forearm, her nose clear of the water, just as the nurse had shown me at the hospital.

Now I am not sure what went wrong. Did we think Felicity had stopped breathing? All I remember is Andy and I jumping about in a panic, and me crying, "Karen is a nurse! Quick, she'll know what to do."

We hurriedly wrapped our baby in the towel and ran outside and thumped on our neighbour's front door. We waited. No answer. Some more panicking and some more thumping. And then we looked down at Felicity.

"Andy, she looks perfectly fine. I don't think there's anything wrong with her at all." We looked at our clean, pink, breathing child. Sheepishly we retraced our steps, hoping no one had seen us. Later, as we dressed our newborn baby, I thought, *There's nothing wrong with Felicity. The problem is her inexperienced parents. How will she ever survive life with us?*

Felicity likes to describe herself as our guinea pig child. She was the one we experimented on as we tried to gain some parenting skills.

I was talking to Felicity on the phone the other day. I retold the baby bath story, and my eldest daughter giggled. "You'll have to write about that, Mum!"

"It must have been hard being the guinea pig child," I said. "All those mistakes that Dad and I made while we were bringing you up. The other kids have it so much easier. These days we are a lot calmer and more confident, and we know what we're doing."

"It wasn't all that bad, Mum," Felicity reassured me. "I had a great childhood."

"So you don't have bad memories of a dragon mother who couldn't cope?"

Felicity laughed. "No."

I have been thinking about the mother I was then and the mother I am now. I have changed so much over the years.

I used to worry about every little thing. I was always rushing down to the doctors with a slightly sick child who seemed to recover in the waiting room. I'd fuss until my children had perfectly clean faces and perfectly brushed hair. They couldn't leave the house unless they were wearing pristine matching clothes. I'd be anxious if they didn't eat and so I spent a lot of time trying to make them swallow food they didn't want. I worried about dirt and mess and an untidy house. Whenever someone accidentally knocked a dinner plate to the floor, I reacted as if it were the end of the world. I became anxious about such things as toilet training and sleeping through the night. The list is endless.

Today I have gone the other way:

"If she's had enough to eat, take her plate away," I'll say.

"But Mum, she's hardly touched her dinner," one of my older children will reply.

"Gemma-Rose is wearing odd socks," someone will observe.

"At least she has socks on. It doesn't matter about the colour," I'll answer.

"Oops! I've knocked the peanut butter jar out of the fridge," someone will confess.

"Go and get the broom and clean up the mess," I'll reply, without even getting up to inspect the damage.

I have to admit I'm not perfect. Some days I get overtired, and the temptation to make a fuss about things that aren't really important threatens to reappear. I had one of those days not so long ago. The girls were cooking a cake, and they got the instructions in a muddle which resulted in all the ingredients going to waste.

After I'd thrown my little wobbly and had my say about "reading instructions properly... and how many eggs did you waste?..." and so on, I immediately began to feel rather bad. What are a few eggs? They don't matter nearly as much as my girls' feelings. Gemma-Rose looked like she was going to cry, and I felt like the worse mother in the world. How could I have forgotten the lessons that have taken so long to learn? I apologised. But all the girls said was, "Don't worry about it, Mum. It's all over. We've already forgotten about it."

Sometimes I wish I could go back and fix up my past mistakes and erase all the not-so-good memories from my children's minds. I don't want that easily overwhelmed, emotional dragon mother to live on inside them.

I wonder if Felicity ever thinks: "Gemma-Rose, you're so lucky. You got the good mother, the calm mother, the gentle mother. She may not be perfect, but she's a whole lot better than the mother I got. She was hopeless. I wish I'd been born last and wasn't the first-born guinea pig child."

Why does it take me so long to learn anything? I have this suspicion that, by the time I have perfected this role of mother, my last child will have finished growing up. She will no longer need a perfect mother. She'll be ready to slap her P plates to her car and drive off out into the big world to live an independent life.

I think again about that seemingly miraculous moment when I was allowed to take a precious baby home from the hospital. I didn't have to present a certificate to the discharge desk, proving I was worthy of the role of mother.

Similarly, God didn't ask me to prove myself before He blessed us with so many beautiful souls. He sent them to us anyway. How could He have done this? It took me a long time to work things out, but eventually, I came to realise that God doesn't expect Andy and me to bring up our children on our own. No. He is always here to give us His strength and His grace. And He doesn't expect us to be perfect. We only have to do our best. That's all God expects. He does the rest.

Isn't that a consoling thought?

Felicity phones for another chat.

"I wrote your baby bath story," I tell my daughter. "It's a post about your very inadequate mother."

"You are a good mother," insists Felicity. "When I was a child, I wanted to grow up to be just like you."

"You did?" I am so surprised. "I didn't know that," I say.

A warm feeling is spreading all through me. Yes, God does indeed fill in all the gaps in our parenting.

"I love you, Felicity!"

And my first-born child replies, "And I love you so very much too, Mum!"

Confessions of a Former Quick-Tempered Mother

A reader stopped by my blog and remarked on how I appear to be a calm and patient mother. And so I have been thinking about how, years ago, I could never have imagined anybody describing me in that way. No, I was a real dragon mother. To be associated with the words 'calm' and 'patient' seems like a miracle.

A dragon mother? Oh yes, I used to have a temper that matched my red hair. And I liked to use it, especially when I was tired and life didn't go to plan, and my kids didn't behave as I hoped.

When my eldest daughter Felicity was about two years old and my second child, Duncan was a baby, I had a real boiling-over day. I can't remember what the circumstances were. Probably the house was a mess, and I was exhausted. Quite possibly, Felicity kept insisting on sitting on top of the baby. All I remember is the pressure cooker feeling that was building up inside me. My head ached. I was hot and bothered. I was going to explode. Would I lose my temper? Shout? Handle my children roughly? I'd done all these before, and I didn't want to do them again. At the last moment, I drew back and burst into tears.

I wondered if there was something physically wrong with me. Perhaps I was anaemic and low on energy. Could this be the reason I never had any patience and why it didn't take much for me to reach breaking point? I made a doctor's appointment. The check-up revealed I was a perfectly healthy mother. I cried.

Could it be I wasn't sick but just an impatient person with a temper that I couldn't control when conditions became trying? I mulled that unpleasant idea over for some time. Maybe I didn't have what it took to be a mother. The problem was I *was* a mother. What was I to do? I knew that if I wanted to bring up my children with love, I'd have to change. I looked into my kids' beautiful eyes and realised I didn't want them to fill with fear every time I came near. No, I had to do something.

Is it possible for a person to change? It certainly is. I look back and see how far I have come. Not much worries me these days. But the journey wasn't easy.

I made a conscious decision: I wanted to be a gentle mother, a calm mother, a mother visibly full of love and peace. But the chances of me changing into that person seemed low. Our family grew, and we began homeschooling, and I wondered how I could be expected to be patient when every day I was given more and more to cope with. I prayed for more patience, but nothing happened. One day I realised patience doesn't arrive like a parcel in the post. We have to work at it. My children were providing me with many opportunities to practise this virtue. I just had to use them. With grace, I sometimes succeeded in remaining calm when faced with a difficult situation. Many times I failed. I fell, but I always made myself get up and try again. And gradually, I did begin to change.

As I became a calmer and gentler person, I noticed something very interesting. My children became calmer and happier too. A mother's mood and attitude and example really do set the tone for the family. All round, life was becoming more peaceful.

But maybe I've made my journey from dragon mother to calm mother sound too simple. When I first told this story, a friend said, "But what did you actually 'do' on a daily/hourly/minute-by-minute basis when your blood was boiling, and nothing was going right?"

And I replied:

I tried to reduce the situations that caused me to become short tempered. I used to get anxious because I thought I had to fulfil outside expectations. Anxiety led to anger with my children when I thought they didn't match up. When I let go of these expectations and started unschooling, listening to my children more, things improved immensely.

Also, I was forever trying to keep up an appearance and wanted to impress others. My children and our home had to look presentable. My children's behaviour had to be impeccable and beyond reproach. One day I decided my kids were more important than the opinions of others, so I relaxed and began putting them first. Appearances no longer seemed important. I stopped trying to change my children and learnt to accept them. Changing my attitude resulted in us being on the same side, and there was less conflict.

Of course, there were, and still are, times when I feel angry. I usually walk away and cool down in my bedroom. It's better than saying words I will regret. I also learnt if nothing is going right, then a change of activity or scene often helps. On bad homeschooling days, we'd pack up a picnic and leave the house and problems behind. Doing this helped me remember what was important: enjoying my children.

Finally and most importantly, I pray. Praying together as a family is good too. And being gentle on myself when I fall. Apologising and starting again is better than wallowing in self-recrimination.

I also look at my children differently these days. They deserve respect and aren't mine to control and treat as I want. I keep coming back to such thoughts to keep myself on track.

Daily/hourly/minute by minute? I pray. I try to reduce stress by getting rid of any attitude or situation, such as worrying about the opinions and expectations of others if it's harming my relationship with my children. I recognise danger signals such as tiredness and am gentle on myself. I abandon a situation that might lead to me boiling over. I don't overload myself. I make sure to plan plenty of special times when we can all enjoy being together. Life shouldn't be all work. I try to be honest and tell others if I'm not coping. I arrange time for myself. I walk off if I'm tempted to react. I go to confession and know God always forgives me. I then try again.

So am I now perfect? No, as I said to my friend, some days I still feel out of sorts and get a bit grouchy. Not very often. Just now and then. Those occasional slips fill me with horror. I feel so terrible and ashamed though I guess it's times like these which prevent me from becoming complacent and proud of myself. But I apologise to my children, and they forgive me. Understanding and forgiveness are so important for all members of a family. When life is full of visible love and peace, everyone can safely weather a storm that suddenly flares up and is quickly acknowledged and dealt with.

I love my children so very much. That love makes me want to be the best mother possible. Love certainly has the power to change people. Love and God's grace transformed me from a hot-tempered mother into a mostly calm and peaceful one. And they allowed me to escape my nickname. Yes, I am no longer known as the dragon mother.

Being a Tired Mother

Today I am very tired. Last night, I lay in bed awake unable to drift off to sleep. Hour after hour passed until it was time for my husband to get out of bed and start his day. Then, just as he disappeared into the shower, I fell asleep.

When the girls heard I'd had a bad night, they said, "You're to rest today, Mum. We'll take care of everything." Imogen drove Charlotte to her piano lesson. Sophie made me a bowl of porridge for breakfast. Gemma-Rose gave me a hug.

Quite often, I have bad nights. There are many days when I feel overtired. It's hard facing the day knowing I haven't got enough energy to do all I need to do, let alone all I'd like to do. It reminds me of when we had babies and toddlers in the family. In those days, I used to dream of a time when I'd be able to sleep the whole night through, without anyone waking me up. I wanted to get out of bed, feeling refreshed. I longed to be able to enjoy my children without feeling weary all the time. I wanted to be able to give them my best.

After Sophie was born, I hit an all-time low. I'd had seven children, five miscarriages, and years and years of constantly having a little person attached to me. I thought I couldn't face any more. I didn't think I could start again with another baby.

A few months later, I fell pregnant. Despite my apprehensions, I decided I could accept one more child after all. Except I didn't have that baby, at least not here on earth. I miscarried again, and I had to deal with more sadness and turmoil while still caring for our other children. But I recovered, and one day I found out another baby was on her way. This baby was Gemma-Rose.

I can't adequately describe the love I feel for Gemma-Rose. What would my life be without her? What if I'd decided that I was too tired to accept one more child? I would have missed out on so much.

Motherhood isn't easy. Sometimes it even seems impossible. We lose control of our lives and often wish things could be different. Surely we won't survive? We wonder if our children will end up suffering because we haven't enough energy to be the perfect mother for them.

I have lots of time to give Gemma-Rose because she is the youngest child in our family. In a way, she is getting a perfect childhood despite my tired days. I can read to her without being interrupted by the cries of a baby. I can give her my full attention. Is she better off than my older children who had to share me, who had a rather frazzled mother? Do my older children wish they were the youngest? No. They had their share of delights. They grew up in exciting times when babies joined our family. They enjoyed little siblings who adored them. Gemma-Rose has never known that. My older children had many natural learning experiences she will never get. They didn't suffer. They saw Andy and I accept more children into our family and hearts, despite the difficulties. They knew they were loved.

So I muddled my way through the baby and toddler years when everyone seemed to need something from me all at the same time, on days when I had little energy to give them. Yes, it was a muddle, but I survived. And looking back, I wouldn't change a thing. I would make those sacrifices all over again. I would give up my time, my freedom, my sleep, my arms, everything. You see, each of my children is a blessing. I now know perfection isn't necessary. A spirit of willing self-sacrifice is far more important.

Times change. My children are now the ones making sacrifices. They are looking after me, freely giving back what I gave to them.

"Did you enjoy your morning tea, Mum?" asks Gemma-Rose.

I smile. "It was delicious. Thank you for cooking the biscuits for me. Thank you for looking after me."

Today I'm very tired. But that's okay because today I feel especially loved.

Why We Live a Life Full of Saturdays

What if every day were a Saturday? There'd be no weekdays to endure before enjoying the delights of the weekend. We'd never say, "I can't wait until the week is over so I can do what I like." We could do whatever we want any day of the week.

Some people have the opportunity to make every day a Saturday, but they don't always choose to do this. Why not? Do they hesitate because they think they don't deserve to live this way? Life isn't meant to be this good. Maybe we need to earn our weekends by working our way through the weekdays?

Some time ago, I was reading the comments attached to an unschooling YouTube video. Most of them were critical of the unschooling lifestyle. Some commenters stated that it doesn't matter whether kids enjoy school or not, they should still have to go. It's character building. It's something we all have to do. We're soft if we allow our kids to stay at home and avoid the sometimes unpleasantness of the system.

Maybe some structured homeschoolers would say similar things: kids need to do their assigned work without question. It's good for them.

Yes, why should kids be allowed to live weeks full of Saturdays? Surely this isn't good preparation for their future lives? Real life has weekdays. Sometimes we have to do things whether we want to or not.

I agree: we all have to do things we don't want to do. But still, I don't make life hard for my kids. There's no need. You see, they freely choose to do unpleasant or difficult things. They need no pushing from me. Why would children do this? Surely if they can spend every day doing whatever they want, they'll choose the easy path? Except they don't.

They'll choose to help with the chores. They'll help each other. They'll tackle an unpleasant task. They'll concentrate and work hard on something they know they need to learn. They'll do these things because they are the right things to do.

With our guidance, our example, and our trust, our unschooled children will become hard-working, self-giving and loving. So we can allow our kids to have seven Saturdays every single week. We don't have to ration out the good times to teach them lessons about discipline and hard work.

So our family does Saturday things every day of the week. I don't limit the special moments, thinking my kids will become spoiled and unappreciative if I give them too much. Every morning, we get up with a feeling of excited anticipation. What will happen today? Of course, we'll work hard. But what else? How can we add joy to our days? Shall we eat pancakes in bed, go on a picnic, swing on the swings, stroll along the banks of the river with our cameras in our hands, curl up in an armchair and read a good book, bake and enjoy a cake, snuggle on the sofa and watch a movie, play a game? Or shall we drink coffee and chat for hours about anything and everything?

Despite my efforts, life isn't always happy. Things happen because not everything is under our control. And so we endure hardships regardless of my attempts to make our days as joyful as possible.

Big sufferings arrive, such as the death of a brother. Then there are the everyday bumps along the way, the ones that occur because we're not perfect people.

And because life is unpredictable and we can't protect our kids from every suffering, searching for joy is essential. It's the joyful times of our lives - the smiles, the fun, the carefree days - that draw us together with strong bonds of love. Those bonds give us the strength to face the difficult times when they arrive. Happy memories give us hope and keep us moving forward when we'd like to give up. They lead us back to joy.

Life isn't perfect. It can be very difficult at times. That's why we live a life full of Saturdays.

Unschooling advocate Sandra Dodd describes a typical "unschool" day as "the best ever Saturday ... the day people dream about when they are stuck in school."

I found this quote in Bridget Bentz Sizer's article Homeschooling 101.

Do You Ever Get Tired of Being a Good Example?

Do you ever get tired of being a good example? I do.

Some days I don't want to hop out of bed as the sun is rising so that I can go for a run. I guess I don't have to. Except my running buddy is counting on me.

There are mornings when I don't want to help with the chores. Instead of grabbing the broom so that I can sweep the floor, I'd rather curl up on the sofa, open my computer and start writing. I want to ignore the housework. Let my kids do it. Maybe I could get away with that because I'm the mother. Yes, I could take advantage of my position in the family.

Other days I feel very lazy. I don't want to think about writing or get involved with any of my other projects. Instead of working, I'd like to do nothing much at all. And I'm not talking about letting myself rest which is good. Instead, I want to fritter away my day deliberately.

And then there are times when I know I should be kind. Maybe someone has said or written something that hurts me deeply. I want to shoot my own sharp words straight back to my attacker. I don't want to think about my response and not get defensive. I want to hurt in my turn instead of trying to do what is right.

Yes, sometimes being a good example is very hard work. And so there are days when we fail.

I think our kids understand when we don't always do what we should. Life can be hard. And we get tired. Maybe there are times when we need a break. Perhaps it's okay if we're not perfect. Instead of struggling on, we could give our kids a chance to look after us.

"You stay in bed, Mum, and rest. I'll make you some breakfast."

"I'll sweep the floor for you, Mum. I know you can't wait to finish that story you're writing."

"Why don't you have a lazy day, Mum. Read a book and do not much at all."

"Words hurt, don't they, Mum? Do you want a hug?"

Why would our kids want to look after us? Why do they understand when we can't keep up, and we fail? Could it have something to do with how we treat them when they also fail to do the right thing?

We don't expect our kids to be perfect. We understand when they're tired or impatient to dive into their work or reluctant to leave something that's absorbing them. We help them out when they're struggling. We empathise. We don't criticise.

I try and be a good example for my kids. Sometimes I fail. But that's okay. When I'm not the person I would like to be, I'm still providing my kids with an example. And it's not a bad one.

I'm showing my children that it's quite okay when we fail to do the right thing. As long as we get back up again and keep trying.

The Less Than Perfect Times

It's been ten years since I last had a bath. Does that sound shocking? I suppose it could be except for the fact that I've had plenty of showers.

Baths or showers are a normal part of life, aren't they? Unless you live in a drought-affected area. My son Callum told me about a small country town in the north of our state that has run completely out of water. Other towns have very little water. The dams are almost dry.

Years ago, we lived in an old cottage on a 100-acre property. We relied on the rainfall for water. Unfortunately, it hardly ever rained. Every drop of water in our tank was precious, so we tried to use as little as possible.

Recently, Callum and I were chatting about that time. He was eight when we moved to that place. We were chasing a dream. We were going to live a self-sufficient, adventurous life. Things didn't turn out as we'd hoped. We had no water to grow our vegetables; mice and rats overran the cottage; the falling-down fences couldn't contain our dog. When we discovered our unborn baby was unlikely to live after birth, we gave up and moved back to town.

I've always thought of that time as a disaster. We made some poor decisions. Our dream didn't become a reality. But Callum told me how he has great memories of living on that property. Our adventures there gave him a desire to have a property of his own with cows to milk and fences to fix. They fuelled a passion. Now Callum is renting a house on a farm, and he's fixing fences, and he has big ideas and plans. Fortunately, at the moment, there's still some water in his tank. He can still take a shower.

We might want our lives to be as good as possible for our kids. We don't realise that sometimes it's the less-than-perfect times that inspire them the most.

Part XVII: Concerns

Responding to Unschooling Critics

I know your heart is in the right place. You're full of love. I can see that. But is that enough? Frankly, my dear, I'm worried. I'm not saying this lightly. I'm not the kind of person who likes to interfere. Everyone knows that. However, don't you think you're putting your kids at risk? They need discipline. Rules. Limits.

The other day, I discovered these words in my notebook, and for a moment, I wondered who'd said them. And then I remembered. A few weeks ago, my friend Amina came over for coffee. "Sue, you won't believe what my neighbour just said to me!" and then she repeated the above words. Later, I wrote them down.

Amina wanted some suggestions on how to respond to critical comments. "Some of my friends and family don't understand what we're doing. They think unschooling is irresponsible. They're worried that my kids are going to become wild and out of control. They think they're not going to learn much."

"Critical words can hurt, can't they?" I said to Amina.

My friend nodded and then she said, "Have you written a blog post about responding to unschooling critics? Perhaps you've got some suggestions about what I could say? I'd like to keep everyone onside, maybe open up a positive discussion. Or is it a waste of time trying to do that? Should I just smile politely and refuse to engage?"

I opened my laptop, did a bit of clicking, and then I turned the screen towards Amina. She started reading:

A few years ago, I received the following comment on my blog:

"Why the hell would you post a picture of your dead baby online? That's just horrible."

The words tore at my mother's heart. That dead person was my son.

I deleted that comment. I didn't even think about it. I just wanted it to disappear as quickly as possible.

It was only later that I wondered if I had done the right thing. I had responded emotionally. I was only concerned about my feelings. But what about the commenter? Why did she say those hurtful words? Was she just a troll not worth worrying about? Or could she have been afraid of death?

If I could go back, this is what I would have replied:

It's rather confronting to see a dead body, isn't it, especially if you're not expecting to see one? I'm sorry the photo of my son disturbed you. I posted it because I don't have any photos of him when he was alive except for the ones that we took when he was hooked up to multiple wires and tubes. Dead bodies used to make me feel uncomfortable too. But after my son died, I realised that I had nothing to be scared of. He was still beautiful, even though he was no longer alive.

With carefully chosen words, we might be able to make connections with people who disagree with us. We can open the way for a possible conversation. When we react emotionally, we lose the chance to change people's opinions or their hearts.

Although you'll probably never have to worry about photos of dead bodies, you might have to defend your decision to unschool. Yes, unschooling has its critics. And many of them have loud voices.

We could choose to ignore these critics, and maybe that's the right thing to do. We don't want to waste time trying to persuade a troll that he's wrong and we're right. But perhaps it's at least worth trying to open up unschooling conversations with our family and friends. Wouldn't it be nice if they could see things through our eyes and support us?

So what do we do?

Instead of reacting to a critical comment, can we find something we can agree with? Can we build a bridge, making a discussion possible?

Yes, unschooling does seem neglectful, doesn't it? I used to think it was too until I read...

Yes, it's not acceptable for children to be undisciplined and selfish. Maybe the family you're describing aren't really unschoolers. Have you heard about unparenting?

Yes, it sounds like kids won't learn if they're not forced to, doesn't it? But they do. Would you like to hear what my kids chose to do this week?

Sometimes our efforts are rewarded. Sometimes they're not. But at least we've tried.

It would be wonderful to have the support of those closest to us, to be praised and told we're doing a fantastic job as a parent and homeschooler. But sometimes we have to do without that. We have to put our kids ahead of other people's opinions and unschool them regardless.

Going it alone is easier when we are confident about what we're doing. If we truly believe in unschooling, no one will be able to discourage us away from this pathway. So we have to be well informed.

And we need to stay away, if possible, from critics. Because sometimes their words can sneak into our heads. They lead to doubts. They make us afraid. And that's just what some people are hoping for, the people who don't understand.

If everyone understood unschooling, would there be no critics? Imagine if there was no need to defend our position.

Amina finished reading my post and then she said, "Yes, words can hurt." She reached for my hand and said, "I'm glad I have a friend who understands."

I'm grateful too. I'm glad I have my pretend friend Amina.

What if Unschooling is Wrong?

Do you ever wonder: what if unschooling is wrong?

We are happy. Life is good. Everything is running along smoothly. And then one day, out of the blue, doubt descends. Our trust begins to waver. We think: *What if the critics are right? What if my kids don't learn all they need to know? What if we're jeopardising their futures? What if...?*

So what do we do if this happens? Do we jump ship quickly while we still have the chance? There's time to try something else.

Or do we think about what unschooling is really all about?

Now some people might think unschooling is just about kids having the freedom to learn what they like when they like. Nice and simple. But that's not the most important part of the story.

Unschooling is about connecting with our kids so that we can guide and encourage them as they grow into the people they are designed to be. We do this by loving them unconditionally.

The question is this: can it be wrong to love our kids unconditionally?

But let's imagine that unschooling is wrong. Then something else must be right. What is that something else? What would we do if we weren't unschooling? Would our alternative to unschooling have to involve such things as unconditional love, respect, trust, self-sacrifice, forgiveness, and kindness? Can we live differently and still incorporate all these unschooling essentials into the foundations of our lives?

Or should we stay with unschooling because these are already part of our lives? Why go looking for something we already have?

Despite our doubts, is unschooling the way we are meant to live? Perhaps all we need to do is trust.

When Unschooling Doesn't Seem to Be Working

We decide to unschool. Everything goes well. Our kids are learning. Our family bonds are strengthening. Life is full of joy.

Then one day, things change. Something happens. Maybe a child makes a mistake. She chooses to go her own way. She does something we're not happy with. We begin to doubt what we're doing. We think: *Perhaps unschooling doesn't work after all.* Maybe the critics are right: *You should have kept tight control over your kids!* Yes, we feel like we've failed.

We hear a lot of positive things from unschoolers. I suppose that's because most parents want to share the good stories. But I'm sure, despite all the amazing things that happen, no unschooling family's life is perfect in every detail.

Our family has certainly had some difficult times. And those times have seemed even worse because I'm a blogger. I've thought: *What if my readers find out that my kids aren't perfect, that they've made mistakes? Maybe I shouldn't write about unschooling. I might be leading people astray.* So I've wanted to delete my blog and run away. Become an ex-unschooling blogger. Become an ex-unschooling family. Yes, I've questioned unschooling.

But we're still here.

While pondering the difficulties, I have always returned to the idea that we have to do what is right, and I'm sure unschooling is the right thing to do. It's the way we are meant to live. We have to respect our kids and love them unconditionally, and not control them but instead trust. We don't have a choice.

And so even if a child goes astray, makes a mistake, does something that we're upset about, we must keep unschooling. We can't change pathways. We must trust that, despite appearances, things will be okay.

Trust is a strange thing. It's easy to trust when things are going just as we want: *As long as my children choose to do what I'd like, I'm happy to pass over control to them and trust they'll be okay*. But can we trust when kids don't act according to our plan? Would we rather forget all about trust and grab back control?

Despite our misgivings, we decide to trust. Who knows? One day, things might fall into place. I know about this. I know how it feels. It's very special.

Yes, it's a special moment when our trust is rewarded, and our children decide for themselves that they're going to live by the values that are important to us. They return stronger and more committed than before.

Children can make mistakes, whether they are unschooling or not. But I think unschooling helps children get back on track.

We have to keep listening, respecting, and loving unconditionally. We have to keep the lines of communication open. Regardless of what our kids do, we can't risk severing or even loosening the bonds between us. It's those bonds that will draw our children back.

There are times when unschooling doesn't appear to be working. What do we do? We need to stay strong, continue to unschool, and trust.

Sibling Rivalry

Sometimes people ask me if my children get on with each other. Have I ever had to deal with sibling rivalry?

I think back through the years, and it wouldn't be true to say my kids have never argued with each other. I don't remember any incidents of physical fighting, but there must have been times when they fought with their words. However, that seems a long time ago. Today, they have no trouble living peacefully together. My children don't compete for my attention. They all feel loved and valued. Everyone has a unique place in the family.

Or perhaps that's only my opinion. Do I see things how I'd like them to be and not as they truly are?

I decide to talk to my daughters Sophie (14) and Imogen (21) separately about sibling rivalry. Do we have a problem within our family?

"Sophie, tell me about your sisters. Do you get on with them?"

"Definitely! They're my best friends."

"So when I say that we don't have any problems with sibling rivalry, I'm speaking the truth?"

"Definitely!"

I ask Imogen: "How do you get on with your siblings? Is there any rivalry?"

"No. People seem to think it's unusual when we say that. But we don't fight. There's no rivalry between us."

I wonder: why don't my kids rival each other for my attention? Perhaps my girls have the answer.

I ask, "Can you remember any times when things weren't quite so good between you?" They come up with a few examples, and I say, "Things got better. Why?" Nobody really knows. It's very hard dissecting relationships and coming up with a list of things we did and didn't do, especially when we're looking back through the years.

But after pondering the topic for a while, we did think of some things that might encourage good relationships between siblings:

- Fulfil each child's individual needs.
- Help kids resolve disputes. Take each child's concerns seriously.
- Foster relationships between kids. Find ways in which they can share talents and work together or help each other. But don't force them.
- Give lots of time to each child. Arrange one-on-one times.
- Don't compare children. Each child is unique. Each child brings something special and valuable to the family.
- Appreciate the differences between children. Encourage siblings to appreciate these differences too.
- Don't have favourites. Or make every child your favourite.
- Encourage kids to be happy for each other. Everyone can take pleasure in each other's achievements. Celebrate each child's achievements regardless of what they are.
- Encourage kids to make allowances for one another. Kids do have off days just like parents, and they sometimes need extra help and consideration.
- Treat our kids how we want them to treat each other. Be a good example.
- Be willing to help a child. This child will then be willing to help a sibling. A parent's example is very important.
- Make sure siblings have their own space, both physical space and the opportunity for quiet times. This is especially important for older siblings.

- Don't tolerate unkind words and meanness. Kids aren't free to say and do whatever they like. Nor are parents. We have to keep each other safe.

- Never criticise a child, especially when she isn't present. Don't allow siblings to criticise each other either.

- Make our homes safe refuges from the world where everyone is accepted.

- Build up a good family team spirit. Enjoy being a family. Do things together. Spend time building bonds between all members. Have fun but also work together. Doing hard and challenging things draws people close.

- Sometimes when one sibling is having trouble getting on with another, they may need extra time and attention rather than critical words. Can we show empathy and listen rather than express disappointment?

- Love unconditionally. Kids need to feel loved at all times. They shouldn't ever fear that we will withdraw our love.

Maybe everything starts with love. I'm not saying parents don't love enough because we do. Could it have more to do with the expression of that love? What are we willing to do to make sure our kids feel loved? The love we give them has a way of spilling over to other people, especially siblings.

Sibling rivalry has long term consequences. It doesn't necessarily disappear when a child grows up, so it's good to talk about it. We have to work on it even if it takes time to see results. Changing relationships doesn't happen overnight.

"Do you feel loved?" I ask Sophie.

"Definitely."

"You don't feel like anybody in the family is loved more than you?"

"No."

"There's no reason to think of your siblings as rivals?"

Sophie shakes her head.

What is the answer to sibling rivalry? How can we avoid it? Perhaps we can start with unconditional love.

Part XVIII: Our Values and Beliefs

What if We Have Differing Beliefs and Opinions?

We're Catholic unschoolers, and maybe you're not. Despite sharing an unschooling way of life, in some ways we might be very different. Is that okay? Can we share and learn from each other even though we're not the same? What if we don't agree with each other's beliefs and values? What about our opinions?

A reader of my blog once linked one of my posts to her blog and added the words: "I don't agree with all her ideas, but I like this one."

Someone liked my post! I smiled. But a small part of me thought, "What's wrong with some of my other ideas?" I wanted the reader to agree with everything I have to say. Is that just a natural reaction? Have you ever felt that way? Maybe most of us want others to accept our opinions.

It feels good when we're exactly in tune with someone else. We don't have to explain ourselves because we understand each other. We know we're not going to have any disagreements so we can relax. We can talk about anything and everything without the fear that we might reveal too much about ourselves. We're kindred spirits. This type of friendship is very special.

But not everyone in our lives has to be a kindred spirit friend. I think we also need people who are different from ourselves.

When I'm willing to look at the world through their eyes, I learn a lot from people who aren't like me. I hear about new things. I ponder fresh ideas. Sometimes I end up giving up my opinion in favour of someone else's. But even if I don't, my life is enriched, and I always grow.

When my daughter Sophie was 14, she said that because she's different from those around her, she's inclined to look for differences in other people. Even when teenagers are trying to be the same so they will fit into the crowd, she searches out the special qualities that make those people unique. Her words gave me much to think about.

If someone is different from us, we shouldn't be quick to dismiss them as a person we don't want to know, someone we can't be friends with, someone we can't learn from. On the contrary, our eyes should light up; our ears should turn towards that person. Who knows what we will see and hear that may enrich our lives?

Is it necessary you agree with all my ideas? Oh no! We don't have to be totally in tune. We can share and ponder and grow because of our differences. We can still be friends.

Life wouldn't be as interesting if we were all the same, would it?

Protecting Kids from Outside Influences

A few years ago, Adelaide knocked on our front door. I directed her into the family room where Imogen and Charlotte were playing, and her eyes opened wide with delight. A huge Barbie game was underway. The floor was awash with Barbies and Kens, Barbie furniture and cars, Barbie clothes and accessories. There was everything a doll and a little girl could wish for.

Adelaide chose several Barbies, and soon, she was immersed in the game. It wasn't long before she was directing the action.

"Let's pretend Ken breaks up with your Barbie. Now he's going out with mine," said Adelaide.

Imogen and Charlotte looked at the little girl with blank faces. Break up? What did that mean? Ken and Barbie were married. They went to Mass and said grace, attended baptisms, went on picnics, and homeschooled their children. Barbie and Ken might have been Andy and me. They certainly didn't 'break up'.

I didn't really want my daughters playing 'breaking up' games with their dolls, but I needn't have worried. The whole concept must have passed over their heads because soon the girls were arranging another wedding. Barbie and Ken were getting married yet again.

A couple of wonderful hours later, Adelaide's mother arrived to take her home. All three little girls had had a great afternoon. I could tell that Adelaide had enjoyed playing with Imogen and Charlotte and all their dolls.

But that was the only time Adelaide came to play. She never knocked on our front door again. I wondered if her mother had forbidden her to visit our house. But why? Weren't we responsible and friendly people? Wasn't our home considered a safe place for children? I pondered these questions for a long time. And then one day I had this thought: maybe Adelaide told her mother about all the Masses Barbie and Ken went to. Perhaps she decided she didn't want us to expose her daughter to our strange Catholic ways.

I smile at that thought. But at the same time, I can understand why Adelaide's mother might have worried. We all have values and beliefs we want to pass onto our children. Perhaps we don't want them picking up something contrary to our way of life. It seems Adelaide's mother might have considered our family as a negative outside influence.

Friends aren't the only outside influence. Music, TV, the Internet, billboards, and books can all adversely affect our children. So how do we protect them?

When children are small, it's relatively easy to isolate them from anything we don't like in the outside world. But what about older kids? We could refuse to let them watch TV and use the Internet. Or we could have strict guidelines they must adhere to. We might insist on previewing every movie and book before we let our children anywhere near them. Perhaps we could make strict rules about friends and places they are allowed to go.

Or is there another way?

"There are a lot of negative influences out in the world. How do parents keep their kids safe," I ask my older children. "Should they make a lot of rules to protect them?"

"Rules don't work," says Imogen. We've talked about this before. "Rules result in a power struggle between parents and children."

"Parents could talk to their children, tell them their concerns, and point out what is right and what is wrong," suggests Charlotte.

"But children might not want to listen," I say. "What makes a child respect her parents' opinions?"

"It's all to do with family loyalty," says Callum.

"Family?"

"Yes, a child needs to have a strong sense of belonging to his or her family. Family must be more important than outsiders. If it is, why shouldn't a child listen to his parents rather than to other people?"

But what gives a child that strong sense of belonging to a family? We did some brainstorming and came up with the following ideas.

We need to:

- Love our children unconditionally.
- Accept each child for who she is.
- Never criticise.
- Never talk about someone in a negative way, especially when they are absent.
- Forgive mistakes.
- Ask for forgiveness when we make our own mistakes.
- Listen to our children's opinions and don’t make them feel stupid or put them down. Discussion keeps communication lines open. Forcing opinions on children closes them off.
- Be willing to hear about and share a child's interests. We must value what's important to them.
- Have interests that are common to all members of the family, so we can do things together and discuss and enjoy working and playing together.
- Make our home a joyful and encouraging place, so everyone wants to spend time together there as a family.
- Have a sense of humour that's unique to our family, that outsiders don't quite understand. This helps create strong bonds.
- Have our own family language that binds us together.
- Create special family traditions.
- Always be willing to help children.

- Respect children.
- Trust children.
- Be trustworthy.
- Pray together as a family.

When it comes to protecting my children from outside influences, I know I have it easier than some. I seem to have fairly quiet homebody kids, and we live away from the city and all its temptations. The only children who live near us are a few preschoolers who are hardly likely to influence my kids.

So are my children safe? Can I be sure that they won't be affected by any negative outside influences? No, I don't think it's possible for any parent to be absolutely sure of that. But I'm confident that a strong sense of family, unconditional love, and prayer will help. I trust that my kids will be okay.

Sharing Our Values and Beliefs With Our Children

Everyone has beliefs. Even if we don't have a religious faith, we still believe in something. We all have values which shape our lives.

Is it okay if we share these beliefs and values with our kids?

I've heard some unschoolers say that we shouldn't influence our children. They should be free to make up their own minds about such things without any input from us. I have a couple of problems with this opinion.

For a start, if our kids don't listen to us, they will listen to someone else. There are lots of voices out there in the world calling for their attention. Isn't it better our kids listen to the people who love and care about them the most rather than listen to those from outside the family? And why shouldn't we share what we believe? If we feel we know the truth, isn't it natural that we share it? Isn't this the right thing to do?

Even if a parent tries not to pass on any beliefs, our kids will pick up something from us whether we want them to or not. Even if they never hear us talking about our beliefs, our actions will give us away. Kids can learn a lot from what we do and what we fail to say.

So if we do have a belief system which we regard as true and fundamentally important, what is the best way of sharing it with our children? Can we share by our example? If our values and beliefs are truly important to us, they will be obvious to our children. They will influence our actions and words. They will be an inseparable part of our lives. Our beliefs will be an integral part of who we are.

Our kids have to see us live our values and beliefs. If they don't, they'll question how important those values are to us. What we believe has to spill over into everything we do, into our decisions, into our speech. Our kids observe. They listen. If we are afraid to talk about these things to our children, maybe they will assume that we aren't sure about our beliefs. Perhaps they are not part of us. Yes, our beliefs and values have to be visible if we want to pass them on.

You might know that we are a Catholic family. Our kids see us going to Mass on Sundays. They see us praying for people who need help. We read spiritual books together. We make decisions based on our beliefs. We filter everything that happens to us through our faith. We talk about religion naturally in our conversations. Of course, these conversations don't run along the lines of "This is what you should believe" and "This is what you should do."

I haven't had to make any rules and say such things as:

"You have to get out of bed (at a particular time) to go to early Mass."

"You have to dress modestly."

"You have to do this."

"You have to do that."

There is no need to say anything. My kids choose to do what we feel is right. Why? I guess they have picked up things from us because we are connected. What is important to us has become important to our children.

I think that living our faith, living our belief system, has to become like breathing. It's the same as learning. We don't have battles over learning because everyone learns. It's a family affair. It's something we all do. It's something we enjoy. And that is what our faith is like in our family. It's just part of our lives. Of course, it's a very important part. It's an inseparable part of everything else. It's what gives joy to our lives. It's not a duty.

Will our children always have the same beliefs as us? Or will they go out there into the bigger world and be influenced by other people? Will they feel they want to do something different from us? Well, I guess there's always that chance, and we'd have to accept that if it happens. But I also feel that even if kids do go along different pathways and explore – which might be good because it could eventually strengthen their faith – when life gets difficult, there's a good chance they will return to their roots. Our faith is all wrapped up in family, love, and acceptance. It's where we go when we are in trouble. It gives us comfort. It gives us joy. And when our kids get into situations where they need that love, that connectedness, that joy, perhaps they will return. That might be in the future. Who knows?

So how do we share our values and beliefs with our children? We make sure we're connected to our kids and then live a life that is a witness to our beliefs.

What if Your Right is My Wrong?

I'm always talking about how important it is that our children develop a sense of right and wrong. But what do we mean by 'right'? Could your idea of what is right be my wrong? Could my right be your wrong?

Although we are all unschoolers, we might not share the same values and beliefs. And this might worry anyone who is thinking about unschooling. What if we give our children the freedom to choose, and they end up following someone else's values instead of ours?

If we're a church-going family, our kids might decide they no longer want to worship with us. What about such issues as marriage and abortion? We might hold strong views about these and, of course, we want our kids to share our beliefs because they are truth to us. So it might feel very risky to unschool. Wouldn't it be better to keep hold of our kids and make them live our way, the way we truly believe is right? Or isn't control necessary?

Our children are very likely to adopt our belief systems if we listen to them, discuss things without pressure, respect their opinions and love them unconditionally. In other words, they are likely to follow us if we are closely connected with them.

Even if we do have our differences, maybe there are a few 'right' things we all have in common.

Perhaps you'll agree that it's right to respect, encourage, trust, and forgive our kids.

And then there's unconditional love. How can it be wrong to love our kids just as they are, regardless of what they do? That's the way we all want to be loved. Wouldn't you agree?

Part XIX: Christian Unschooling

An Impossible Adventure

When Andy asked me to marry him, of course, I said yes. "But I'll never become a Catholic," I added. I had to make it clear. Just in case. What if my cradle Catholic husband had plans to drag me into his church?

I'd heard stories about the Catholic Church. Bad ones. The Church controls people's lives. Tells them what to do. It's just a big institution, similar to schools, designed to take away people's freedom. Once you get entangled with Catholicism, there's no hope for you. Much better to stay well away. So I did.

And then our daughter Felicity was born, and 17 months later, Duncan joined our family. And despite not wanting to, I started thinking about baptisms. Babies are baptised. Why? Does baptism mean anything? Or is it just an empty celebration that parents arrange because it's the expected thing to do?

One day, I said to Andy, "If we were to get our children baptised, what church would you choose?"

He gave me the expected answer: "The Catholic Church."

Did I want our children tied to the Church? Did I want to burden them with Catholic beliefs? I hesitated. Perhaps baptism wasn't a good idea. Or maybe it was essential? I just didn't know. Finally, I decided it wouldn't hurt to find out more about the Church and what baptism actually is before making a decision.

So I arranged to meet the local parish priest. He was the first priest I'd ever spoken to. I felt a bit nervous. And a bit daring too. I was brave enough to meet a Catholic priest! What would he be like? Strange, for sure. But he wasn't. He was perfectly normal. He was kind and friendly and willing to help me.

"I'd like to know more about the Catholic Church. We might get our children baptised." And then I quickly added, "But then again, we might not."

Yes, I was only investigating. If I didn't like what I was about to find out, I would walk away. The Church wouldn't get my children. I made that perfectly clear.

Although I was prickly and defensive, the priest pretended not to notice. He was magnificent. He smiled as if he met mothers like me every day of the week. He searched his shelves for a book that explained the faith for non-Catholics and gently offered an invitation to answer any questions at a later date.

It wasn't long before I did have a question: "Can you baptise our children?" And then a few months later: "How do I become a Catholic?"

So what changed my mind about the Church? God. He spoke to me as I turned the pages of the Catholic book. He showed me where to find the missing pieces of my life. He flooded me with love. By the time I got to the last chapter, I wanted someone to open the Church door and invite me in.

And so I became a Catholic.

Did I lose my freedom? Were huge burdens heaped upon my shoulders? Is my life dictated by the rules of the Church? No. I needn't have worried. The Catholic Church isn't what I'd assumed it to be.

I didn't understand Catholicism. I didn't even want to. Then God began whispering the word *baptism* in my ear. That word led me on an impossible adventure.

In the same way that I didn't understand the Church, many people don't understand unschooling. They hear the negative stories that people pass around. And they say: "I'll never unschool!" But maybe they will.

When we're willing to learn more, and then ponder with an open mind, amazing things happen. Impossible things. I've discovered that. Perhaps you have too.

Letting Go of Control

On Saturday evening, Jessie, Quinn's sister, died. A two-metre-long brown snake bit my son Callum's Shar Pei/Great Dane puppy.

Her death wasn't in The Plan. She should have lived for years. Instead, the Jessie stories have suddenly come to an end. They'll be no more comparisons: "Is Jessie much bigger than Quinn? Send us a photo!" No more *I'll protect you!* barks from a warrior puppy. No more soggy doggy kisses.

We make plans. We think we know what's ahead. And then something happens. In an instant, life flies out of our control. Without turning the page, or even moving to a new paragraph, the story changes.

Callum digs a big puppy-sized grave under the tree in his backyard.

We lower our one-day-old son into the cemetery ground.

A routine ultrasound. "I'm sorry there's a problem with your baby." As these few words hit our ears, our story changes. Just like that. No warning.

Our son Thomas died. There was nothing we could do about it. Sunk in my pit of grief, I cried, "My plan for my life was better than this one!" But I know, deep down, it wasn't.

I survived the death of a child. I could never have done that on my own. Oh, at first, I tried to. But a day arrived when I knew that only God could help me. And so I let go of control. I had no choice. I threw myself into His arms. And I trusted that I'd emerge on the other side of grief.

Joy and sorrow. How can the world contain both? When does one turn into the other? Which one is ahead? I just don't know. And does it even matter? We're not in control. God is.

These days we don't look too far ahead. Instead, we try to live life as we should. Right now.

Live. Give. Forgive. Love until it hurts. Trust.

In other words: unschool.

It'll all work out. It always does. Because we're God's.

Faith and Trust

I never wanted to be in a position where I had to trust God. I preferred to rely on my resources. I wanted to be totally in control of my own life. That seemed easier to do because trusting is very difficult. Or so it can seem.

Then one day, at a time when I was feeling rather proud of the way I was handling my life and my family, my world fell apart.

"I'm very sorry, but I don't think your unborn baby will survive after birth."

It's strange how everything can change with a few words. The reins of my life jerked from my hands. My life began galloping along, totally out of my control. Five agonising months of waiting passed and Thomas was born. A day later, he died in my arms. I wanted to die too. How was I ever to survive the grief? I wasn't as strong and as perfect as I had previously believed. I turned to God because I had nowhere else to go.

For month after month, grief gripped my heart tightly, refusing to loosen its fingers. Again and again, I fell into a pit of near-despair. Many, many times, I no longer wanted to fight the pain. I just wanted to lie down and give up.

I knew I had to trust that God was helping me, even though He felt so remote. The words *Jesus, I trust in You* were constantly on my lips, as I battled the thought that He might have abandoned me. I had to believe God would bring me through the grief, that the suffering had meaning and that joy would return to my life.

Nearly two years after Thomas died, we erected a headstone over his grave. On that stone are the words: *Jesus, I trust in You.* They are words of thanksgiving. God did indeed bring us through that sorrow.

There have been many other times since the loss of our son when we've had to trust God. Today, I'm still trusting. You see, we don't live a perfect life. There is so much I can't fix on my own. I have to place everything in God's hands and trust He will sort things out as they are meant to be.

Unschoolers talk about trust all the time. Do we have enough trust to unschool? I wonder what that means. Is it a case of putting trust in the unschooling process alone? Or do we trust because we feel unschooling is what God wants us to do? It could be both. I know there are many people without any faith who successfully unschool. It's not necessarily a religious thing to do. But I also feel an unschooling life can be completely compatible with a life lived for God. Doesn't God want everyone, regardless of their situation, to trust Him? He wants all of us to live in the moment, accepting His plan and not our own for our lives, relying on Him and not ourselves: abandonment to Divine Providence. Trust is something we all have to do.

I think back to that time when I didn't want to trust and hand over control of my life to God. I thought I could do everything by myself. And I now wonder why I wanted to be in control. That's a lot of responsibility. It involves many worries. Isn't it better to follow where God leads? Isn't it better to trust?

Why is it so hard to trust? Why did my world have to spin out of control before I was willing to place my life properly in God's hands? I have no idea. If I'd known the peace, the joy, and the love that was waiting for me, I'd never have hesitated. But then again, if I'd known all about these, there would have been no reason to trust.

Is trust all about love? How much do we love? Do we appreciate how much God loves us?

The Trust Problem

Why do we have such a problem with trust? Have we just got out of the habit of trusting? Because who needs to trust when we have the Internet?

Whenever anyone has an illness or an injury, most people head straight to the Internet to do a bit of self-diagnosis. As a second step, we might visit our doctor and see if his diagnosis matches up with ours. If we don't like what he says, we do some more research, and then we make our own decisions about the care we need. It's good to be informed and to know about the various options. However, does having access to so much information give us the feeling that we know as much as our doctor? Or maybe more because it's our body, not his? Perhaps we no longer have the same respect for the medical profession as people did in days gone by. Do we need to listen to our doctor's advice? Trust his opinion? Isn't it better to rely on our own?

When I had a Facebook account, my feed was full of posts warning me about all kinds of things from fluoride in toothpaste and town water, to terrorists and refugees, to the dangers associated with eating too much sugar, grains or gluten. An endless stream of negative stories warning me about this, that, and the other.

Many of these warnings come too late for me. I've already trusted a lot of people and made decisions based on that trust. For example, my children are vaccinated. I decided to go down this pathway a long time ago.

We often judge each other's decisions. Vaccinate, and you're judged. Don't vaccinate, and you're judged. Emotions run high on issues like this one.

All those anti-vaccination posts eventually made me feel guilty. What if the decision I made for my children ends up adversely affecting their well-being? Should I have done my research better? I thought I knew the facts. I'd listened to my doctor. I'd asked questions. But could I have done more? I accepted the doctor's opinion because I trusted him. Was that wrong? Even if it was, there is nothing I can do about it now. I can't go back and change the situation.

What if I hadn't trusted the doctor? What if I don't trust anyone ever again? I could decide that I'm never going to rely on anyone but myself. Yes, I'll be in total control of my life and the lives of my children. But is that possible? No. Even if we research and make our own decisions, things still happen. We could still get cancer even if we've reduced the risks by changing our food and environment. Or we might eat well, avoid alcohol, rest and look after ourselves, do everything right during pregnancy, and still not have a perfectly healthy baby. Our child might even die. Like my son Thomas.

I used to think that I lived my life for God. But I didn't really. Oh yes, I went to church and tried to avoid sin and do good instead. But I did things my way. When I prayed, I told God exactly what I needed. I didn't want to put my life entirely in His hands and trust. And then our baby was born and died a day later, and as I held his small still body close to my heart, I was absolutely certain that my plan for my life was better than God's. Mine wouldn't have included such unbearable grief. How could God have done this to me? It was hard to accept.

But I did accept it. I had to. My life was out of control, and I knew there was nothing I could do about it. I had to trust God and let Him guide me through the pain.

So I learnt about trust the hard way. Or maybe it was easy because I had no choice. When we are at the end of our resources, we know we have to give up our battle to stay in control, and then trust. If we don't, we won't survive.

Many people don't trust God. Maybe they think they don't need Him. We're a society of independent people. We can make our own decisions and run our lives without relying on God or anyone else. Trust has gone out of fashion. We don't trust each other. We don't trust our children. We don't trust God. We have a trust problem. This is rather unfortunate because unschooling is all about trust.

We might like the idea of unschooling, but will we be able to do it? Will we be able to trust? And what if we do and things don't turn out as we hope? Will we think we were wrong to trust? No, because the outcome doesn't necessarily depend upon us.

We make our decisions with good intentions. We do what we think is right. And even if things don't turn out quite as we expect, it will be okay. If we let Him, God will work everything out. Just like He did all those years ago when I lost a child and learnt about trust.

I wonder why we want to be in control. Why do we fight so hard to do things alone? Surely it is better to trust?

What if Our Kids Don't Want to Go to Church?

What if our unschooled children don't want to go to church with us? Should we make them go?

It can be quite a dilemma, can't it? As unschoolers, we want to give our kids the freedom to make their own choices, but can we do this with our faith? Could going to church be different from everything else? It's all very well letting kids choose what they eat and when they go to bed. But what if they choose not to go to church? They might not fulfil their religious commitments. They could end up not being in a state of grace.

So should we make our kids go to church? Is it our duty to do this even if it conflicts with our unschooling principles? Perhaps these are questions that we should consider. Or is there another question worth pondering first? Could it be better to start with this one: *why don't our kids want to go to church?* Has it got something to do with us?

Maybe we give our kids the impression that we go to church because it's our duty. Do we grumble about having to get up early to go? Do our kids think we go because we *have* to?

Perhaps our kids need to hear that we go to church because we *want* to. Regardless of our obligations, we choose to go. Our faith is the source of our joy. It's the centre of our lives. We recognise that we need to go to church. We can't wait to go. We are grateful that we can go.

Sometimes kids aren't interested in going to church because they don't understand what's going on. The service might not feel relevant. Kids might think it's boring. Maybe we need to share what going to church is all about.

We need to weave our faith into our family life. It should be an integral part of it. The foundation of everything we do. But is it?

Do we talk about our faith in a natural way? Do our kids see us making decisions based on our faith? Do we invite them to pray with us?

Most importantly, do we visibly love our faith?

We could make our kids go to church, but what if they end up saying, "As soon as I can, when I can make my own decisions, I'm no longer going"? Forcing our kids to do what we think is right might make us feel good. We've done our duty. No one can say we haven't. But wouldn't it be better if our kids freely choose to go? Because they love their faith? Because they have felt the love and joy of God within our homes? Because the people that they love and trust show them that it's important by making it the foundation of their lives?

I once listened to a spiritual talk with some advice about keeping kids faithful. I expected the speaker to say we have to drum the catechism into our kids, make rules about such things as going to church, make sure we do our parental duty. But he didn't say this. He said, first and foremost, we have to make sure our family homes are happy places. We must live our faith with joy. I guess that's what I've been trying to say. It doesn't matter whether we are Catholic or not, the same principle applies.

We have to live whatever we believe with joy.

So if our kids don't want to go to church, we could make them go. Because it's our duty. Or maybe it's worth pondering this thought: is it time to rediscover our wonder, awe, and love for our faith?

Can Unschooling Be a Christian Thing to Do?

When a child has been controlled all her life, she might grow into the kind of adult who says, "Nobody is ever going to make me do what *they* want ever again. From now on, I'm going to do what *I* want." She might close herself off, stand well back, not let anyone get too close. Because you never know what other people might want her to do. Even someone she declares she loves.

"If you think I'm going to do your washing for you, you're wrong! You can do it yourself."

And it's not just physical work she will refuse to do for someone else. She'll keep a guard on her emotions too. She might grow into a prickly independent person, not trusting, suspicious of any overtures of real love.

"I can do that for myself! I don't need anyone!"

She'll want to be the one in control.

How do I know this? Amina told me. This is her story.

My friend thought a lot about her experiences, and then one day, she realised something: "How can there ever be real love when there is control?"

We were all born free, and we all have great dignity, which should be respected. We don't have the right to control anyone.

Real love is all about giving ourselves freely to other people, without counting the cost to ourselves, without expecting something back. No one has to make us do what is right. We choose to do it.

I want my children to grow up to be loving and giving. I don't want them to be concerned only with themselves, not willing to reach out to others. But I can't make them into that kind of person, by force. I have to give my children the freedom to choose, and in so doing, they receive the opportunity to give freely of themselves.

Sometimes people question whether unschooling is a Christian thing to do. Isn't it irresponsible? Surely all that freedom will make children self-centred and concerned only for themselves? We should tighten up, do our parental duty properly, instead of taking the easy way out.

But what could be more Christian than respecting another person and loving them freely? And what could be more difficult? Because our children will only learn what true love is all about, by observing our example of self-giving.

I think unschooling is compatible with the Christian way of life. Not everyone who unschools is a Christian. But every Christian can unschool.

At least that's what I believe. And so does my pretend friend Amina.

Experience, Wisdom and Original Sin

Why do we have trouble trusting kids? Why do we think that left to themselves, they will choose to be lazy and not want to do much at all? Why do we have trouble believing they will want to do what's right rather than what is wrong?

If we have a faith, we might believe that original sin weakens our kids. Because of this sin, they will be more inclined to choose the easy options. They will lack the strength to work hard and to do what is right and necessary. Therefore they can't be given the freedom to decide for themselves what they're going to learn or do.

Parents have experience and wisdom their children haven't got. Do they need to use these to push their children to do what is right? Perhaps it's their duty. Children might have to accept that they aren't in a position to make the best decisions, and so they have to be willing to do what their parents tell them. Perhaps if we give control to our kids, we are negligent?

But parents have faults too. We are also tempted to do what is wrong. If we recognise this, we could say, "I can't be trusted, so why should I trust my child? I sometimes feel lazy, so why shouldn't my child be lazy too? She needs me to push her along to make sure she does what she needs to do."

But instead of using our self-awareness as a reason to control our kids, perhaps we can use it to make connections with them. Parents know what it feels like to struggle to do what is right. It's hard to do what is necessary constantly. Knowing this should give us empathy for our kids. It doesn't give us permission to take over and make decisions for them.

Whether we believe in original sin or not, we all know our kids will make mistakes. Perhaps we think parents are in a position to prevent these mistakes. If we can use our control, to keep our kids from failing, isn't it our duty to do this? And if we agree with this idea, how long will we try and protect them? As long as they are at home with us? Do we not believe that children can overcome their faults?

Kids may have faults, but we can't just say, "That's the way they are. I can't trust them." Kids have to try and overcome their faults. But how do they become stronger? By trying and failing and trying again. One step forward at a time. If we are always interfering, taking the reins out of their hands, they will have no opportunity to try. They will never make progress. We have to let our kids make mistakes.

But some mistakes seem huge. Is it too risky to hand over control? What if our kids do something big that they'll later regret? They could make the wrong choices that end up affecting such things as their career opportunities or worse, their personal lives. Or are the risks not as big as we might think?

Kids don't do things in isolation. We can't step back and say, "Hey, do what you like. I'll let you make mistakes, but if you fail, you'll have to deal with it. It has nothing to do with us."

Kids belong to families who care about them. Parents might not take control, but we are there to help them as they learn and grow and develop. We build up strong connections by trusting, loving unconditionally and forgiving. We show empathy; we listen and discuss. Also, our children observe us trying to overcome our faults. Because of the strong bonds between us, they will look to us for guidance. There's a good chance they will want to adopt our values and follow our example.

If we do take over and control our kids, making them follow the pathway we feel is best, who says it's all going to work out? Do we really have enough wisdom and experience to determine without a doubt what our kids need? Do we know our kids better than they know themselves? Perhaps we remember, as children, not knowing who we were and what we needed. (Perhaps we're still searching for these answers even though we are now adults.) But what if we'd been allowed to discover who we were? We could give our children the opportunity that we were denied. We could trust them to know their needs instead of assuming we know better and taking over.

But what if we don't do this? What if we make the wrong choices for our children? We might feel bad if we don't do our 'duty', but we'll also feel bad if our plans fail, especially if our control results in a rift between our children and us.

Our role is to believe in our kids. Encourage them to become the best people they can be. If we tell them they are incapable of being responsible for themselves, they will come to believe it. When they get to adulthood after a childhood of control, how will they have the skills to make the right decisions on their own?

Yes, kids might be weak. But this doesn't mean we have to control them. Weakness needs empathy and understanding, kindness and encouragement. We can become better people together. We shouldn't want to control our kids or break their wills but instead, turn them in the right direction: towards love.

Love? Isn't that the best reason to do what is right? It's much better than doing something because we have no choice.

Part XX: When a Child Finds Life Difficult

Not all children will have a mental illness like my eldest child. But many will find life difficult. How will we feel if we discover that our children's lives aren't the ones we dreamed about the day they were born? Will we grieve? Will we be able to give our kids the help they need? Will we make mistakes? Will we feel like we're failing? And what about love? Will love bring us through the pain?

This is my daughter Felicity's story. It's also mine

The Beginning

Felicity phones home. We chat. One thing leads to another, and we find ourselves talking about the difficult years when my eldest daughter was suffering from undiagnosed bipolar disorder, and I was an inexperienced mother, not understanding her needs.

I have never written about those times because only so much can be shared publicly. Sometimes the whole story can't be told. "I haven't wanted to invade your privacy," I say to Felicity.

"I don't mind if you write about me," she replies. "Go ahead."

So I have Felicity's permission and I'm going to write about my daughter, those difficult teenage years, bipolar disorder, all the mistakes I made, the pain of the years when Felicity was living an enclosed life in a convent, and how we grew apart and then made it back to being mother and daughter.

Where shall I begin? I shall begin at the beginning.

When I was expecting our first child, I hoped our baby was a girl. "It doesn't matter if the baby is a boy or a girl," I told everyone. But it did matter, just a little bit. I had always dreamt of having a daughter. I grew up, the eldest of three sisters. Yes, life in our house was girl-orientated. I wanted to share all those feminine experiences with a child of my own. I hoped for sons too. They would be a wonderful new experience. But a girl? Having a girl first would be perfect.

A couple of weeks before our baby was due, I decided to fill in some of the waiting time by knitting a tiny little cardigan. I debated which colour wool to use. It would have been sensible to have bought a unisex colour like white, yellow or mint green as we didn't know whether our child was a girl or a boy, but I found myself selecting a delicate pale pink. I hoped.

"You have a daughter!" announced the doctor, as soon as Felicity was born. A daughter? Really? I had a huge grin on my face for weeks.

Felicity, of course, was absolutely gorgeous. I looked at her, and my heart ached with love. I wanted to be a perfect mother for my child. She deserved the best. Yes, I was going to raise her well. I was going to look after her and keep her safe. I wanted to give her the best start I could in life.

But I didn't always go about things in the right way. It's no wonder really. I had no mothering experience, and so I had a lot to learn. Many times I found myself butting heads with my strong-willed daughter. But we survived, and Felicity did grow into a beautiful person, despite my poor mothering skills.

By the time Felicity was 12, she was a very capable child whom I depended on. She could cook and run a house and look after her younger siblings. She was clever and talented and outgoing. She was funny and good to talk to. In fact, life couldn't have been running more smoothly.

And then unexpectedly, things began to fall apart.

"I think everything started to happen about the time Thomas died," said Felicity. "That's when the bipolar started to affect me."

Thomas is our sixth child. He died when he was one day old. Felicity was 12 at the time. I remember how she held us together during those difficult days. My mother-in-law was staying with us, but it was Felicity who was really in charge. She kept family and friends informed and cooked and cleaned and helped in any way she could while I was grieving. But was she grieving too?

I assumed all my children were grieving in some way or other. Duncan grieved most openly. I worried about him. But Felicity? I thought she was coping.

As an adult, Felicity wrote these words:

I have a crushing sense of guilt, one that seizes on any occasion to make me feel sad, worthless and powerless. I don't quite know how this all started. Maybe it began when my brother Thomas died? He was one day old when he died of a birth defect. I remember how we found out he had a birth defect before he was born. I remember how upset my mum was. I even remember lying in bed, unable to sleep, trying to bargain with God. If He took me, maybe he could heal Thomas? I wanted more than anything else to have my family happy and whole again, and if that meant me dying so that my brother lived, I was okay with that.

Of course, God notoriously doesn't do bargains, and I found myself stubbornly alive while my brother died one day after birth. In the time that followed, I tried my hardest to hold the family together, to be a good big sister and daughter. I remember trying to take over as much cooking as possible, trying to keep my siblings happy and trying not to bother my heart-broken mother. I resolutely crushed down my own feelings of grief out of a sense of responsibility towards my family.

All my efforts seemed to be in vain, however. I couldn't mend broken hearts no matter how much cooking I did. I felt guilty that I couldn't do more. And, as I grew up, this sense of guilt grew and expanded. Looking back, I realise I was developing bipolar disorder, which was causing havoc with my emotions. But at the time, all I could see was me betraying my stoic, responsible ideal with these stupid emotions. I wanted so much to be good, to be the perfect daughter, but I felt so bad.

These words make me want to cry. I had no idea what Felicity was experiencing at the time of Thomas' death. She needed help, and I was so wrapped up in my own sorrow, I didn't realise. I had absolutely no idea until 13 years later. Guilt? I felt guilty. What did I do that made Felicity feel she had to fix my broken heart in such a way? How could she have thought I'd be happy having Thomas but not her?

Felicity turned 13 and, of course, we officially pronounced her a teenager. I prepared myself for a hard time, and yes, it arrived. My capable daughter fell apart. I thought Felicity was just acting like a 'normal' teenager. It seems she wasn't. I shall write about those years in the next story.

The Teenage Years

When my eldest daughter Felicity was a teenager, she could be moody and sullen and emotional. She was very hard to live with. I thought she was a 'normal' teenager.

We tend to judge other people's experiences by what we know, what we have experienced ourselves. Most people label teenagers as difficult. Felicity was our first child. Of course, her behaviour was typical of a child her age, or so I thought.

I tried to put myself into Felicity's shoes, to think back to when I was her age. I remembered being sullen myself. I'd withdraw into a mood and refuse to be enticed back to happiness by my very patient mother. It was my way of responding to those hard years of being almost grown up but not being allowed the freedom or trust I felt I was ready for. I was drifting between childhood and adulthood, and yes, it was difficult. I assumed Felicity was going through a similar experience.

Some days Felicity was 'normal'. I'd watch her carefully when she got up in the morning. Was this going to be a bad day or a good one? When she smiled and was chatty, I sighed with relief. On those days, we'd sit around the table sipping coffee, talking about all sorts of things. Felicity was very open, and our conversations were deep and satisfying. She was delightful company, and I thought, "If only all days were like this one."

Sometimes Felicity would be in a good mood but then all of a sudden, I'd realise she was slipping away into her moody world. When I talked to her, she responded in short, curt sentences. I could feel her emotions becoming cooler and more remote. At these moments, my heart sank. I did everything I could to draw her back into our warm and loving world where we could communicate properly. I'd smile and offer love, say nice things. I'd ask her if she'd like to do something special with me. Felicity would shrug her shoulders, and I'd find myself driving her to town so we could have mother-daughter time in a café. After ordering coffee and huge cakes - which she didn't need, but I was willing to buy if it helped - I'd try to talk to Felicity and keep her engaged. My efforts didn't often work.

There were many days when I ended up frustrated. I'd shout such things as "I spend so much time with you. I try so hard, and you refuse to respond. Do you realise everyone is going to get fed up with you if you continue like this? What more can I do?"

The huge amount of time I gave to Felicity was time I didn't give to our other children. I resented this, especially as my efforts didn't seem to be appreciated.

Felicity is a talented person. She is musical. She can write. She can draw. And she is clever in so many other ways. During her teenage years, she played the piano and clarinet, and she sang.

Sometimes when Felicity was practising the piano, I'd walk by and, as soon as she realised I was there, her hand would jerk, and a book would disappear out of sight. Felicity would resume her practice instantly as if she'd been playing all along and not reading the first book that came to hand. "Felicity's lazy. She knows nothing about commitment," I'd say with frustration. "Haven't I taught her to be hard working? We've paid for all those lessons. She wants to study music at the conservatorium, but she'd rather read than work hard. She'll never make it."

Felicity didn't make it to the conservatorium. Her confidence seeped away. Her commitment disappeared. Even her ability seemed to desert her. I listened to her practising the piano the day before a big exam. She made so many silly mistakes over and over again. In the end, she asked if she could miss the exam. We agreed. It was a relief for all of us.

But there were times when Felicity's ability and confidence were awe-inspiring. When she was in the examination room doing her 6th-grade clarinet exam, she discovered her teacher hadn't prepared her to play enough of the set pieces. She was one piece short. The examiner pointed out an appropriate piece of music in her book and asked her to give it a try even though she hadn't worked on it. Felicity came home with a triumphant look on her face and a grade A result.

And there were many times when Felicity stood up in front of hundreds of people at Mass and sang solo beautifully. Yes, I thought God had given her extraordinary talents. I was afraid she was wasting them due to a lack of self-discipline.

So Felicity changed her mind about studying music at the conservatorium. What was she to do instead? I tried to help her by making some suggestions. Could she do a Bachelor of Arts degree and study writing? She'd always enjoyed writing and was good at it. She'd completed a few Open University units and achieved distinctions and high distinctions. I knew Felicity would be able to cope with the work.

Somehow we found ourselves talking about a horticulture course that was offered at TAFE (Technical and Further Education). It wasn't necessary to get high grades to be accepted on this course. I thought Felicity was aiming too low. She had the talent to achieve so much more. It wasn't as if she had shown a passion for plants either. But after Felicity began talking about making a career out of being a checkout assistant in a supermarket, I said, "Find out the course details."

Felicity never did enrol in that course. She continued to cry, "What shall I do? I just don't know."

"You don't have to decide right now," I replied. "You're young. There's plenty of time to make a decision." But this didn't help. Felicity seemed to have a real need to know what she was expected to do right then and there. And I couldn't help her.

While all this was going on, Felicity worked as a casual at a supermarket. She got the job with the aim of saving money to buy herself a better clarinet, and for a time, her savings grew. Then she started frittering her money away. Before all her money disappeared, I dragged her down to the music shop, and we bought the clarinet. I don't think she ever used it.

One thing she did buy was lollies and chocolate, family-sized packets which she ate by herself. We'd find the lolly wrappers hidden away under her bed. Rather, her sisters would find the evidence. I guess our family started to divide, with Felicity on one side and us on the other. No one else would consider eating a big packet of lollies on their own. Why did she? I suggested Felicity bought sweet treats openly and shared them around. But this wouldn't have satisfied her need, the need we didn't understand.

Of course, Felicity's weight steadily increased. I began to worry about this. I tried to talk to her about it. It wasn't healthy. She'd regret it later when she realised she'd have to diet. She should exercise more. I'd say, "Come on, we're going for a walk." Felicity would reluctantly put down her book and follow me outside. She'd walk behind me, her head down, barely lifting her feet off the ground. However slowly I walked, she could go slower. In the end, I'd shout at her, "You are impossible to help!" before heading for home.

There were times when Felicity cried, "I have no friends!" Her crying was always dramatic and noisy, with tears rolling down her face in torrents. Actually, Felicity had more friends than her siblings have ever had. We took her to every possible homeschooling gathering. She invited friends for sleep-overs. She visited her friends in return.

During her homeschooling years, I said, "Do you want to go to school? You'd see a lot of people there. You could make some new friends." But just like every other suggestion I made, this one was rejected. It was as if I could never help Felicity however hard I tried. I thought she wanted to complain but wasn't interested in finding a solution. And so I got frustrated. I can remember many times when I gave up, and my mood of trying to help turned into one of anger. I'd yell. We'd both yell. I'd leave her, slamming the door on the way out. A moment later, I'd return wanting to say more. Didn't Felicity know how difficult she was making my life?

I could tell you so much more about those years. I could write an individual story about every paragraph of this one. But perhaps I have recorded enough.

I thought Felicity was a normal teenager exhibiting normal teenage behaviour. She had good days. She had bad days. Very bad days. I thought she was sullen and moody, lazy and undisciplined.

I tried to help but got so frustrated when I thought Felicity wouldn't let herself be helped. I yelled and wanted to give up. I invaded her privacy. I didn't trust her. I didn't show her unconditional love. I didn't parent her at all in an unschooling kind of way.

Do you think that would have made any difference? Maybe it would have alerted me to the fact that Felicity was suffering from more than the need for respect and trust. It might have made me realise she wasn't a 'normal' teenager but one with special needs. And even if I'd never worked it out, doesn't everyone deserve to be treated with kindness, respect and love?

Felicity had a very difficult time as a teenager. She didn't understand why. I didn't either. We both didn't know.

We weren't aware that Felicity had an undiagnosed mental illness.

Making a Teenager's Life Difficult

My teenage daughter Felicity asks, "Can I wear jeans, Mum?" She looks at me with pleading eyes. She must know what I'm going to say. I've said it so many times before: "Jeans are unfeminine. You're a girl. You should wear a skirt."

When Felicity was younger, clothes weren't an issue. She had dresses and pants and jeans, and she wore whatever suited the occasion. I didn't think too much about it. Then we moved house, and I made some new friends. They introduced me to some new ideas.

Girls are different from boys. They should look and act like girls.

Yes, girls are different from boys. I agreed. I listened some more and observed. Other mothers were dressing their girls in skirts and dresses. Some weren't allowing their girls to participate in activities traditionally associated with boys. Perhaps I shouldn't either.

So I decided not to allow Felicity to wear jeans or join in with the rough soccer games that were enjoyed by the boys. Instead, she stood on the sidelines, yearning to kick the ball with all the other kids.

Occasionally Felicity would defy me. She'd sneak off when I wasn't watching, and play soccer anyway.

"Hey, your daughter Felicity is a powerful kicker!" someone would later tell me, not realising his words would get her into trouble.

"What were you doing playing soccer?" I'd ask my daughter.

Soccer? Jeans? Did it really matter if Felicity pulled on a pair of jeans and kicked a ball with the boys?

I have to admit jeans and soccer weren't the real issues, though I pretended they were. I only adopted the standards of the other mothers because I liked these women. I wanted to belong to their group. I wanted them to like me in return, to approve of me, and to accept my family. So I did things their way instead of listening to my child and making decisions more appropriate for my own family.

If I'd encouraged Felicity to participate in sporting activities she enjoyed, would this have prevented her inactive lifestyle of later years? If I hadn't had constant battles with her over her clothes, would she have felt better about her appearance? Would she never have written the following words?

I also took my rising desire to prove myself as an individual, to have different looks and hobbies and interests to my mum's, as a very bad thing. I felt guilty about wanting to be different, so I would take any criticism of my appearance or interests very badly.

Would I have made the life of my child, who was suffering from undiagnosed mental illness just a little bit easier? Maybe a healthy child would have felt resentment because of my rules. It seems my child ended up feeling bad.

I don't think it matters whether a teenager is dealing with a health issue or not; we should avoid battling with them over unimportant things.

We should be prepared to trust and accept, rather than constantly control our young people. We have to value their opinions and who they are. They don't have to be just like us. And they certainly don't have to conform to the ideas of our friends.

All these years later, I'm wondering: would our friends have accepted us just as we were? Perhaps it hadn't been necessary to change. Why do we find it so hard to be ourselves?

Losing My Mothering Role

My daughter Felicity was going to be a musician and then a writer. She considered studying horticulture, and then decided she wanted to do no more than work as a checkout operator in a supermarket. I could see she was having a great interior battle, trying to decide what God wanted her to do with her life.

Then one day, Felicity announced, "I think God might be calling me to the religious life. Perhaps I should visit some convents." So she spent a few days with a teaching order of nuns. We knew these women. I could imagine Felicity joining them and using her talents in music and English to help other people. Yes, I could accept she might become a teaching nun. It made sense.

But then Felicity arranged to visit an enclosed order: "Just to compare orders, Mum!" She might have looked lightly upon this visit, but it concerned me: "She's going to come back and tell us she wants to be a contemplative nun," I said to my husband, Andy.

As soon as Felicity arrived home, she did indeed announce this intention, and a sharp pain instantly gripped my heart. I am not exaggerating, being overly dramatic. It hurt to a depth even I hadn't anticipated. The tears started flowing despite my efforts to hold them back. I wanted to smile and say, "I'm proud of you for wanting to give up your life for God." But it was hard. So hard.

"When are you leaving?" I asked.

"Mother Prioress says I should return to the convent as soon as possible, maybe in two weeks."

There was so much to do. First, I had to let everyone know about Felicity's decision. Maybe friends and family would like to visit and say goodbye. So I picked up the phone and began a round of "I'm just phoning to let you know Felicity has decided to enter an enclosed order of nuns."

The reactions were diverse. Some friends congratulated us. Isn't it every Catholic parent's dream to have a daughter who is willing to embrace the religious life?

Some people were happy but thought Felicity was too hasty. Shouldn't she get a university degree first? If it were meant to be, waiting a bit longer wouldn't hurt. Why did she have to hurry back to the convent so soon?

And then there were those who just didn't understand. Why would a beautiful, talented, young girl want to give up her life and shut herself away from the world in a convent? Some people were very upset with Felicity's decision, and I bore the brunt of it, trying to explain, trying to support my daughter. It wasn't as if I was exactly happy about the decision either, not because I didn't understand, but because my heart was breaking.

I imagined the future, which was hurtling towards us, without Felicity. She'd never be part of our family life again. We wouldn't be able to do simple things with her like chat over a cup of coffee. I watched Felicity sorting out her clothes and possessions, deciding who to give them to. I would never see her dressed in her colourful skirts and dresses again. She wouldn't wear her huge hoop earrings. I wouldn't be able to enjoy listening to her funny stories as the kids washed the dishes together each evening. No more sharing a pew at Mass. Felicity would never again enter our home once she passed out the front door, on her way to the convent.

The tears flowed on and off for that last two weeks. I felt like I was grieving. I guess I was. I wanted to say, "Couldn't you wait until you're a little older?" but Felicity said, "You're not going to try and stop me going as well, are you, Mum?" No, I've always told my children we have to be prepared to do God's will whatever that involves. I had to support my daughter's decision.

"If Felicity is running away from an unhappy home life, she can live with us." These words cut deep. Unhappy home life? Felicity wasn't running away. Or was she? Felicity wrote:

I remember a particularly bad time of depression when I was 17. I was very focused on music at the time, and I pushed myself extremely hard to do an advanced and difficult clarinet exam. The plan was for me to continue with my clarinet studies after that, and gain entrance into the Conservatorium of Music. I wanted to be in an orchestra. But after completing (and doing very well in) my exam, I lost all motivation. I couldn't settle down to practice. I couldn't seem to do anything. I gave up on music. I tried to decide on another course of action – horticulture, part-time work, anything, but nothing seemed to stick._Well, at the age of 18, I ran away to a convent.

As I began my teens, I wanted to be perfect. Throughout my teen years, I think I would have settled for normality or stability. As I ended my teens, I thought I would achieve peace by sacrificing my life in the convent.

I don't think Felicity was running away from her family and home life, but maybe she was running away from the confusion and pain of her mental condition. Perhaps she thought she'd find peace in the religious life.

The day arrived for Felicity to leave. Andy was going to drive her to the convent, and several of our children were going along for the ride. I couldn't go with them because Charlotte wasn't well. Gemma-Rose had been sick too. I was so glad of an excuse to avoid a public goodbye at the convent. The one at home was hard enough.

We had morning tea together around the kitchen table. As I watched my eldest daughter sipping coffee, I kept thinking, "This is the last time..." We tried to keep the conversation light as if the day were just like any other day. But then Andy said, "Shall we go?" and our time together ran out.

The tears flowed down my cheeks as I hugged Felicity close. She said, "Oh, Mum!" but didn't cry herself. And then she was gone.

Of course, life carried on. We adjusted. But the pain remained quietly in the background.

We were allowed to visit Felicity every month or so. Mother Prioress was kind, recognising it was difficult to break the family ties so quickly. None of the other nuns had young siblings. Mother made an exception for us, and we were allowed more visits than usual. I knew it wouldn't always be that way, but it helped at the beginning.

We always visited on a Saturday afternoon between 1 pm and 3 pm, not a minute longer. Two precious hours. We met in the guests' library. One of the nuns always brought us a jug of cordial and plates of biscuits. There was tea and also coffee. But only for us. Felicity wasn't allowed to eat or drink with her family.

"How are you doing?" I'd ask.

Felicity would smile and say, "Everything's fine." She told us funny stories of her new life like the one about the magpie. It flew into the chapel, and the nuns had to chase it out. She showed us some drawings she'd been allowed to work on. She described the Bible and other lessons she was involved with. "Mother says you gave me a wonderful education. She is impressed by my Latin." And we told Felicity all the latest news from home. It was all very polite and all very meaningless: light, happy conversation about nothing important.

After six months, Felicity was accepted as a novice. She received a religious name. But I never used it. My daughter was always Felicity or Tissie to me. There were other things I had a hard time accepting. Maybe they were silly things. Why did my daughter's hair have to be hacked off? Couldn't she have special cleansers for her skin? The rough soap was causing irritation and inflammation. Did the nuns set aside time for exercise? I had a lot of concerns, but I had no right to voice them.

I wrote to Mother Prioress. "Could you please tell me what obligations, if any, Felicity has towards her family. I am no longer certain what role I play in her life. Do we need to let go of Felicity completely and not expect anything of her?"

She wrote back telling me that Felicity was expected to pray for her family, but that was the extent of her obligations. Mother Prioress was now her mother. She assured me she would look after her in my place.

I was no longer Felicity's mother. My role had been handed over to another woman. I tried to talk about this with friends, and they said such things as:

"You should feel grateful she is somewhere safe."

"You should be happy that she has a religious vocation."

"It would be the same if she got married."

"We all have to give up our children one day."

But having a married daughter is nothing like having a daughter in the convent. I have experienced both. And children do grow up, but that doesn't mean we don't still care. And I know we have to do God's will, but that doesn't mean it's easy. It sometimes involves great sacrifice.

So I stopped talking about my feelings because I thought people would think I was complaining. But there was one person who was an enormous help. A priest, who knew the nuns well, would phone occasionally and ask how I was going. He acknowledged it wasn't easy for a mother to give up a daughter.

The months passed. Then in the autumn of Felicity's second year at the convent, we arrived to discover our afternoon tea was going to be served outside. "It's such a glorious day," Mother Prioress smiled. "I thought you would enjoy having your visit in the garden."

We spread a rug on the grass, and the children ran along the paths enjoying the sunshine. Mother Prioress looked at them and said, "The girls are all so beautiful. I want every single one of them." I tried not to imagine losing five daughters to the convent. Instead, I concentrated on taking lots of photos as Felicity gave piggyback rides to Gemma-Rose and Sophie. Then I took out my camcorder and recorded a few minutes of video as usual. I have photographic and video records of every single one of our visits to the convent. And like the video of our son Thomas' funeral, I have never watched a single minute of any of them.

It was an enjoyable afternoon. Felicity looked well and happy. "Look, Mum! I've lost weight. I had to ask Sister to put a new hole in my belt." Yes, things were going well, and I was adjusting. Maybe it would be okay. Could the joy that we receive from accepting God's will be on its way?

But then we had a phone call.

Back in the Mothering Seat

I was snuggled up in bed, still half-asleep, my head buried under the quilt. I could hear Andy moving about the room, getting dressed. Soon he would bring me a cup of tea, say goodbye, and leave for work. It was just another weekday morning. And then the peace of the early hour was shattered by the sound of the phone intruding upon our day. Andy disappeared out the bedroom door, towards the kitchen, to answer it. I swung my legs over the side of the bed and hurried after him. "Who was that?" I asked as he replaced the phone in its handset. Who would phone at this time of day?

"It was Mother Prioress. She wants me to collect Felicity later this morning."

Collect Felicity? My eldest daughter, who'd been enclosed in the convent for more than a year, was coming home?

"Why? What's wrong? Is she sick?" The questions tumbled out, one after another.

"Mother said Felicity should come home for a while. She'll explain more when I arrive at the convent."

We'd thought our eldest daughter would never come through our front door ever again. But in a few hours, she'd be doing just that. A few hours? So much to do. Where would she sleep? Our youngest child, Gemma-Rose, had taken over Felicity's bed.

For several hours, I was busy cleaning bedrooms, rearranging furniture, tucking in sheets. My mind was racing. Thoughts whirled around my mind: "Felicity's coming home. Why? She'll walk through the door. She'll eat dinner with us tonight. Is she okay?"

About lunchtime, the car pulled onto the driveway. Andy got out and opened the boot to retrieve a small bag. Then the passenger door opened and Felicity appeared. The children ran down the back steps to greet her. With much excitement, they practically dragged her into the house. Felicity looked around and noticed some changes. We looked at her. She had changed too. She looked so small and thin and uncertain. Her head was covered with a scarf. Of course, she needed it because she didn't have much hair.

Andy thrust a letter at me. "From Mother Prioress. I'm sorry, but I have to go to work."

I read the letter. It explained why Mother Prioress was sending Felicity home. I don't know if I still have that letter. Probably not. It contained painful words, words I didn't want to preserve. But I remember what Mother wanted to tell me.

She was apologetic but firm. She couldn't have Felicity at the convent. She was too volatile and emotional. She was making life difficult for the other nuns because of her moods. If she could learn to control her temper, she could return. Maybe six months at home would give Felicity a chance to think about whether she really wanted to be a nun or not. She could use that time to modify her behaviour.

I read the letter, then turned to Felicity and said, "How could you? Didn't I teach you anything about getting on with people? You can't take out your temper on others! I thought you had more control than that."

I took Mother Prioress' words very personally. I hadn't taught Felicity the skills she needed to get on with people. I had failed as a mother. And what would people think? Felicity had disgraced our family.

I have often heard parents say such things to their children as "Whatever you do, don't bring shame upon our family. Your behaviour is a reflection of your parents and your upbringing. Remember that, and do nothing that will hurt our reputation." Of course, I've said similar things many times myself. Children have to be loyal to their family, don't they? And maybe they do, but I think it's equally important that parents show complete loyalty towards their children. Family loyalty means rallying around and supporting each of the family's members, regardless of the mistakes they make, supporting them when outsiders start to criticise, making sure they feel loved regardless of the circumstances. We are a family, and we stick together whatever happens. And I should have rallied around Felicity better, instead of imagining what others were going to say about her, and therefore us.

I thought back to our last visit to the convent, that happy afternoon we'd spent in the garden. That hadn't been very long ago. We'd seen Mother Prioress. We'd spoken to her. Why hadn't she given us at least a hint of what was to come? Why hadn't someone told us long ago that Felicity was experiencing problems? I knew the answer: it was none of our business. Except now it *was* our business. Mother had sent Felicity home to us. I was back in the mothering seat.

I tried to work out what had gone wrong. Why had Felicity got so upset at the convent? She must have told me a little of what she'd experienced, but I can only remember a couple of incidents. "I fell asleep when it was my turn for adoration." That didn't seem such a big deal to me, especially for a young girl who had to sacrifice a lot of sleep during the night. But Felicity seemed unable to forgive herself.

Felicity told me how she had tried to relieve her feelings by taking out her frustrations on her pillow in her cell. But the sisters complained. That was no way for a nun to behave. They have to be in control, even in private, all the time.

So my eldest daughter was home again. Her siblings excitedly tried to show her everything she'd missed while she'd been gone: "You must watch this movie with us! We have some new books!" I wonder if they noticed their sister was so very different to that girl who'd left home maybe eighteen months before?

I wonder what it's like to suddenly find yourself back in the world.

"Mother Prioress asked me to come and see her this morning after prayers. She told me she'd asked Dad to collect me. She was sending me home."

"So you had no warning?"

"No. I didn't even get to say goodbye to the other nuns. I guess they know by now." And then after a moment, she added, "But I'll see them again. I'm going back."

But Felicity had to gain control over her temper before Mother Prioress would admit her to the convent once more. And until that time, she had to live back in the world.

I must say I admire Felicity's courage. Maybe her natural inclination was to hide away at home, but she didn't. She found a hat to cover her bare head and accompanied me to the shops and the other places I had to go. Everyone was very curious. "Was that Felicity I saw you with? Is she home? What happened?" I guess we provided some very interesting gossip for quite some time.

"Felicity couldn't adjust to the rigorous convent routine," I would say. I didn't mention her moods or her anger. Was I protecting my daughter or myself? Anyway, it was none of their business.

Some people were exceptionally kind. When Felicity came with me to the swim school, where the younger girls had lessons, the owner/manager remembered her. She offered Felicity a job. So a few days after re-entering the world, my daughter had employment. She was going to be a swim teacher for the next two school terms.

A few people said, "Felicity's home! How wonderful! I'm glad she changed her mind. You must be so happy."

But Felicity hadn't changed her mind, and I wasn't happy. How could I be happy when Felicity so obviously wasn't?

Mother Prioress had passed Felicity back to me. I was once again her mother, and I wanted to help her. But Felicity wouldn't listen to me. Everything I said was wrong. I suspect we might have had many arguments. She might have yelled at me, and I would probably have yelled back at her. But Felicity was on her best behaviour. She couldn't afford to show any emotion. She had to prove she was in control of her temper so that she would be allowed to return to her other mother as soon as possible.

Mother Prioress had given Felicity permission to phone her at regular intervals. "Can I phone Mother tonight? I have lots to talk to Mother about." Mother and not Mum. Mother Prioress was still the most important person in Felicity's life even though she'd sent her home. She was the person my daughter wanted to pour her heart out to.

So the months went by. Felicity's hair grew. She abandoned the hat, and it looked, from the outside, like she was becoming part of the world again. But in reality, she was ticking off the weeks until her six months at home were up. There was no way Mother wasn't going to accept her back. Felicity was counting on that. She couldn't face any other possibility.

I decided to book a family beach holiday for the month before Felicity's possible return. We'd never been on such a holiday, all nine of us. I found a luxury beach house right across from the sand. We were all excited. Felicity's suspension from the convent would give us an unexpected opportunity to enjoy some special time together.

Then one day, Felicity put down the phone after speaking to Mother Prioress and announced, "I can go back!" Her eyes were shining. "I'm going as soon as possible."

"But what about our beach holiday? What about your job? You committed yourself to teach until the end of the spring term."

Felicity shrugged her shoulders. "The swim school will understand. The holiday is weeks away. I don't want to wait that long."

The swim school owners were very polite and accepted Felicity's resignation without complaint, but I knew they felt hurt. These kind people had helped Felicity when she was at her lowest, and now she was leaving them in the lurch, one teacher short for the third term of the school year, and she didn't even seem to care. I apologised on Felicity's behalf. I felt responsible. Again, I felt like I'd failed as a mother. My reputation was beginning to look very tattered, or so I thought.

So Felicity packed up her few belongings once again. She hugged us and said goodbye and Andy drove her back to the convent. This time our goodbyes, although tearful on my part, weren't so distressing. We'd done it all before. I just felt all-over, low-key sad. Keeping Felicity home wasn't the answer. She wasn't happy with us. I just wanted her to find peace. I hoped she'd find it this time round in the religious life.

We enjoyed our family beach holiday, even though Felicity wasn't with us. We came home, and our lives continued. The weeks passed quickly, and before we knew it, we were talking about Christmas. When would we make our Christmas visit to the convent, our third one since Felicity had entered the enclosed life? We were looking forward to seeing our daughter again. I don't think we'd seen her since her return.

We didn't end up visiting Felicity that Christmas. There was no need. She spent that Christmas at home with us.

One morning the phone rang. It was Felicity: "Mother Prioress says I can come home. Can Dad collect me?"

This time Felicity had decided to leave the convent herself. "I'm having panic attacks. I keep thinking Mother Prioress is going to say, 'I'm sending you home.' I can't take any more."

So Andy drove to the convent to pick up our daughter. It seemed like her days as a nun were over. How would she readjust to life at home? But first, what state would Felicity be in when she arrived home for the second time? I didn't anticipate my reaction to what I saw when she came back through our front door.

A Difficult Time

We were looking out of the window, waiting for my husband Andy to arrive home with our eldest daughter Felicity. The younger girls were hopping up and down. "When will they be here? When will they be here?" they said, again and again.

And then we could see the car coming along the driveway. Everyone rushed helter-skelter down the back steps into the garden. The car doors opened. Felicity was here. I looked at her. And I was shocked.

It had only been a few months since we'd last seen Felicity. When Andy had returned her to the convent, she had looked fit and healthy. She had been excited and hopeful and eager. Now she was a changed person.

Felicity was wearing someone else's clothes: a plain skirt and shirt, probably cast-offs of a woman who'd swapped her ordinary clothing for a habit. They were big clothes. They needed to be. Felicity had put on a lot of weight. A scarf once again covered her head. I looked at her face. Not only was it blemished, but it also showed signs of stress. My daughter was suffering.

Of course, we were all excited to see Felicity. We kissed and hugged. Someone filled the kettle and made some coffee. We asked about the journey. Then Andy went to work, and I asked the other children to give Felicity some space. "Let her settle in," I said. "She'll still be here later."

We went to her bedroom where we could chat. I wanted to make her comfortable, find out what she needed. Her first need was clothes. It was obvious all her old ones that we'd packed away wouldn't fit her. Felicity's size was a huge surprise. How had she put on so much weight in such a short time?

"Mother Prioress made me the cook."

Felicity cooked the meals for the nuns as well as those of any guests who were making retreats at the convent. The nuns had discovered she is an excellent cook. Felicity knows how to turn ordinary ingredients into something spectacular. No wonder her efforts were appreciated.

I thought about Felicity cooking and the nuns enjoying her meals, and I clenched my fists. I would never have given that job to Felicity, despite her obvious skills. I know my daughter. I know the kitchen would have been the worst place to send her to several times a day. When Felicity is stressed, she comfort eats. I knew that. But I wasn't Felicity's mother at the time, so no one consulted me about what was best for her. She was instead under the care of Mother Prioress. "I'll look after your daughter," she'd said.

"How could she have sent Felicity home in that state?" I later asked my husband. "Couldn't she see there was something wrong with her? Didn't she notice she was putting on weight? Why didn't she give her another job?" Andy tried to soothe me as I poured out all my frustrations.

But her weight wasn't the only problem. Felicity needed help with her skin. Was it irreversibly blemished? And her scalp was very dry with skin flaking off. "What's wrong with using proper cleansers and shampoo?" I asked. "Soap is far too harsh."

"It's the same for everyone, Mum," replied Felicity. "No one worries about their appearance. We are taught not to pay it any attention. It's not important."

Blemishes and itchy scalps might be acceptable in the cloister but not at home. I wanted to soothe Felicity's skin, see her glow with health and take pride in her appearance again. But she didn't seem to care about all that. Her physical state didn't matter when she was so distressed spiritually.

There was so much I needed to know. Why had Felicity decided to come home? "Every time I saw Mother Prioress, I imagined she was about to say, 'I've phoned your father. I've asked him to take you home.' It was too stressful. I had panic attacks. Mother didn't take them seriously. She just thought I was calling attention to myself."

Tears ran down Felicity's face. I could barely make out her words as she added, "I was willing to give up my life for God, and He just didn't want me. I failed. I failed twice."

What does a mother say at such times? I hugged my daughter close. I didn't dismiss how she was feeling. I knew enough not to do that.

"You'll feel better when you've had a good night's sleep."

"Things will improve. Just wait and see."

"Some new clothes will help."

"I'll help you lose some weight. That will make you feel good."

"Cheer up. At least you're at home."

All these would have been stupid things to say when I could see the agony my daughter was suffering.

But still, I wanted to do something. I wanted to take away Felicity's pain, or at least help her to deal with it. I thought back to when I was at the point of despair after our son Thomas died. Each day felt like a never-ending marathon, which I had to endure. I had to force myself to get out of bed each morning and plod through the day, putting one foot in front of the other. I found myself telling Felicity about this, suggesting some prayers and even some spiritual reading. With great enthusiasm, I found a couple of books I thought might help her. She didn't even glance at them. It was all too much, far too soon. All Felicity needed at that moment was to be hugged and to be listened to. She didn't need an overenthusiastic mother ready to solve her problems, problems I felt could, at least in part, have been avoided by proper care and attention.

I wanted to tell Mother Prioress how I was feeling. She'd promised to look after my daughter but had she really done all she could to take care of her? Perhaps she didn't understand the needs of young women. I thought they needed regular opportunities for exercise and a diet that maintained a healthy weight. Surely health and fitness should be a priority in any situation, even a convent?

After she passed out through the cloister door for the last time, Felicity never again heard from anyone in the convent. No one phoned to check on her. There was no debriefing session. She went back out into the world, and as far as the convent was concerned, she no longer existed. That's just the way it was. But even if Felicity had never been given the opportunity to discuss the whole experience with Mother Prioress, I felt I was entitled to have my say.

I wrote Mother a long letter. I didn't end up posting it though. I decided it wasn't my right to tell a nun how to run her convent. I wouldn't like anyone telling me how to run my family. And Felicity had entered the convent of her own free will. But it took a long time for my anger to seep away.

Soon it was Christmas. I can't remember many details. Probably this celebration was a distraction for all of us. Then it was the start of a new year. What was Felicity going to do next?

Someone phoned asking if Felicity would like a job looking after a family whose mother had just died, a kind of nanny/housekeeper. I don't know what Felicity thought of this idea. I refused the job on her behalf. How could she be expected to look after a grieving family when she was so needy herself? This time I was in charge and I made the decision.

Then one day, Felicity announced, "I think I might join a youth mission team, Mum." We knew some other young people who'd spent a year or more mentoring young Catholics. They'd enjoyed their time visiting schools and arranging retreats and other activities for young people. Maybe this would be something good for Felicity to do while she waited for an answer to her plea: "What am I supposed to do with my life?"

Felicity was accepted on a team, and before we knew it, she was packing her bag and leaving us once more. She'd hoped she would be sent to Sydney so she could be fairly close to home. Instead, she found herself on a plane flying towards Perth. This city is right on the other side of Australia from us, about as far away as you can go without leaving the country. "I'll be home mid-year, Mum. We all get a week's break during the winter."

Felicity phoned home now and then. She sounded happy enough. She had a part-time job in a café. She was sharing a house with two young women who were part of her team. "They call me Mum because I look after them." Everything sounded fine. Just occasionally she'd report an upset she'd had with her housemates or with her boss at work. Teething problems, I thought. She'll work it out.

Mid-year the team flew back to Sydney for World Youth Day, and when that finished, Felicity caught a train home. We were going to have her to ourselves for a whole week.

Are all mothers like me? Do you look at your children carefully when they've been away? Do you notice differences? I looked at Felicity, and my heart sank. She was still having weight problems. I tried to bring up the subject in a sensitive way. Could I help her? Then Felicity said something I have never forgotten.

"I'm sure you'd love me more if I were slim like you."

Aren't these shocking words? Of course, I loved Felicity just as she was, but somehow the subject of weight was standing there like a boulder, causing tension between us. Why do our weight and appearance seem to matter so much? Oh, I could write so much about this topic. Maybe it deserves a few stories of its own.

"I'm worried about your health," I defended myself.

"I haven't got time to deal with my weight problem at the moment," said Felicity. "I have too much else that needs sorting out."

I didn't understand what she meant by 'too much else that needs sorting out', but it was obvious Felicity still wasn't happy within herself. And it was obvious I'd just had yet another conversation where I'd said all the wrong things. It seemed I had a talent for doing that. Felicity and I couldn't seem to slip back into our old comfortable roles of mother and daughter.

The leader of the youth mission team phoned to arrange a time to get together with Felicity. "He meets up with all the team members to see how they're going before we head back to Perth," she told me.

When Felicity returned from her meeting, I could see something was wrong. By this time, I guess I wasn't surprised.

"The other girls have complained about me. They say I'm hard to get on with and want me off the team." Felicity felt she had failed yet again.

So did Felicity return home to live? No, she went back to Perth with the team. She still had her café job. She was hoping to find somewhere to live. She wanted to make a life for herself in a new place, rather than rely on us at home. I am very proud of Felicity for doing this. She'd always lived at home or in the convent. Now she wanted to live an independent life.

I'm a bit hazy about the details of the next year or so. I know Felicity and I talked on the phone now and then: polite talk where I tried not to offer suggestions or say anything that might cause her to back away from me. Felicity faced many challenges. She had trouble with landlords and bosses. There were times when she cried and had panic attacks. Nothing seemed to last very long. I was concerned that when life became a bit difficult, Felicity caved in and gave up. Perhaps if she tried a little harder, persevered, was a little less concerned with herself and her feelings, tried to get on better with others... Oh, I had many such thoughts. It's just as well I kept them to myself.

But it wasn't all bad. I heard good stories about the skills Felicity had and was using. She made a few close friends, despite her problems.

And she discovered something important. She found out why her life has been so difficult, why she was unable to cope as a teenager, why she couldn't adapt to life in the convent and why even living with other young women was such a challenge. She wasn't a bad person. She wasn't self-centred and bad-tempered by nature. She wasn't unfriendly or socially maladjusted. No, there was another reason.

Mother and Daughter Again

The phone rang, and all the girls ran to answer it. Gemma-Rose got there first. "It's Felicity!" she shouted. My eldest daughter wanted to speak to me. She had some significant news to share.

"I have depression! It's been diagnosed." Felicity didn't sound depressed at all. Actually, she sounded rather excited.

"Depression? Are you sure?"

"I told a friend about my problems. She said I sounded depressed and suggested I see a doctor."

A few days later, Felicity rang home again: "The doctor has upgraded my diagnosis to clinical depression."

And then not long after that: "I have bipolar disorder."

Felicity sounded happy that someone was taking her problems seriously, that there could be a physical cause for her failure to cope. But as far as I was concerned, it was all bad news. Every time my daughter called home, the news seemed to get worse and worse. I started to dread the phone ringing. What would she tell me next?

I remember a friend once speaking to me about her teenage son's bipolar condition: "He's gone away to a camp for children with mental illness. He's making jokes with the other kids about how weird they all are but how good it feels to be 'normal' for once." I felt so glad my children weren't affected like hers. I couldn't understand how she could talk about it so openly. Wasn't mental illness something people kept to themselves? What would everyone think?

And now Felicity was telling me that she had bipolar disorder too.

I knew nothing about mental illness. I wasn't even sure mental illness really existed. Surely if everyone bucked up and got on with life, they'd be okay? Maybe Felicity just had to face the fact she needed to work on her self-control. When I was a young person, I had a hot temper, but no one diagnosed me as having a mental illness. I just faced my problem, worked hard and overcame it. (I make it sound easy, don't I?) I changed. Why couldn't Felicity do the same?

But I remembered my friend's son. I'd heard about other people who'd had a hard time coping with life. Yes, maybe mental illness was a valid condition. But still, I couldn't accept my child had it. I rejected the diagnosis because I didn't want it to be true.

I thought about how I'd felt when I'd held Felicity in my arms for the first time. All the dreams and hopes I had for her didn't include mental illness. I had wanted to keep her safe and bring her up well. She was going to develop her talents and use them. I was sure she would do spectacular things, change the world. Most of all, I wanted her to be happy. Yes, bipolar disorder had no place in my plan for my daughter.

"The doctor has prescribed some medications," Felicity told me.

I had a lot of questions. “Are the medications addictive?” Wouldn't it be better, even if the diagnosis was true, not to become dependent on drugs? I didn't like to think that once Felicity started taking them, she would need them for the rest of her life. "Will they affect your health? What about if you ever have children? Will they harm an unborn child?"

Did Felicity really need the medications? I didn't want her to take them. But my opinion didn't matter. She took the drugs anyway.

At regular intervals, Felicity would phone home.

"How are you doing?"

"I had to have my medication adjusted. I felt manic for a while. I'm okay now."

I'd listen politely, not saying much. I didn't know what to say. I'd learnt that keeping quiet and standing well back was the safest option when talking to my daughter.

Then Felicity came home to celebrate Christmas with us. One evening, we all gathered as a family to sing carols together. Like usual, everyone sang a favourite by herself. Felicity seemed reluctant when it was her turn.

"Come on! You're a good singer!" I encouraged. "We'd love to hear you sing."

Under protest, Felicity started singing, but before she'd got too far, she made a mistake and lost confidence. She looked upset and refused to sing another word.

"Don't be silly, Felicity," I said. "Carry on!"

But she wouldn't. I sighed deeply and rolled my eyes. Any moment now, I expected her to burst into tears. I didn't take Felicity seriously. I just wanted her to pull herself together and get on with things. I wasn't very sensitive. I didn't understand her problem.

So life continued like this for a long time. I guess I gradually came to accept Felicity's condition even though I didn't want to. I accepted her need for medication. I know she did what she felt she needed to do. Maybe she couldn't endure the condition any longer. Perhaps she hoped she could live a normal life like everyone else. Sometimes people don't have much choice.

But even with acceptance, I couldn't seem to connect with Felicity properly. Oh yes, things looked okay from the outside. We talked regularly and said all the right things. But something was missing. The past few years were definitely getting in the way of our relationship.

Then Felicity created a blog. She started writing about herself, her thoughts, what she'd experienced. And suddenly I was seeing inside her head. I understood. I left a couple of comments on her posts. Then Felicity picked up the phone, and we started talking, really talking for the first time in years. Oh, there is so much we keep hidden within us, so much it feels safer not to reveal. But when we are brave enough to talk, we can begin to move towards healing.

It's still not easy in some respects. I don't like getting phone calls where Felicity says, "I'm phoning from the mental unit of the hospital. I've been admitted because I'm hearing voices. I need my medication adjusted."

What do I say? "I hope you feel better soon"?

It's frightening, especially when my child tells me that she is under 24-hour surveillance. Surely she isn't at risk? She'd never take her own life, would she?

I once ventured onto a bipolar disorder Facebook page to understand the condition better. I hated being there. I hated, even more, the thought that my daughter was one of these people. "Stay away from people with bipolar. They'll make you more depressed," I yearned to say. But then I remembered the comfort it gives me to talk with other bereaved parents. Everyone needs others who understand. They can help, and I admit I can't.

So Felicity has bipolar disorder. She's had it for a long time. It has caused her a lot of confusion and mental anguish. Because of it, she has been misunderstood and judged. She hasn't understood herself. Now her disorder is controlled by medications. Even with them, she can't function like me. She has many talents, but she isn't always mentally healthy enough to use them. But she tries, and one day I hope she will feel able to do all she wants. For her sake, not mine. I love her just the way she is.

You know, I think it's love that brings us through such difficult times. Sometimes it seems to get buried under a whole pile of problems, but it's still there. It won't let us give up on each other. And eventually, it starts to emerge again, as we begin to heal. I know Felicity's and my love will keep on growing. You see, we're mother and daughter again. I really am Felicity's mother.

And so I come to the end of this story. It's not really the end. It's only the beginning. For when we ignore our fears and step out of our comfort zone, facing the mistakes of the past, miracles can happen.

I'm hoping for a miracle for my daughter, the daughter I love very much.

Part XXI: Some Last Thoughts

How Do We Want to Be Free?

Unschoolers are always talking about freedom. We all want to be free. But what does that mean?

Do we want to be free to do whatever we want? Or is that not possible? Perhaps it's not even desirable because we'd end up living very self-centred lives if there were no limits, wouldn't we?

Maybe there are better ways of being free. Imagine being free of the old flawed ideas about parenting and education, the ones that sometimes echo in our heads, preventing us from moving forward. Wouldn't it be good to be free of our fears, free of the worry about what others think of us, free of our need to be liked and approved of, free of our impatience and anger and critical nature, free of our need to control?

Wouldn't it be good to be free of whatever it is that interferes with our relationships with our children and other people?

Perhaps we want to be free to love unconditionally and trust and live this unschooling life fully with our kids.

Discovering Radical Unschool Love

Over the years, I have discovered many things.

Here are a few of them:

Kids will learn if they are surrounded by a rich environment, as long as we don't get in the way of their natural curiosity.

Learning isn't just for school-aged children. It's for everyone. It's important that parents are excited about learning. We need to be curious people too.

We can't expect our kids to do anything we're not prepared to do ourselves. We have to be good examples.

Kids are wonderfully unique people. They don't need to be who we think they should be. They're perfectly designed just the way they are.

Despite any negative messages we might have heard when we were children, we're okay too.

We all have talents. These are bound up with our missions in life, so it's essential that we use them while we're exploring the things that interest us.

There's a second reason why we should follow our interests and do the things that are important to us: they bring us joy.

Talking of joy, we should live life in the moment, searching out and appreciating each delight.

But, of course, life isn't always happy. Things happen that are out of our control. Sometimes life is very difficult. But with the help of our family - and our faith - we can get through anything.

Our family is our safe place, our refuge from the world. It's where we are accepted just as we are.

Our family is also our team. We are each other's cheer-squads. We delight in everyone's achievements. We pick each other up when we fail. We forgive. We help each other as we try to become the people we are meant to be. We do this not with criticism but with love.

Love results in strong family bonds. We're the most important people in each other's lives. We chat and discuss and listen and treat one other with respect. We all try and do what is right without imposing control. Connection, not rules, is the key.

There are no guarantees in life. Regardless of how we bring up and educate our kids, there's always the chance a child will go astray. But when we keep the lines of communication open, when we love regardless of the situation, we open the way for our kids to return.

Family loyalty means rallying around when anyone is in trouble, regardless of the mistakes they may have made.

We shouldn't worry about other people's opinions. Our kids don't have to fulfil outside expectations.

We'll all find our place in the world. Everyone can make a difference. We just have to trust.

And love

Live radically. Love unconditionally.

Years ago, when we first set out on our homeschooling journey, we were searching for the perfect method of education for our children. We never found that method, but we found something better. Somehow we arrived at radical unschooling, and we discovered unconditional love.

Is there anything more important than love?

Completing Some Serious Work

I once posted the following words on Instagram:

> My daughter Sophie and I were talking about how fast technology changes. Not that many years ago, most people wore watches, and then when smartphones became popular, watches went out of fashion. But now loads of people are wearing fitness trackers and Apple watches on their wrists. The watch is back.
>
> "I wonder what kind of technology we will be carrying around with us in the future," I said to Sophie. We couldn't imagine what's ahead of us so I said, "Remember this exact moment and this conversation and then when you're my age, we can talk about how we used to wear fitness trackers on our wrists. I'm sure they'll seem very old-fashioned compared to what we'll be using in the years to come."
>
> And then I was struck by a thought: I probably won't be alive when Sophie is my age. Her life will continue on, and I won't be part of it.
>
> So I've been thinking about time and how I've already used up more than half my lifetime. The years have passed much too quickly. What do I still want to achieve with those I have left? Lots of things.
>
> Maybe many people think unschoolers drift through their days doing nothing much at all. They go from one thing to another as they feel like it, not achieving anything. But that's not the way it is. We're always talking about our projects, what we want to do, and how we're going to do it. And then we work hard to achieve our goals. At least that's what my children do. Recently, I haven't been as focused as they are. I have found myself ambling through my days, thinking I have all the time in the world. But I don't.

> Perhaps it's time for me to get off Instagram and go do some serious work. I don't want Sophie to look back when she is my age and say, "I remember fitness trackers. I also remember how my mother was writing an unschooling book. It's a pity she never finished it."

Well, I stopped drifting. I finished my unschooling book. And then I wrote a second one. It looks like I can now spend as much time as I like on Instagram.

Or I could finish the third book in my children's Angels novel series. Or how about a book about homeschool record keeping for unschoolers?

Pursuing our passions, developing our talents, following our dreams, doing work that matters.

Don't you love how unschooling isn't just for kids?

Continuing This Unschooling Conversation

So you've come to the end of my unschooling book. You've read all my stories. What do you think? Have all the puzzle pieces fallen into place? Do you now have a concrete picture of unschooling?

Of course, this is my family's unschooling story. Maybe yours will look a little bit different, at least on the surface. But deep down, our stories could be the same. Are they all based on unconditional love?

I hope you feel excited by the words in my books. But what if you're don't? What if you disagree with my ideas?

It could be that there's nothing wrong with what I've written. Ideas sometimes need pondering. With time, we often change our minds and accept ideas we previously felt uncomfortable with. Maybe when we do hear something we disagree with, we need to keep an open mind. Take our time to think about the idea and not dismiss it straight-away.

But what if you ponder further what I've shared in this book and then conclude that I'm wrong? Well, maybe, I am. Perhaps I've got something more to learn. I can accept that. I'm sure that I've still got many things to discover about unschooling. That's why it's so interesting. Peel back one unschooling layer, and another one appears. There's always something new to explore. It's very exciting.

If you do think my ideas are offtrack, should you dismiss my book and say, "That was a waste of time and money!"? I hope not. Instead, maybe we can discuss the ideas I've written about. You could share your thoughts. We might learn from each other. Go deeper.

I want my book to open up a conversation.

Where You Can Find Us

If you'd like to continue the unschooling conversation, you can find us in these places:

My blog: *Stories of an Unschooling Family*

My podcast: *Stories of an Unschooling Family*

My YouTube channel: *Sue Elvis*

My Instagram account: stories_ofan_unschoolingfamily

My first unschooling book: *Curious Unschoolers*

My children's novels:

The Angels of Abbey Creek

The Angels of Gum Tree Road

Imogen's book: *The Crystal Tree*

Imogen's website: *Write. Rewrite. Read*

Imogen's Instagram Account: write.rewrite.read

Imogen's music on YouTube: *Imogen Elvis*

Notes

Forcing a Child to Do What He is Afraid to Do / Aiming for Love Not Perfection

Quotes by John Holt

Books by John Holt

How Children Learn

How Children Fail

Learning All the Time

Teach Your Own

Hold on Tight

My children's novel: *The Angels of Abbey Creek*

Keeping Our Teenagers Safe From the World

Stories of an Unschooling Family podcast, episode 18: *Resolutions, Reading, Writing and Coarse Language*

Speed Angel Joy

Book: *I Believe in Love* by Fr d'Elbee

Why We Live a Life Full of Saturdays

Quote from *Unschooling 101* by Bridget Bentz Sizer

Sandra Dodd's website: *Sandra Dodd*

Acknowledgements

Thank you to my daughter Imogen for proofreading and formatting this book. And thank you to my daughter Charlotte for creating its fabulous cover.

Thank you to my friend, Jacqueline Brack, for helping me rediscover my love of writing.

Thank you to my friend, Venisa, for your help with the proof copy. I'm so glad you were happy to be part of the process.

And a huge thank you to my brilliant family Andy, Felicity, Duncan, Callum, Imogen, Charlotte, Thomas, Sophie and Gemma-Rose for letting me write your stories. Without you, there would be no book.

Sue Elvis is a long time unschooling mother who lives with her husband Andy and some of their eight children somewhere south of Sydney, Australia.

Sue enjoys running through the beautiful Australian bush with her children and her dogs, Nora and Quinn. While she is racing up and down the hills, she thinks up new ways to spread the word about unschooling.

When she's not having fantastic learning adventures with her family, Sue can found at her computer tapping out books and blog posts, recording podcasts, and uploading videos to YouTube.

Printed in Great Britain
by Amazon

59188247R00232